The Media,
Social Science,
and Social Policy
for Children

Child And Family Policy

Series Editors
James J. Gallagher and Ron Haskins

Volume I

MODELS FOR ANALYSIS OF SOCIAL POLICY:
AN INTRODUCTION

Ron Haskins and James J. Gallagher

Volume II

CHILD HEALTH POLICY
IN AN AGE OF FISCAL AUSTERITY:
CRITIQUES OF THE
SELECT PANEL REPORT

Ron Haskins

Volume III

PARENT EDUCATION
AND PUBLIC POLICY

Ron Haskins and Diane Adams

Volume IV

FOSTER CARE: CURRENT ISSUES, POLICIES, AND PRACTICES

Martha J. Cox and Roger D. Cox

Volume V

THE MEDIA, SOCIAL SCIENCE, AND SOCIAL POLICY FOR CHILDREN

Eli A. Rubinstein and Jane Brown

The Media, Social Science, and Social Policy for Children

ELI A. RUBINSTEIN and JANE D. BROWN

University of North Carolina

EDITORS

Ablex Publishing Corporation
Norwood, New Jersey 07648

Library of Congress Cataloging in Publication Data
Main entry under title:

The Media, social science, and social policy for children.

Includes bibliographies and index.
1. Family policy—United States—Addresses, essays,
lectures. 2. United States—Social policy—Addresses,
essays, lectures. 3. Mass media—Social aspects—United
States—Addresses, essays, lectures. 4. Child welfare—
United States—Addresses, essays, lectures.
I. Rubinstein, Eli Abraham. II. Brown, Jane, 1950-
HV699.M465   1985   362.7'95'0973   85-1393
ISBN 0-89391-229-8

Ablex Publishing Corporation
355 Chestnut Street
Norwood, New Jersey 07648

Contents

PREFACE TO THE SERIES

JAMES J. GALLAGHER

Emergence of the new field of social policy analysis, starting in the 1960s, but accelerating in the 1970s, is an intriguing phenomenon in the academic world that is worthy of study in its own right. This evolving discipline is clearly multidisciplinary in nature, drawing interest and contributions from such diverse bedfellows as the health sciences, economics, sociology, psychology, and education, among others.

Even more interesting than this multidisciplinary thrust from the academic community is that those in positions of power seem to be aware of this new movement and are generally attentive. The relationship between the keepers of knowledge and holders of power has always been a strained one. Truth, particularly when unpleasant, has rarely been welcomed by those at the seat of power. Those messengers who deliver such unpleasant truths run some very real risks, more psychological than physical these days. On the other hand, the academician rarely has a sense of the multitude of conflicting pressures and compromises that are the daily menu of the practicing politician, and often doesn't appreciate the many changes in directions that often must be taken to reach a political (policy) goal.

To appreciate this continued strain between knowledge and power, one need not invoke the memories of Galileo or Sir Thomas More. The current difficulties are well expressed in the agonies of the atomic scientists, aptly delineated in an extraordinary series of novels by C. P. Snow. Given this obvious and continued strain, why is there a current interest in pursuing what academia can bring to social policy formulation and implementation?

My own view is that the public policies of the 1960s are the stimuli for this review of relationships. Those policies were, by and large, designed to lead to a better life for all our citizens through improving the delivery of health, social, and educational services. The consensus held by both the political community and the lay public appears to be that after 15 years, the programs have largely come to grief, or have attained much less than was originally intended. Whether this outcome is the result of unrealistic expectations, poor policy formulation, or inadequate policy implementation is still a matter of personal interpretation.

Currently, there is a growing realization that attempts to improve American society can no longer be based on a "seat-of-the-pants," largely uncorrelated, and uncontrolled set of innovations. Such a strategy yields uncontrolled budgets and a corrosive cycle of over-expectation, disappointment, and despair. There appears to be a new willingness, tinged with some skepticism, to pursue what academia has to offer in improving policy design and implementation. What does academia have to offer? What it always has—the ability to organize systems of ideas into a pattern that allows us to bring order and new insights to the phenomenon under study.

This series on social policy analysis summarizes some of the latest ideas and methods that are being utilized by those social and health scientists most directly concerned with policy relating to children and families. Each volume in the series will be built around a particular theme so that contributors to a given volume will be focusing on a common topic. In this first volume, the theme is the development of models for analyzing social policy. Such model development is presented from a multidisciplinary perspective as we seek some usable procedures to bring clarity and comprehension to complex policy topics. In subsequent volumes, we will focus upon policy issues such as parent education, the needs of handicapped children and their families, maternal and child health, and children and families in poverty. In each of these volumes, there will be a mixture of general descriptions on the topic area plus the inclusion of specific policy analyses that attempt to bring insight into particular topics within the theme.

It would be inappropriate to conclude these introductory remarks without giving credit to the Bush Foundation of St. Paul, Minnesota, whose forward thinking has provided financial support for much of the analytic work that will be included in these volumes. The Bush Foundation has established training programs at four major universities—Michigan, Yale, UCLA, and North Carolina—and while the papers in this series will be based, to a large degree, on the work at North Carolina, the ideas and concepts in this series will undoubtedly reflect the interests of all four Bush centers.

Preface to Volume V

JAMES J. GALLAGHER

This volume, *The Media, Social Science, and Social Policy for Children*, is the fifth in a series of child and family policy books produced by the Bush Institute for Child and Family Policy at the University of North Carolina. Previous volumes have dealt with foster care, parent education, child health policy, and models for analysis of social policy.

Through the 6 years of the existence of the Bush Institute, we have increasingly come to an understanding of what is necessary in order for the social sciences to impact upon public policy and decision making. There are three major steps. Each of these steps is complex and difficult in its own right. Having all three work appropriately is a rare thing indeed.

The first step involves a careful consideration of social science's contribution to the issue in question such as foster care, or the impact of the media upon children. We should ask if the knowledge is sufficient in the various social science disciplines to allow us to bring special insight to the condition or to the issue at hand. Many of the issues of public interest are extraordinarily complex with many interactions between variables. There are few outstanding forces or variables we study that dominate the issue itself and clearly reveal themselves to the social scientist and the public policymakers' attention. So the first step is to find out if social scientists know enough about the topic to make a significant contribution.

The second step is, having understood the problem, for the social scientist to devise alternative strategies that might provide a partial or complete solution to the problem. Since any solution would likely change the status quo and involve a number of negatives such as increased costs, it becomes important for the social scientist to understand, not only the issue, but the societal dynamics in which the issue is embedded. For example, many educational reformers may have interesting ideas about what to do about the general problem of American education, but find that their ideas break apart upon the rocks of the educational establishment and its current operation. So the objective is to determine whether we can devise productive and implementable strategies that will complement our increased understanding of the issue.

One example of this problem lies in the familiar strategy to form a blue ribbon commission to study a prickly issue and deliver some recommendations to the public decision makers.

One of the flaws of the comission approach is that while the commission members may analyze existing information fairly well and state the problem well, they do not have either the resources or the techniques for pilot testing their recommendations. It is the recommendations that often make a well-documented commission report look foolish because of the lack of practicality of the solutions. Often the commission comes up with these recommendations in the last days of its existence ater having spent many months defining the problem. It is becoming clear that the developing field of policy analysis can help social and health scientists analyze the available alternative strategies as well as identify the flaws in an existing program or strategy.

The third major step then is for social scientists to communicate these issues and strategies effectively to decision makers and to resource allocators. It is at this point that the media become important. The media operate as both an amplifier and a filter of information, as is discussed in some of the papers in this volume. The media's approach to such issues as pornography or desegregation often distorts or even changes the basic message that was delivered by the social scientist. Since the decision makers get most of their information through reading popular news magazines, the daily newspaper, and the T.V. news programs, it is through those vehicles that the judgment is made on what the social scientists are trying to say.

It becomes critically important, therefore, that the media and the social sciences gain some rapport with one another. The media should never be the passive tool of social scientists, nor should the social scientists' work be distorted or sensationalized to the needs of the media in search for more readers or viewers. This volume, providing as it does a variety of perspectives on this relationship, offers one useful contribution in this attempt to find a bridge between these important elements in our society. Hopefully, that bridge can aid in the development of more effective social policy.

Dedicated to Minnie S. Rubinstein, 1919–1985
Dear Friend and Loving Wife

INTRODUCTION

ELI A. RUBINSTEIN and JANE D. BROWN

What happens to a scientific conclusion on the way to the marketplace of social policy? This book explores that question from three different perspectives: (a) the development of the scientific conclusions as they relate to social policy, (b) case histories of the implementation of that social policy, and (c) how the media get involved in this complex trans-formation.

While our emphasis here is on social science and social policy for children, the total process is not dissimilar from that involving other sciences and other policy areas. Indeed, in our modern society, one could compare the process of utilizing scientific ideas to the production, distribution, and marketing of tangible goods. In today's information society scientific knowledge has become a tangible good, as much in the economic sense as in the ethical context.

We have tried to examine areas that best illustrate this triangulation from scientific knowledge to social policy to media involvement. All of the contributing authors were selected because they themselves have been intimately concerned with the specific aspect of the total process which they discuss.

Since this process is so intimately interactive, we could have se-quenced the three perspectives in almost any order. We chose to begin with the case histories of major national social policy efforts because each reveals within its respective unfolding the way the complete sequence develops. For example, a major survey of school quality by an eminent sociologist, James Coleman, immediately upon publication in 1966, becomes a political football. Indeed, the initiation of the study, a year earlier, drew media attention that, in turn, produced anticipatory bureaucratic reactions and influenced the way the report itself was received. And, even today, subsequent "Coleman Reports" continue to stimulate new public arguments and political debates as to implications for public policy. Thus, almost 20 years after the first report was produced, it is clear that neither the scholarly arguments about quality of the research, nor the public debate about the policy implications therein have been resolved.

A major effort to reexamine federal mental health programs is initiated with White House participation and thus becomes an object of media scrutiny from its inception to its final report. In this sequence, the passage of time itself brings changes in priorities and the inevitable erosion of impetus as action is stalled in the ponderous bureaucratic process.

A commission appointed by President Johnson in 1968 to look at obscenity and pornography produces much research documentation for a series of policy recommendations and then finds its entire report later repudiated by President Nixon on the basis of conservative political reaction to only one of the many final recommendations.

It is clear from all three case studies that the inevitable changes over time in the political environment have critical influences on both the scientific documentation and the resulting policy outcomes.

In the second section of this volume we look at an earlier stage of this complex evolution of knowledge into action. These chapters show how the slow accumulation of scientific information provides the nutrient top soil from which the social policy hopefully draws its factual strength. Our examples are from research on the effects of television on children, studies of the effectiveness of health education, and research concerned with child mental health.

In each instance, it becomes unarguably clear that the sheer accumulation of scientific knowledge is never sufficient unto itself to point unequivocally toward appropriate social policy, let alone carry the strength of argument to bring such social policy to fruition. While the social scientist has the luxury of time to debate the scholarly argument, the policymaker must, at some point, make a decision. Almost always that decision precedes the conclusion of the scholarly investigation. And, it would be disingenuous not to recognize that, too often, that policy decision influences the scholarly evaluation.

Finally, we look more directly at the role of the media. How do social scientists and journalists learn to talk each other's language? What are their conflicting self-interests in pursuing their respective professions? When social scientists try consciously and conscientiously to communicate research findings to the public through the media, what pitfalls emerge and how can these problems be overcome?

Furthermore, are there ways that a common framework can be established? Two of our colleagues in the Bush Institute at the University of North Carolina describe a series of workshops held over a 4-year period to build communications bridges between media professionals and social scientists. The workshops were moderately successful. They have proven, however, that those bridges need stronger foundations to prevent them from swaying in the cross-winds of self-interest and differing priorities.

We come away from this examination of the media, social science, and social policy with some optimism that we can learn from all this prior effort and experience. What is perhaps a bit discouraging is that some of the problems in this process of converting knowledge into social action emerge as often from procedural difficulties as they do from substantive complexities. We must simultaneously be aware of: (a) what we are trying to learn, (b) how we can use that knowledge to shape policy, and (c) how best to bring the meaning and the message to public awareness. That is a juggling act we are barely beginning to master. We hope that this volume will help the reader to understand what it takes to cope successfully with this complex process.

PART ONE

FROM THE SOCIAL POLICY PERSPECTIVE

ONE

JAMES COLEMAN AND THE COLEMAN REPORTS*

GERALD GRANT and CHRISTINE MURRAY
Syracuse University

There is perhaps no better introduction to this study of the politics of
the Coleman Report (Coleman, Campbell, Hobson, McPartland, Mood,
Weinfeld, & York, 1966; henceforth referred to as the Report) than James
Coleman's own informal summary of his findings in testimony before
a Senate committee 4 years after the original publication of the Report.
His Report, formally titled *Equality of Educational Opportunity*, had been
based on one of the most extensive surveys of the schools ever undertaken. The results, as he noted, "were not at all what was anticipated":

School Quality—Racial Differences

First, all the standard measures of school quality were compared, for
schools attended by whites, by Negroes, by American Indians, Oriental
Americans, by persons of Puerto Rican origin, and by persons of Mexican-
American origin. The schools attended by Negroes had slightly lower
levels of these measures of quality than those attended by whites. The
same was true of the comparison between whites and other minority
groups that I mentioned, as well, but what was striking and surprising
was the relatively small size of these differences.

School Quality—Regional Differences

For example, there was a much greater difference between regions
than between races within a region; and there was a larger difference
between rural and urban than between races within urban areas or within
rural areas.
In short, the degree of inequality of opportunity by race, as classically measured

---

*Parts of this paper were published earlier in *Harvard Educational Review* &
the *Teachers College Record*.

by "school quality" indices, was not very great, and, in fact, less great than many persons had anticipated, including me.

School Resources and Achievement

The second conception of equality of educational opportunity, that is, equality of effective school resources, showed equally surprising results.

Very briefly, it showed that equality or inequality in the various measures of school quality that educators have traditionally used was not very important for achievement.

School Quality and Achievement

What was most striking about all this, however, was the relatively small differences in achievement related to any measures of school quality. Thus, one might say that schools of Negroes and those of whites were rather close to equality, but equality in precisely those things which were not very important for school achievement. In fact, the element in which the schools differed most—qualities of teachers—was the one element that showed a non-negligible relation to children's performance.

Social Class Composition

There is, however, another set of resources in the school which is not measured by educators' school quality measures. This is the educational resources brought to the school by other children, as a result of their home influences.

These resources are things like the reading material in the home, the amount and level of discussion in the home, the parents' level of education, the parents' interest in the child's education.

What appears to happen is that the educational resources held by other children are more important in increasing the child's own achievement than those that are allocated by the school board.

Social Class Resources—Racial Differences

The practical importance of this result as it relates to policy is enormous, because of two simple facts: Children from middle classes ordinarily have greater educational resources in their homes than children from working classes; and white children ordinarily have greater educational resources in their homes than do Negro children, or Puerto Rican children, or Mexican-American children.

Segregation—Cumulative Effect

Thus, if schools are racially homogeneous or economically homogeneous, the disadvantages a working-class or Negro child, or a Puerto Rican child, or a Mexican child experiences in his home environment are multiplied by the disadvantages he experiences in his school environment. (Coleman, 1971, p. 88; emphasis in the original)

This is what Coleman declared his Report was about from the beginning. But it bears little resemblance to the government's first biased summary of the Report. And in the 4 years that elapsed between the publication of the Report and this testimony, the Report was bent to serve remarkably different uses in the government. It was misconstrued by the press and became the subject of major squabbles among social scientists.

The Johnson Administration had issued a misleading summary of the Report in order to play down the negative implications it held for President Johnson's prized Elementary and Secondary Education Act. As Daniel P. Moynihan said later, Coleman's work suggested that the Great Society education legislation "may turn out to be a very bad idea. Gilding the cage in the urban ghetto doesn't work."

The Johnson Administration tried to soften the impact of the Report insofar as it might undermine the funding of Great Society programs. Instead, it selectively used the Report as a document that could help to advance the school desegregation struggle in the South, an action then under strident attack in Congress. But even in this use of the Report, the Johnson civil rights advocates distorted it by exaggerating alleged differences between black and white schools, when the real news was that there were fewer differences than anyone had thought. Either because the social-class findings were not fully understood, or because such arguments were deemed politically risky, the Administration did not emphasize the very powerful case the Report made for the benefits of socioeconomic integration.

The Nixon Administration took nearly the exact opposite attitude toward Coleman's Report. The Nixon White House initially softpedaled the Report's integration findings and championed it as a document that justified cutting inflationary federal aid to education programs. Here again the outcomes were otherwise: The Nixon Administration achieved unprecedented breakthroughs in school desegregation (which it steadfastly refused to boast about as part of its strategy of building better political bridges in the South). Furthermore, Nixon was unable to stem the flow of education dollars into old programs. Instead, the President found himself "reluctantly" signing the largest federal aid to education bill ever passed by Congress.

The selective emphasis of the Coleman Report by the Johnson Administration occurred during a time when there was a wide divergence of scholarly interpretations of the Report. But reanalysis of its extensive data continued in the Office of Education, at Harvard, Johns Hopkins, and other places. The Nixon Administration initially played down Coleman's integration findings, but it found it could not discount them in the face of the emerging consensus among scholars and the forceful advocacy of those findings by Daniel P. Moynihan and James Coleman himself, who became a presidential adviser at a crucial policymaking period. Eventually, President Nixon based Administration policy on the integration findings as well as the more politically appealing findings in the Report that could be used to justify his proposed budget reductions for some traditional school programs.

This study suggests that while a large-scale empirical study may be abused by policymakers in the short run, it will not be ignored if (a) it rests on a solid base of evidence, (b) a consensus emerges among scholars about the major policy implications of the research, and (c) these policy implications are presented in an authoritative way in policy-making councils.

LEGISLATIVE HISTORY

The rather obscure origins of the Coleman Report lie in the Civil Rights Act of 1964. This was the law that was conceived following Kennedy's death, partly as a testament to him.

At the time, the section of the bill authorizing what eventually became the Coleman Report received virtually no notice. Public attention was focused on the voting rights and public accommodations titles of the bill. During the lengthy hearings before the Judiciary Committee (the bill had been introduced by Representative Emmanuel Celler, chairman of that committee), the whole education title attracted little interest. There were few questions about the section authorizing the commissioner of education to make grants to school boards and other agencies to provide training institutes to deal with desegregation problems.

The authorization for what became the Coleman Report was found in section 402 of the bill. It had originally been written in rather punitive language, giving the Commissioner of Education power to ''conduct investigations'' of ''the extent to which equal educational opportunities are denied to individuals. . . .''

In last-minute compromises in the Justice Department and on Capitol Hill, large sections of the bill were rewritten and toned down to gain support for its passage. Section 402 was amended to read:

> The Commissioner shall conduct a survey and make a report to the President and the Congress within two years of the enactment of this title, concerning the lack of availability of equal educational opportunity for individuals by reason of race, color, religion or national origin in public educational institutions at all levels in the U.S., its territories, and possessions, and the District of Columbia.

A decade earlier, such a survey would have been unthinkable. The U.S. Office of Education had traditionally been an inventory-taking agency—counting the number of pupils, schools, and teachers. It seldom dared ask how well anyone was doing with what they had. It was influenced to a surprising degree by the then more politically conservative National Education Association. And it had a strong aversion to projecting an image that would smack of federal meddling in the schools.

But Commissioner Francis Keppel clearly had a fresh mandate when he was appointed as head of the agency by President Kennedy. One of the few commissioners who had not been handpicked by the NEA, Keppel worked hard to overcome the traditional educator's antipathy to his bluestocking, Harvard background. He knew that many school superintendents would be strongly opposed to any kind of achievement tests. James Coleman, a sociologist then at Johns Hopkins, was asked to undertake the major responsibility for the survey. Time was running short, however. Congress had stipulated that the Commissioner should report within 2 years. That meant July, 1966. The project had languished for nearly a year and it was April, 1965, when Keppel called together a group of superintendents to test their reaction to the survey proposal. The meeting was a catastrophe. The superintendents recited the litany of complaints about testing. It would be an administrative mess. Tests would lead to unsophisticated and invidious comparisons between school districts. Civil rights leaders in northern cities would subpoena the data for use in court suits then beginning to challenge patterns of de facto segregation in the North. Several of the participants continued their opposition to the point of refusing to participate in the survey that fall.

Keppel, apparently concerned about any possible political repercussions that might affect the passage of the historic federal school aid bill then nearing final action in the Congress, temporarily put the survey on ice. It was another month, with the school bill safely enacted, before he gave Coleman the go-ahead.

THE SURVEY BEGINS

Preparations then began in earnest to put tests and questionnaires into the hands of thousands of teachers and pupils that fall. That summer, Coleman attempted to head off opposition among the superintendents. He relied heavily on his Congressional mandate, and once the project was committed, received full backing from Keppel. In retrospect, however, Coleman believes that greater cooperation could have been obtained (more than one tenth of the target school districts refused to cooperate, including Chicago, Los Angeles, and the entire state of Florida). He blames this on poor relations between the U.S. Office of Education and the states, a small liaison staff, and inadequate sensitivity to political problems. It may be that greater effort to involve local superintendents in planning the survey and painstaking attempts to brief school personnel through regional meetings may have paid off in terms of increased participation. On the other hand, Coleman himself admits, it is equally likely that it would have increased grass roots opposition to the survey and might even have killed it altogether.

The tests and questionnaires—standardized versions developed by one of the nation's largest testmakers, Educational Testing Service (ETS)—were scheduled to be administered nationwide on three days in October. There were one or two horrible mixups, including a batch of forms filled out by school superintendents that had to be mailed out all over again after it was discovered that ETS had failed to code them properly. This did not increase the superintendents' confidence in the survey.

A controversy began to develop in the press about some of the attitudinal questions in the survey. Questions designed to elicit information about white children's racial attitudes were singled out by critics. Inquiries about background factors (e.g., "Who acts as your father?") also enraged opponents of the survey. A plaintive headline over a story in the *Cincinnati Enquirer* was not untypical of adverse press comment: "Must Johnny Tell All?"

In Washington, the fuss produced a number of inquiries from the press and Congressional representatives that worried the survey staff. Since the data had already been collected, the controversy did not upset the survey. But it absorbed a considerable amount of staff time in reassurances about the confidentiality and anonymity of the data. The contretemps also had a subtle but important impact on other parts of the bureaucracy in that it magnified fears about the possible political kickback. There was a feeling among many of those connected with the Coleman survey that they had just barely escaped the political rapids without upsetting their boat. It is quite likely that the experience also made Coleman more willing to listen to those who would later warn of the dangers that might grow out of a misinterpretation of their work.

It took months for the masses of data that Coleman collected to be processed for computers so that sophisticated analyses and comparisons could be made. The early correspondence during this period between Coleman's staff and the advisory committee appointed by Keppel shows that Coleman expected to find major differences in the kinds of schools attended by whites and blacks, and that these school characteristics would be highly related to differences in achievement between the two groups. As Coleman put it in an interview published in the *Southern Education Report* of November–December, 1965:

the study will show the difference in the equality of schools that the average Negro child and the average white child are exposed to. You know yourself that the difference is going to be striking. And even though everybody knows there is a lot of difference between suburban and inner-city schools, once the statistics are there in black and white, they will have a lot more impact.

This, of course, turned out eventually not to be the case at all. Indeed, it was the major controversial finding of the study, upsetting many traditional notions, although readers of the summary of Coleman's findings as published the following July would be hard put to discover it. The preparation of the summary document, which one reviewer later called a "political rather than a profession document" (Moynihan, 1968) and another said "omits some of the most interesting findings of the larger report" (Jencks, 1966), constitutes one of the most fascinating chapters in the varied life of the Coleman Report.

THE SUMMARY

The peculiar form of group journalism by which the highly misleading summary of the Coleman Report was constructed involved an unusual range of forces within the Department of Health, Education, and Welfare. Names of two of the most instrumental in this inside battle appear nowhere on the Report. One was Howard Nemerovsky, a San Francisco lawyer and White House Fellow who was an aide to HEW Secretary John Gardner. Another was David Seeley, who came to the Office of Education as a special assistant to Keppel and at this time headed the politically sensitive and embattled office that was charged with enforcement of the federal school desegregation guidelines. It was largely through their efforts that three different versions of the summary came to be written.

An understanding of the political context is crucial to understanding the forces that were working to shape the public view of Coleman's findings. Clearly, the overarching political pressure was the matter of desegregation. Mounting attacks from Southern Congressmen over the school guidelines and Mayor Richard Daley's ire over Keppel's attempt to cut off federal funds for Chicago, because segregation in the public schools there contributed to Keppel's decision to step down as commissioner in December, 1965. Harold Howe, II, who succeeded him in January, 1966, proved as committed to integrationist goals as Keppel. Howe, if anything, was even more outspoken. That spring, as the Coleman report was beginning to take shape, Howe issued stronger desegregation guidelines, requiring Southern school districts to show percentage progress in pupil desegregation and demanding integration of faculties as well.

In addition to the clear legal mandate for desegregation, civil rights activists wanted to buttress their guidelines fight by emphasizing the disparities in school facilities and programs between white and black schools. It was important to show that schools were not only separate but also grossly unequal.

In the North, it was argued that the promise of modern superschools with the latest equipment and modern curriculums (and implied higher achievement for all) would be the sugar-coating that would induce middle-class white parents to swallow the integration pill.

A report that said not only that there were no major differences between schools attended by blacks and whites but that even those school differences that did exist did not markedly affect achievement, well, this was no help to these activists. Furthermore, the report said it was not race but socioeconomic class that mattered when it came to integration. This was no argument for the racial integration of *poor* blacks and *poor* whites in the rural South—a principal target of integration at that time. And the conventional politics in America required one to pretend there were no "social classes" in this egalitarian nation.

Consequently, the summary of the report intended for the press underwent three revisions. Nothing was overly misstated in the final summary, but it was cast in such a way as to all but erase the heart of the survey. The really crucial finding was buried in the text following pages of blown-up bar graphs illustrating the degree of segregation in the schools, which was hardly news to anyone.

MEET THE PRESS

The press conference was set for July 1 at 1:30 p.m. There was no press release highlighting what the Office of Education felt was the news of Coleman's survey. One reporter who had been attending government press conferences for seven years, noted this was the first time he had been handed a report without a covering press release. The summary itself (there was no full report until weeks later) was not available to journalists until just before the press conference itself began. Usually, the government allows several days for reporters to absorb the contents of complex technical reports.

Howe, who had the reputation of being an unflappable man, seemed nervous to some observers. He stuck very close to the text of the document. In fact, the press conference consisted largely of his reading excerpts from each section of the Report. He gave prominence to none and refused to entertain any questions about the policy implications of what was being presented.

Although there really wasn't much news in the fact that American schools were highly segregated, it seemed to a number of journalists to be the most prudent news peg. Certainly it was safer than drawing the wrong inference from the rest of the data. The survey came about as a result of the Civil Rights Act, didn't it? It was titled "Equality of Educational Opportunity." So it must be about segregation. Nice charts, too.

The story written by the Associated Press's Tom Seppy which appeared in hundreds of American newspapers that depend on the wire services was not atypical:

> Washington (AP)—The Office of Education has told President Johnson and Congress that a nation-wide survey of education shows American children are attending public schools which are largely segregated.
>
> "We have now documented what we always believed," Education Commissioner Harold Howe II said, "American children attend schools where almost all of their fellow students are of the same racial background as they are." (*Biloxi Herald*, 1966)

In a column in *The New York Times*, John Herbers (1966) noted in one paragraph that "differences in schools had very little effect on the achievement scores of children with a strong educational background in the home." The headline, lead, and the rest of his story conformed perfectly with the structured emphasis of the official summary:

> Washington—A survey of educational opportunities ordered by Congress has shown that predominantly Negro schools are inferior to those attended largely by whites and that this tends to widen the achievement gap between the races.
>
> In achievement tests conducted as part of the survey, average Negro scored lower than average white at every level. The difference was greater in 12th grade than in the first.
>
> The U.S. Commissioner of Education, Harold Howe II, said in releasing results of the survey today that these findings had not been unexpected but would be useful to documenting what was already known or suspected. (Herbers, 1966)

A memo written by Leroy Goodman, director of public information at the U.S. Office of Education, quietly exults over the press coup:

> The summary as it ultimately emerged plus your press briefing analysis of the significant aspects of the EEO report evidently convinced reporters that a sound case had been made for the Negro student. Obviously, it was extremely useful to get over the basic points of the survey to the press early in the game. My impression is that with the foundation of favorable

opinion that now exists, we will not be subject to *adverse reaction by the press* to the full report.

In general the news media have taken the point of view that the EEO survey provides "convincing statistical proof that the Nation's schools are still segregated—and that the result is inequality of educational opportunity for Negro children. . . ."

The conclusion that schools account for only small differences in achievement produced no noticable reaction. Perhaps this is because it was coupled with two other findings: (1) That achievements of minority groups are more dependent on the schools they attend than is the case with white children and (2) A strong relationship exists between the achievement of Negro pupils and the educational backgrounds and aspirations of their fellow students. The effect on Congress is not ascertainable at this time. The report came too late to be a factor in the Congressional hearings on pending elementary and secondary education legislation. . . .

What can be said from a public information point of view is that in the months since its issuance the report has created no public relations problems. On the credit side, it has provided you with some telling points for your speeches and has reinforced the Office of Education effort to accelerate school desegregation. (Goodman, undated)

IMPLICATIONS AND CONCLUSIONS

A student of bureaucracy pondering this brief case history is attempted to lean on the theories of Anthony Downs (1966) in *Inside Bureaucracy*. The struggle over the Coleman report seems to highlight the typologies of self-interested bureaucrats suggested by Downs. By this mode of analysis, we might conclude that the event should be placed in the context of bureaucratic conflict. The civil rights advocates working with public relations allies outmanuevered the opposition (Coleman) to successfully convince the statesman (Howe) that their view of the Coleman Report should prevail. While there is some truth in this analysis, it may obscure as much as it reveals. The principal fault is the assumption that all are bureaucrats.

Let us place Downs's insights in a wider context. A more useful scheme of analysis lies in a consideration of the relationships between knowledge and action, between the outside experts and the policymakers. Much of what happened can be explained as a result of the different perceptions, inclinations, and motivations of administrators and policymakers on the one hand, and the experts or social scientists on the other.

1. Competitive drives are strong among key executives in the bureaucracy who have an opportunity to influence policy, which leads them to become early advocates of one of a number of policy options. Lyman Bryson (1952) has noted that whereas in scholarly debates opin-

ions are merely that and are seldom settled in any final sense, "In practical matters, the question almost always gets settled but it is a man and not an opinion that wins. Every member of the staff wants to be that man, or to be associated with him" (p. 49).

2. The policymaker's inclination to place his bet early and to look for guides to action has another outcome. It leads to a focus on the conclusions of research rather than the reasoning or analysis behind it. Hence, most of the debate centered on what shape the summary would take rather than the broader implications of Coleman's analysis. But Coleman's conclusions gave no clear guide for action. On the contrary, the Report upset much conventional thinking about remedies for inequality of education without offering any prescriptions as to what might be the right remedies. In this sense, the conclusions were negative. The Report indicated that no known technology seemed to exist that would enable the Office of Education to achieve one of its major objectives. It said: *Our science has proved your intuition faulty and the job is tougher than anyone thought, but we can't tell you what you should do.* In the absence of any clear-cut guidelines, the policymakers sought to impose their own view in the summary.

3. The policymaker and the scholar respond to different constituencies. The policymaker is naturally concerned with defending the agency against external attack and in advancing the goals of the agency as he or she defines them. The expert values his scholarly reputation and the judgment of his professional colleagues. Thus, the Office of Education was most sensitive to the political realities of its major goal of achieving desegregation; Coleman with generalized findings about what constitutes equal educational opportunity. Essentially, the result was a compromise designed to satisfy both. Mood and Coleman bargained away the public impact of the summary and the press conference—with all that implied about the posture the government assumed toward the Report—for editorial control of the final, less immediately visible product.

4. Policymakers and experts tend to define problems in a way that best suits their own interest. The policymaker gives up his or her definition with great reluctance. The scholar often redefines the problem without obtaining either the necessary understanding or cooperation of the policymaker.

5. A major consequence of Coleman's definition of the problem was to cast the policy options into a broader framework than the agency that sponsored his research was capable of considering. For Coleman's work indicated that equality of educational opportunity may not rest in any significant way on *school* resources or *school* policies. This raised issues far beyond the normal concern of the educational bureaucracy. It asked

those concerned about equal educational opportunity to consider what happened to a child outside of school and during the preschool period as perhaps the key factors determining equality of opportunity. The policy implications cut across many department of government, including such questions as the need for a family allowance, consideration of what factors affect a child's environment and peer group outside of school. This, perhaps, was a key reason for the lethargic bureaucratic response to the real news of the Coleman report.

THE GOVERNMENT: A REPORT WITHOUT A FORUM

It was not until August, 1966, nearly 5 weeks after the misleading summary was released to the press, that the full, 737-page document, *Equality of Educational Opportunity*, was published. Coleman's voluminous raw data was also made available to qualified researchers and scholars.

Within the Office of Education, Commissioner Harold Howe, II, circulated a memorandum to his bureau heads requesting their reaction to the Report and its policy implications. With few exceptions, he received cautious, unimaginative replies from men who viewed the report piecemeal, attempting to assess its particular impact on their bureau's programs, or expressing satisfaction that it had not caused any problems on Capitol Hill.

The Report was published just as the House Education and Labor Committee was meeting in executive session, wrapping up its work on a 2-year extension of the historic Elementary and Secondary Education Act of 1965. Hearings had been concluded several weeks earlier, and the Committee staff was burdened with the job of publishing testimony, determining fine points of legislation, ironing out differences within the Committee, and readying the bill for the floor of the House. When Coleman's volume arrived on their desks with its complicated tables and rather obscure summary, it was promptly filed and forgotten.

Committee staff might have been stimulated to pay more attention to the controversial aspects of the Report had the press emphasized its controversial aspects. But most of the press misread the Report as a result of the deadpan, elliptical nature of the summary as published by the U.S. Office of Education, and treated it simply as a segregation survey. Few Congressmen have time to read reports; their response is usually determined by what the press says about a report.

The Office of Education (USOE) itself, seeing plenty of risks but few chances for gain in the Coleman Report, never marketed it on Capitol Hill. If the USOE felt any piece of research buttressed its legislative program, it would take special pains to brief relevant Congressional representatives and staff. It ought to come as no surprise that in the case of the Coleman report, no briefings were held. And in Washington, where reports are all too plentiful, most legislators still depend more on their ears for information than on their eyes.

Thus, the Report was virtually ignored by Congress which had requested it in the first place. Commissioner Howe, however, did not let the matter drop. Although the summary report issued by his own agency was a seriously compromised document, this happened rather in spite of Howe than because of him. On his own initiative, Howe decided that he needed a wider perspective on the Report than he was receiving within his own agency.

Accordingly, he invited a small panel of social scientists and educators to Washington to advise him on what response the government should make to Coleman's work. This meeting was to be confidential, and it was Howe's intention that it should be a continuing advisory group.

The meeting was held October 2 at the Dupont Plaza. All the invitees came: Henry Dyer of the Educational Testing Service; Daniel Moynihan of Harvard; Philip Hauser of the University of Chicago; Kenneth B. Clark of The City University of New York; Samuel D. Proctor of the Institute for Service to Education; and Sidney P. Marland, superintendent of Pittsburgh schools. Coleman, abroad on a sabbatical, was not invited.

On October 2, Howe opened the meeting with a review of the social-class findings and noted that there were larger achievement differences across socioeconomic levels than among racial groups. Howe said the Report indicated to him that changes in social environment would do more than changes in the physical environment in the schools. This was certainly quite a different summary of the Report than his own agency produced.

The record of the discussion that followed does not reflect well on the social scientists, however. Moynihan revealed that he was still concerned about the bureaucracy sitting on the Report: "There is a sense this is a dangerous document and a corresponding reluctance to face it if a problem is more difficult than you thought." Hauser pressed for more attention to teacher training. He was supported by Dyer, who felt Coleman's finding about teacher attitudes had not received enough attention. But most of the conversation was pedestrian, and the social scientists did not exhibit a very profound grasp of the Report. Some of them even might not have read it. By midafternoon Howe's disappointment began to show, as he appealed for some useful advice. "We have a lack of imagination," he declared.

The meeting ended with very little evidence of concrete suggestions. Almost none of the questions posed by Howe had led to any fruitful advice, even insofar as to suggest further research. At the end of the day, Howe concluded that the session had been of little value, and he never called the group together again.

THE PRESS AND THE PUNDITS

Most of the nation's mass press was misled by the summary that had been issued in July and found the full Report impenetrable when it arrived 6 weeks later. But the press (and elite journalists in particular) is sensitive to other indicators. Three articles that appeared in the fall of 1966 were instrumental in altering the consciousness of the press about the Coleman report.

The first was Coleman's own review appearing on the stands in September in *The Public Interest*. He stated his findings more vividly, raised some of the policy implications, and added the hint of intrigue that the summary was misleading (Coleman, 1966).

More influential, perhaps, because it was more widely read among journalists was Christopher Jencks's (1966) cogent review in the *New Republic*.

The third was Robert C. Nichols's (1966) analysis in the December issue of *Science*, a magazine to which more intellectually inclined journalists in Washington pay close attention. And Nichols, director of Research of the National Merit Scholarship Corporation, wrote his view in a lucid question-and-answer format. He concluded that Coleman's findings "stand like a spear pointed at the heart of the cherished American belief that equality of educational opportunity will increase the equality of intellectual achievement" (Nichols, 1966).

The Washington Post, one of the few papers to catch the significance of Coleman's Report in July, now picked up Coleman's trail more forcefully. In a December article, headlined "An Educational Time Bomb: Coleman Report Jolts Some Time-Honored Premises," the *Post*'s education editor wrote:

> The nearest thing to an educational bomb shell to come out of the Federl Government in a long time is a 737-page document known as the Coleman Report, or, more formally, "Equality of Educational Opportunity."
> . . . It has been a delayed time bomb with many of its implications just beginning to hit with full force, although a 33-page summary of the full report was released last summer.
> The massive report challenges some of the most basic premises upon which educators have traditionally operated American schools. For example, it indicates that virtually no improvement in the achievement of pupils can be traced to increased expenditures for facilities and equipment.
> It also provides convincing documentation for what have long been

perhaps only strong suspicions—for example, that slum schools have not been able to overcome the handicaps dealt to a child who is born into a poor and battered family. On the contrary, exhaustive testing shows that slum children tend to fall further behind their middle class counterparts the longer they stay in school. (Grant, 1966)

Joseph Alsop, one of the nation's most heavily syndicated columnists, joined the fray in a series of three columns in January, 1967 (Alsop, 1967a). One of Alsop's themes for some time previously had been the idea that blacks were increasingly concentrated in the big city ghettos and that it made little sense to attempt any major integration plans. He wrote that the Civil Rights Commission had made an "ass" of itself in suggesting such moves. Alsop thought President Johnson's compensatory education legislation his finest domestic achievement. In his usual understated fashion, Alsop said his reading of the Coleman Report recalled to him H. L. Mencken's opinion of pedagogues: "To hell with the 'gogues." The Coleman Report "has already done profound though still invisible harm," he concluded. To Alsop, "the Coleman Report does not address itself to the really key question: what can be achieved by separate but unequal education . . . in the sense of much better, more costly education. . . . The worst of it is that radical school improvement, now partially discredited by the wrong interpretation of the Coleman Report, is the only practical way to offer a more hopeful future to the children of the ghettos" (Alsop, 1967b). Alsop (1967d) pressed these themes further in the *New Republic*, pointing to New York's more effective schools as evidence for his argument. Alsop received a sharp retort in a later issue from Robert Schwartz, Thomas Pettigrew, and Marshall Smith (1967).

A NEW SPOKESMAN AT THE WHITE HOUSE

Accident, chance, even a touch of irrationality play a role in the development of any science, though these factors may escape the analyst in his neat search for paradigms and causal relationships. Certainly these elements marked the history of the Coleman Report, and there is perhaps no better illustration of it than the extraordinary influence that Daniel P. Moynihan had upon the Report.

Moynihan probably had more to do with the way the Report was received, analyzed, and subsequently made an instrument of policy than any social scientist other than James Coleman himself.

In addition to his interest in the Coleman Report for the additional evidence it might provide to support his theories about the breakdown in the black family, Moynihan had an instinctive response to the Coleman Report as a document that flew in the face of the conventional wisdom about the schools. And in an early and revealing commentary about the Report, he jabbed with the force of a dockworker swinging his book at the bureaucracies and educators who were complacently ignoring the Report.

There was another unscientific element, and it had particular importance when Moynihan found himself in a position to do something about the Report under the Nixon Administration. To say it was personal pique would make it sound too trifling. To call it revenge would be overdoing it. But Moynihan was smarting from his treatment under the Johnson Administration when his report on the black family was misinterpreted, and he was called a racist for his efforts. That experience provided a sharp edge to his interest in the Coleman Report.

Moynihan had heard about the Coleman Report from Professor Seymour Martin Lipset in a casual conversation at the Harvard Faculty Club during the spring of 1966. Both Lipset and Moynihan had been invited to a meeting by Douglass Cater and Joseph Califano, White House aides under President Johnson, who were seeking new ideas to refuel the Great Society. The Coleman Report had not yet been published, but it was far enough along for Lipset to inform Moynihan that it appeared to have a significant finding bearing on Moynihan's black family thesis.

Moynihan had left the government and was wearing two hats at Harvard—a professor at the Graduate School of Education and director of the Joint Center (with MIT) for Urban Affairs. He was casting about for something to do and recalled that his interest in the Coleman Report "grew partly as the response grew." With Thomas Pettigrew as co-chairman, he hit upon the idea of beginning a faculty seminar on the Coleman Report.

Thus began one of the most extended reanalyses of Coleman's work, initiated by a man who admits he knew very little about the sophisticated statistical methodology that is essential to a thorough understanding of the Report.

The seminar brought the Coleman study further into the main stream of intellectual inquiry and eventually provided significant confirmation of its major themes. Moynihan publicized the findings of the Report in his provocative fashion in a number of speeches and articles.

That would probably have been the end of Moynihan's involvement, if it had not been for some other accidents. As the 1968 presidential campaign heated up, there were rumors that Moynihan would eventually find a prominent role in Robert Kennedy's inner circle. That was not to be.

It may be that no one was more surprised than Daniel P. Moynihan, a liberal Democrat, to find himself sitting in the White House in January, 1969, as the key adviser to President Nixon on urban affairs. He sat, in fact, at the same desk that Douglass Cater had occupied as President Johnson's principal assistant for educational affairs. Cater had taken a dim view of the Coleman Report.

In this role, Moynihan was the principal author of President Nixon's message on education reform on March 3, 1970. The message was grounded on research evidence as no previous education message from the White House had been. It was the Coleman Report writ large. And in terms of officially stated policy—not, of course, the same thing as an actual change of existing law and practice—it was a dramatic reversal of the whole thrust of the federal education programs of the Kennedy–Johnson years. The message was a primer for the American people on the meaning of the Coleman Report, and from the first line, the emphasis was on reform and the need for a new yardstick by which to assess the nation's schools:

American education is in urgent need of reform.

A nation justly proud of the dedicated efforts of its millions of teachers and educators must join them in a searching reexamination of our entire approach to learning.

We must stop thinking of primary and secondary education as the school system alone—when we now have reason to believe that young people may be learning much more *outside* school than they learn in school.

What makes a "good" school? The old answer was a school that maintained high standards of plant and equipment; that had a reasonable number of children per classroom; whose teachers had good college and often graduate training; a school that kept up to date with new curriculum developments, and was alert to new techniques in instruction. This was a fair enough definition so long as it was assumed that there was a direct connection between these "school characteristics" and the actual amount of learning that takes place in a school.

Years of educational research, culminating in the Equal Educational Opportunity Survey of 1966, have, however, demonstrated that this direct, uncomplicated relationship does not exist.

Apart from the general public interest in providing teachers an honorable and well paid professional career, there is only one important question to be asked about education: *What do the children learn?*

The *outcome* of schooling—what children learn—is profoundly different for different groups of children and different parts of the country. Although we do not seem to understand just what it is in one school or school system that produces a different outcome from another, one conclusion is inescapable: *We do not yet have equal educational opportunity in America.*

The purpose of the National Institute of Education would be to begin the serious, systematic search for new knowledge needed to make educational opportunity truly equal.

The National Institute of Education
   As the first step toward reform, we need a coherent approach to research and experimentation. Local schools need an objective national body to evaluate new departures in teaching that are being conducted here and abroad and a means of disseminating information about projects that show promise.
   The National Institute of Education would be located in the Department of Health, Education, and Welfare under the Assistant Secretary for Education, with a permanent staff of outstanding scholars from such disciplines as psychology, biology and the social sciences, as well as education.
   Here are a few of the areas the National Institute of Education would explore:
   (a) *Compensatory Education.* The most glaring shortcoming in American education today continues to be the lag in essential learning skills in large numbers of children of poor families.
   In the last decade, the Government launched a series of ambitious, idealistic, and costly programs for the disadvantaged, based on the assumption that extra resources would equalize learning opportunity and eventually help eliminate poverty.
   In some instances, such programs have dramatically improved children's educational achievement. In many cases, the programs have provided important auxiliary services such as medical care and improved nutrition. They may also have helped prevent some children from falling even further behind.
   However, the best available evidence indicates that most of the compensatory education programs have not measurably helped poor children catch up.
   While our understanding of what works in compensatory education is still inadequate, we do know that the social and economic environment which surrounds a child at home and outside of school probably has more effect on what he learns than the quality of the school he now attends. Therefore, the major expansion of income support proposed in the Family Assistance Plan should also have an important educational effect. (White House Press Office, 1970)

Even this primer was not without error, however. At one point Nixon noted: "We will often find our most devoted, most talented, hardest working teachers in those very schools where the general level of achievement is lowest." The Coleman Report showed the opposite.

More importantly, one can ask whether this was a triumph of policy or just a very convenient fit between available research and the political goals Nixon wished to achieve. Nixon was an economy-minded president, and a convenient outcome of the line of argument in his speech was that it required little in the way of funds and justified budget cutting in growing federal-aid-to-education programs. Coleman himself, obviously pleased that *his* message had finally reached the White House after a 4-year delay, was among those who said, "We'll just have to wait and see if the speech is not just a simple rationalization for spending less money."

The editorial reaction to the President's message was highly skeptical. *The New York Times* ("memo entitled education," 1970) found the message "replete with delayed action rhetoric." And *The Washington Post*, which like the *Times* had been a booster of the Great Society education programs, saw it as "a political play, a stall, an evasion" ("memo entitled the never-never land," 1970). In addition *The Washington Post* (1970) editorial revealed that the writer had no basic understanding of the Coleman Report by such bombast as, "It is indisputable that a high ratio of pupils to teacher impedes learning."

Spokesmen for the National Education Association and other lobbies were similarly incensed. "The President seems to think the schools can wait while somebody does more research or sits on a commission," said a leader of the Education Association. "But we don't have the time to wait for that sort of thing any more" ("memo entitled delayed impact," 1970).

How much of Nixon's embrace of the Coleman Report was political expediency and how much was the result of Moynihan's advocacy of the idea as a powerful piece of evidence that could not be discounted. The answer cannot be given with much certitude. But assuming it was all expediency, what would be the point of developing the argument in such detail? Why risk alienating the powerful educational bureaucracies who do not like being told their rationales for huge federal aid-to-education programs are a house of cards? If one is using research merely as rationalization, one does not need to develop such a detailed argument.

The irony of the President's message was that in the area where he leaned most heavily on the Coleman Report, he was least successful in achieving his goals. The Johnsonian education legislation had become bread-and-butter school programs in every Congressional district in the country, and Congress seldom shuts down popular bakeries.

A month later *The New York Times* (Semple, 1971) reported: "With considerable reluctance, President Nixon signed today the most expensive education legislation ever passed by Congress—a bill authorizing $26.4 billion over three years for elementary and secondary education."

Whereas the Coleman Report was virtually unknown in the Johnson years, it now was not only known but argued about. Coleman made several appearances on Capitol Hill that spring, and he appeared in the news so often that *The New York Times* ran a "Man in the News" profile about him.

The kind of visibility Coleman and his research had achieved in

Washington, DC, gave the Report more weight elsewhere. But it had already gained a firm foothold. Education writers on even small dailies knew about the Report in at least a rudimentary way. It was cited so frequently, if not always accurately, that those who had a hand in educational policy at any level—and who felt an elemental sense of intellectual responsibility—were compelled to inform themselves about it. Coleman was asked to advise many local school boards, and the Report's influence also grew as it was introduced as evidence in the courts.

JAMES COLEMAN AND THE "NIXON STRATEGY"

Whether the policy on school desegregation was ever as muddied in President Nixon's mind as it seemed at the outset may remain a mystery even to his closest advisers. But the policy gave every appearance of being in flux during the first year of Nixon's Administration and was further confused by much of the press's analysis of Nixon's "southern Strategy."

In a word, Nixon's strategy was in many ways to take the zeal out of the federal enforcement effort. In effecting this strategy, the Coleman Report, and Coleman himself played an important role, although the implications of the Report for integration were initially soft-pedaled by the White House in an ironic twist of the use Coleman had been put to under the Johnson Administration. Under the Johnson Administration, the Coleman Report had been trumpeted to the point of distortion by both the Department of Health, Education, and Welfare (HEW) and the Civil Rights Commission to make it as powerful a weapon as they could in the desegregation effort.

Final tabulation of HEW's second national survey of racial enrollment showed an astonishing result. The numbers of black students in white-majority schools in the deep South more than doubled from 1968 to 1970, far outstripping the North in this regard. In 1968, 18% of the South's black pupils were enrolled in predominantly white schools, and two years later the figure had jumped to 39%.

Compared to the South's 39%, only 28% of black pupils in the North and West attended predominately white schools.

These were dramatic results, but they were not ballyhooed by the Nixon Administration. On the contrary, jubilation and credit-seeking were eschewed. This was the first point of the Administration's low-profile strategy: Lower the rhetoric that would antagonize the South and take as much sting out of the communication process as possible. The second was a shift of personnel in the bureaucracy designed to facilitate that communication, combined with a political thrust to enlist moderate biracial leadership in the effort within the southern states. Third, the emphasis was shifted from enforcement and punishment to enticement and reward—accompanied by an effort to provide financial aid to ease the desegregation process. And finally, the overall strategy was to shift as much as possible the burden of edicts and compulsion to the courts.

President Nixon's major education message on March 3, 1970 made only passing reference to desegregation. The following day, while the White House policy appeared to be in an unsettled state, John D. Ehrlichman, assistant to the president for domestic affairs and the president's chief domestic adviser, met informally with reporters at breakfast. He leaked the news that the White House would issue a major policy statement on school integration because there was "a lot of confusion in some people's minds."

A week later, a liberal presidential adviser, Leonard Garment, called Coleman on Nixon's instructions and asked him to be a consultant to a new Cabinet Committee on Desegregation. He went to work with characteristic energy and began to counterbalance more conservative forces that were then shaping the forthcoming message. On March 19, Coleman spent several hours talking directly with the President in his forceful but unassuming way. A White House official who was impressed with his intellectual performance joked about his professional style of dress: "You think he might have gotten his pants pressed before he went in to see the President."

Nixon's policy was outlined in an 8,000-word statement (the president's statement, 1970) on school desegregation on March 24, 1970. It was a document of a centrist president, and it had something in it for Strom Thurmond, Roy Wilkins, and even black separatist Roy Innis.

But its major themes were keyed to assuaging the South, rewarding desegregation efforts, and putting the responsibility for increased busing on the courts. Nixon went out of his way to assure the South that he understood their difficulties and that desegregation could no longer be regarded as a sectional problem; in his follow-up message two months later he stressed that 500 Northern school districts would soon be under review to determine their compliance with the law.

In his review of developments in the courts, he generally indicated he would use strong Presidential initiative only when the Supreme Court had spoken. He regarded as "untypical" those lower court decisions that "have raised widespread fears that the nation might face disruption of the public education: that wholesale compulsory busing may be ordered and the neighborhood school virtually doomed."

In his statement of policy there was more reassurance for ruffled southern egos: "In devising local compliance plans, primary weight should be given to the considered judgment of local school boards—provided they act in good faith." He gently slapped zealous federal enforcement officials: "Federal advice and assistance will be made available on request, but federal officials should not go beyond the requirements of law in attempting to impose their own judgment on the local school districts."

He emphasized his opposition to busing in order "to achieve racial balance" and pointedly noted that while the Supreme Court had required the South to take affirmative steps to eliminate segregated schools "root and branch . . . at once," "this positive integration . . . does not necessarily have to result in 'racial balance' throughout the system."

The impact of Coleman's research and his work with the Cabinet committee was evident in two ways. The message contained the first clear Nixon statement of the educational benefit of integration, although it was buried in the middle of the text and explained in a manner to strongly dissociate it from the idea of racial balances:

> Available data on the educational effects of integration are neither definitive nor comprehensive. But such data as we have suggest strongly that under appropriate conditions, racial integration in the classroom can be a significant factor in improving the quality of education for the disadvantaged. At the same time the data lead us into several more of the complexities that surround the desegregation issue.
>
> For one thing, they serve as a reminder that, from an education standpoint, to approach school questions solely in terms of race is to go astray. The data tells us that in educational terms, the significant factor is not race but rather the educational environment in the home—and indeed, that the single most important educational factor in a school is the kind of home environment its pupils come from. As a general rule, children from families whose home environment encourages learning—whatever their race—are higher achievers; those from homes offering little encouragement are lower achievers. . . .
>
> The data strongly suggest, also, that in order for the positive benefits of integration to be achieved, the school must have a majority of children from environments that encourage learning—recognizing, again, that the key factor is not race but the kind of home the child comes from. The greater concentration of pupils whose homes encourage learning—of whatever race—the higher the achievement levels not only of those pupils, but also of others in the same school.
>
> Students learn from students. The reverse is also true: The greater concentration of pupils from homes that discourage learning, the lower the achievement levels of all.
>
> We should bear very carefully in mind, therefore, the distinctions between educational difficulty as a result of race and educational difficulty as a result of social or economic levels, of family background, of cultural patterns, or simply of bad schools. Providing a better education for the disadvantaged requires a more sophisticated approach than mere racial mathematics.

Coleman's second major input came through his advice to the Cabinet Committee on School Desegregation on new ways to achieve integration. The President noted:

> Most public discussion of overcoming racial isolation centers on such concerns as compulsory "busing"—taking children out of the schools they would normally attend, and forcing them instead to attend others more distant, often in strange or even hostile neighborhoods. Massive "busing" is seen by some as the only alternative to massive racial isolation.
>
> However, a number of new education ideas are being developed, designed to provide the educational benefits of integration without depriving the student of his own neighborhood school.
>
> For example, rather than attempting dislocation of whole schools, a portion of a child's educational activities may be shared with children from other schools. Some of his education is in a "home-base" school, but some outside it.
>
> This "outside learning" is in settings that are designed neither as black nor white and sometimes in settings that are not even in traditional school buildings. It may range all the way from intensive work in reading to training in technical skills, and to joint efforts such as drama and athletics.
>
> By bringing children together on neutral territory friction may be dispelled; by limiting it to part-time activities no one would be deprived of his own neighborhood school; and the activities themselves provide the children with better education.
>
> This sort of innovative approach demonstrates that the alternative is not limited to perpetuating racial isolation on the one hand, and massive disrupting of existing school patterns on the other. Without uprooting students, devices of this kind can provide an additional educational experience within an integrated setting. The child gains both ways.

A day after reading the President's full statement, Coleman sat down and wrote a letter to *The New York Times*. Coleman had obviously pushed his views forcefully within the White House policy staff. He saw that he had won half a loaf. In a brief and eloquent letter (Coleman, 1970), he appealed to the President to adopt a more "farseeing" and historic policy:

> The President's message on school desegregation has been subject to widely differing interpretations. The reason for these differences, I believe, is that the message takes two major policy positions, which go in opposite directions.
>
> The first is that the Administration will limit its enforcement of school desegregation to what is described as the *de jure* component of racial segregation in districts that have maintained dual systems and will thus disregard the *de facto* component of segregation in these districts. This policy is applicable principally to Southern cities. The second major policy position which goes in the opposite direction, is that the Administration regards racial integration of schools as a highly desirable social goal, and

will commit the major portion of $1.5 billion toward aiding the implementation of school integration.

I strongly disagree with the first of these policies, and I strongly agree with the second. The first is an affirmation of the recently emerging Administration policy toward enforcement of desegregation, and I believe it to be unwise.

The rationale for this policy presumably is as follows: Why should Southern schools undergo desegregation which is not regarded as illegal in the North? I would give two answers: first, in a system with a history of legal racial separation, it is not possible to distinguish *de facto* from *de jure* segregation. Second, recent court decisions have begun to regard Northern *de facto* segregation as illegal under the 14th Amendment—correctly, I believe—and there are many signs that they will increasingly do so, even across school system lines.

A more farseeing policy would have anticipated the extension to the North of enforcement now being applied in the South rather than limit enforcement in the South to current pattern in the North.

The second policy direction, which I strongly support, is a new one for any Administration. No President in the sixteen years since the Brown case has seen fit to commit resources to the goal of effective and stable racial integration in American schools.

It is important for two reasons to bring about stable racial integration in schools: to create school environments that provide equal opportunity to learn, regardless of race, income, or residence; and second, to induce those habits of thought and attitude among black and white children that are cohesive rather than divisive—a development that this country sorely needs.

Finally, after sixteen years, there is some commitment of resources by a President of the United States to this goal. I strongly applaud this, just as strongly as I oppose the other half of the message. Which of these two policies will ultimately be more effective is difficult at this point to determine.

But it is possible, I believe, to help shape the outcome: to work against that part which represents a backward step in enforcement of desegregation in dual systems of the South; and to work for that part which commits the Federal Government to encouraging and strengthening school integration, with serious application of resources.

Coleman's views were also reiterated and amplified in Congress in the hearings that began a month later under Senator Walter Mondale's Subcommittee on Equal Educational Opportunity.

The key legislation that translated the President's general policy statement of March into specific, money-backed programs emerged two months later. The Emergency School Aid Act was announced by the White House on May 21, and it very clearly put the emphasis where Coleman hoped it would. Most of the money was now earmarked for assisting schools undergoing court-ordered desegregation (primarily in the South) and to encourage voluntary plans to achieve more integration in the North.

It also provided some funds for ghetto schools, but even here the emphasis was "for special interracial or intercultural educational programs," although it would also allow, "where these proved impracticable, for unusually promising pilot or demonstration programs to help overcome the adverse educational impact of racial isolation [i.e., compensatory education in segregated northern schools]" (White House, 1970).

The bill also included a special sweetener for the South that meant districts under court-ordered desegregation plans would receive twice as much money, because eligible pupils would then be "double-counted" for the purpose of determining their share of the money. This was the frosting on the Nixon's reward strategy.

The Administration's strategy of putting the stick in the hands of the courts, which was evident to many careful observers months earlier, was formally announced in August by the new secretary of Health, Education, and Welfare, Elliot Richardson. "The Department of Health, Education, and Welfare has ceased cutting off federal funds and is supporting court action instead in dealing with the remaining hard-core holdouts on school integration," Richardson said. And there were indications that the courts might yet provide the most significant forum for Coleman's findings. For Coleman had begun to be cited in significant court opinions in both the North and the South.

THE SECOND GENERATION OF COLEMAN REPORTS

In the next decade *Equality of Educational Opportunity* continued to exert a broad influence through the courts, in the hands of educational policymakers, and in the scholarly community. In 1981, 15 years after its original publication, it was cited 120 times in the journals surveyed by the *Social Science Citation Index*. It influenced scores of studies on inequality and educational opportunity. It led to Coleman being described ("Stoning the prophet," 1981) as "the most widely known of contemporary American sociologists." The report came to be called Coleman I, after Coleman authored two other major reports that were seen in part as reinterpretations of his original findings. Debate about both James Coleman and the reports continued. The controversy—fueled by new evidence and Coleman's response to it—followed two main policy implications of the 1966 report: The first had to do with the finding that poor black children do better in schools that are predominantly white and middle class—this was widely used by integrationists to promote and later defend "forced busing." The second line of debate flowed from the finding that school quality as traditionally measured did not account for much of the variance in the outcomes of schooling, which was interpreted (too simply) as "schools don't matter."

Remember, however, that the Coleman I Report did not contain any policy recommendations when it was published in 1966. In an interview for *The High School Journal* ("Conversation," 1979), Coleman took pains to stress at three separate points that the report "was a study of existing conditions, and the results were not intended to be used as direct inputs to policy."

As the research findings were introduced in court cases and considered by school boards and legislators, the Report was cited in behalf of a variety of policies. The primary policy which seemed to be supported by socioeconomic findings of the Report, however, was the highly emotional issue of busing. Throughout the United States busing became the primary means of integrating schools and of providing the opportunity for low-income black children to attend school with middle-income white children. James Coleman became so associated with this policy that *Time* magazine ("Coleman on the griddle," 1976) referred to him as "a sort of godfather to busing."

It is not surprising, therefore, that the probusing community was stunned in the spring of 1975 with the news that James Coleman (1975) had issued a new report whose findings suggested that involuntary busing was resulting in resegregation because of the "white flight" from the cities to surrounding suburbs and the placement of white children in private schools to avoid the integrated public school system. The report, *Trends in School Segregation, 1968–1973*, analyzed data from the Office for Civil Rights on the percentage of white students in the school systems of the 20 largest U.S. cities over a 5-year period.

In it and in subsequent articles, Coleman stated that busing was not a problem in smaller school systems and where black students were assigned to predominantly white schools, but outmigration occurred when white students were bussed to predominantly black schools in black neighborhoods. Consequently, two-way busing, or compulsory assignment of white children to schools in black neighborhoods, had not worked. Coleman (1977) concluded from this study that the only form of busing which would have a chance of succeeding was voluntary busing, and his subsequent policy recommendations reflected this view. For Coleman the critical issue was that of the compulsory nature of most desegregation plans. Increasingly, he sided with antibusing groups when the issue was involuntary busing.

Despite this opinion, Coleman did not retreat from the *Equality of Educational Opportunity* finding that poor black children achieve better in a classroom with middle-class children. As an alternative to compulsory busing, Coleman advocated the development of "magnet schools" which would accept 15% of their students from outside the school district on a voluntary basis. Parents would have an incentive to bus their children in order to qualify for special enrichment programs in the magnet schools.

Trends in School Segregation, also called Coleman II by some writers, was reported under the headline "Second Thoughts" in *Newsweek* (Sheils & Comper, 1975). Although Coleman had not retreated from his position that a mix in socioeconomic groups was important for the achievement levels of minority students, he was generally charged with having abandoned integration. The distinction Coleman was trying to make between beneficial desegregation through voluntary involvement and destructive desegregation through mandatory busing was largely ignored. For example, Charles V. Willie (1975) a Harvard sociologist, wrote:

> James Coleman is urging the nation to go slow on school desegregation to prevent white flight from cities. What Coleman and his supporters are doing is urging this nation to violate its Constitution, as if a system of racial segregation could coexist with the legal requirements for integration. (p. 46)

Willie went on to criticize Coleman for viewing the benefit of integration in a racist manner:

> Coleman has ignored the mutual benefits of integration and has conceptualized it as a one-directional benefit for blacks and other racial minorities. . . . Coleman expresses concern about white flight from the cities but not about white segregation in the suburbs. The former he sees as a threat to the education of blacks; he is silent about the latter as a threat to the education of whites. (p. 46)

Another criticism which developed as a consequence of the *Trends* report and Coleman's presentation of it was the charge that Coleman was now mixing his research findings with his own pronouncements on education policy. *The Washington Post* education editor, Noel Epstein (1977) in an article titled "The Scholar as Confuser," later reprinted in *Society*, wrote about the reaction to *Trends in School Segregation*, saying:

> The reason Coleman's message has been misunderstood is that the scholar has been engaging in a perilous exercise that is not uncommon among social scientists or for that matter, among their brethren in the physical sciences. He has, as he will tell you himself, been mixing rhetoric and research in many recent pronouncements, and few people know which is which. . . . He has seriously affected our debate on a critical national issue. His misconstrued words are being echoed in the Congress, the presidential primaries, the corridors of the bureaucracy, the meetings and streets of volatile places like Louisville and Boston.

Of course, a social scientist who avoided making any interpretations of his data or who refused to reflect on the policy implications of his work would be naive at best. In Coleman's case, however, his unabashed approach to highly sensitive policy questions, combined with his career as White House policy adviser and frequent Congressional witness, gave special weight to his pronouncements—particularly if he seemed to be changing his mind. Was this a scholar looking at new data, or was Coleman bending to new political pressures? In our view, there is no doubt that it was the former; but not everyone in the scholarly community would agree.

Hence, it was a major news event when in 1978 Coleman appeared to reject his own earlier findings that low-income black children perform better in middle-class classrooms. Under the heading "Desegregation Discounted, Scant Benefits Found For Black Pupils" (1978), *The Washington Post* noted: "Sociologist James S. Coleman now says it is a 'mistaken belief' that black children learn better in integrated classrooms."

Subsequent commentaries in *The Washington Post* (1978) and in the *New Republic* (Marshall, 1978) discounted his change of opinion, arguing that the 1966 report's findings on the percent of improvement among blacks attending middle-class schools was terribly small in any event and that desegregation was not done primarily to improve achievement but because it was morally right. Unfortunately, Coleman's major point (that mandatory desegregation, carried out primarily through busing plans, did not seem to improve achievement) was for the most part overlooked. In a later interview, asked whether he had made an about-face, Coleman ("Conversation with. . . ," 1979) replied:

> The media coverage of the hearings chose approximately two and a half minutes out of extended testimony before the committee and greatly simplified my position. I made no about face. I still believe that the conclusions that we reported in the 1966 study are accurate for schools at that time, before major desegregation actions had taken place. Subsequent studies of achievement in districts that have desegregated show considerably less achievement benefit for black children than was evident in our data. . . . I wholeheartedly support policies which will promote long-term, stable, and the important consideration is stable—school desegregation. (p. 57)

PUBLIC AND PRIVATE SCHOOLS—"SCHOOLS DO MATTER"

The second persistent, if oversimplified, point in Coleman I was that schools don't matter. This view remained strong enough to provide the major contrasting commentary between Coleman I and his 1981 report, *Public and Private Schools* (Coleman, Hoffer, & Kilgore, 1981). Both a *Wall*

Street Journal and a *Washington Post* commentary indicated that unlike the 1966 report, the new study showed that "schools can make a big difference after all." The 1981 Report, completed under contract for the National Center for Education Statistics as part of a larger study, *High School and Beyond*, produced such a dramatic reaction from the press and educational organizations that it, too, has been referred to frequently as Coleman II. *Public and Private Schools* analyzed responses from 58,000 students in 1,015 public and private secondary schools. Comparisons were made among public schools, Roman Catholic schools, and other private schools on the racial and economic composition of the schools within each of the sectors, the resources and functioning of the schools, and the outcomes for students.

The Report concluded that the Catholic or parochial schools produced better cognitive outcomes for poor blacks than public schools, and that they provided a more disciplined environment. The authors also concluded that Catholic schools more nearly approximated the "common school" ideal of American education than do public schools in that they were more racially and economically integrated than were public schools, and student aspirations differed less by social class origin. In addition to these comparisons, the authors also concluded that a policy of tuition tax credits would facilitate the use of private schools by minorities and lower-income students and consequently would decrease segregation.

The Report received wide press coverage immediately in both the newspapers and news magazines. The emphasis of most of the first news reports was on the superior schooling provided by the private institutions largely as a result of greater discipline and higher academic demands. However, after the Report had been presented and critiqued by a scholarly panel at a Washington meeting organized by the sponsoring agency, the controversial nature of the Report quickly surfaced. Public school supporters began to attack the Report and James Coleman. Albert Shanker (1981) of the United Federation of Teachers wrote:

> Like Coleman I, Coleman II leads us to very wrong conclusions. For example, the public schools are made to look worse because Coleman knocks points off their achievement to take into account the lower scores which dropouts would have made had they remained in school. . . . It's not hard to see how Coleman achieved his results. It's hard to understand why he wasted his time, or why anybody would pay attention to the obvious. Just as there is a much higher percentage of sick people in hospitals, there's a much higher percentage of good students in private schools, because if you admit good students, reject poor students, and expel those who don't meet standards, you're bound to end up with better students than schools which accept everyone.

The Columbus (Ohio) school superintendent, Joseph L. Davis, said: "Once again James Coleman has produced an opportunistic piece of research. I find it difficult to believe that his findings can be stated with the apparent level of confidence he has attributed to them. . . . Coleman has tied his research wagon to the private school star" (Sobovich, 1981).

At the American Educational Research Association meeting in Los Angeles, Coleman was criticized both on methodological grounds and for having made the Report public prior to the opportunity for extended scholarly review. These criticisms were further developed by the academic community in special issues of the *Harvard Education Review* and *Phi Delta Kappan* in November, 1981, and in the Spring, 1982 edition of the *Sociology of Education*.

Politically, the Report was published at a time to lend support to President Reagan's effort to have tuition tax credits adopted by Congress. In some quarters, this raised the question of whether the research results had been made to fit Coleman's preconceptions, because he was seen as a supporter of aid to parochial schools. In a response to an editorial in *The New York Times* which implied as much, Coleman (Coleman, 1981) said that he did not favor tuition tax credits and that while personal values do influence some aspects of analysis it is far more critical for the analysis to be correct. However, in an interview, Coleman indicated that were he to write the Report again, he would focus more on the finding that "good public schools do just as well as those in the private sector," and he would have addressed the question of how public policy could help schools in both sectors be more effective (Fiske, 1981).

There can be little doubt that James Coleman came to occupy a critical position as both social scientist and, eventually, as a policy actor as well as adviser. He did not shrink from the role, and some would say he grew to relish it. Certainly, he cast *Public and Private Schools* in the most provocative and policy-oriented language in contrast to the style of *Equality of Educational Opportunity*, which was tedious and circumspect. Historically, both in the development of social science and of federal social policy in education, he occupies a unique position. No one was more aware of that than Coleman (1976) himself:

> After the discipline of physics had come to be seen as a powerful force in society—as a result of the creation of the first atomic bomb—there was a long period before society learned that physicists' opinions on matters of nuclear policy were not to be regarded as conclusive, that their technical skills did not provide perfect wisdom in matters in which physics intersected with public policy. I believe we are in a similar period now in social science, not because the social sciences enjoyed success comparable to the discovery of atomic power, but because of the power that social research and social scientists in some cases have had in the creation of policy. Only

slowly does the general public come to realize that the technical capabilities of the social scientist do not make his opinions conclusive on issues where social science intersects with policy. But in time that realization does come, just as in time there comes a broader set of skills by non social scientists to draw their own implications from research results. And as these changes occur, the role of the social scientist in social policy will come to be less important, even as the role of social research in informing public policy becomes more important. (p. 338)

Given his belief that at the present state of development of social science few were as qualified to draw policy implications from his work as he was himself, and given the early manipulation and misinterpretation of *Equal Education Opportunity* in 1966, Coleman apparently concluded that he had a duty to act as he did. Hence, Coleman took an increasingly larger role in the politics of the Coleman Reports. In 1966, Coleman's major problem with *Equality of Educational Opportunity* was to rescue the Report from the misleading summary issued by the Johnson Administration. In the case of the Coleman II Reports—both *Trends in School Segregation* and *Public and Private Schools*—the major problem was to defend the reports from attacks by other social scientists, integrationists, and public school advocates who disagreed with the now bluntly stated policy implication of those reports. Some would argue that the quality of his research declined as it became more sharply focused on policy questions. We do not have the space here to rehearse the scholarly arguments in any detail. And the verdict is not in. But we suspect that in the end, Coleman will be confirmed in the large outlines of his work and that it will set the terms of the debate for some years to come.

REFERENCES

Alsop, J. (1967a, January 23). Coleman and Plowden. *The Washington Post.*

Alsop, J. (1967b, January 25). To hell with the Gogues. *The Washington Post.*

Alsop, J. (1967c, January 27). A modest proposal. *The Washington Post.*

Alsop, J. (1967d, July 22). No more nonsense about ghetto education. *The New Republic*, 18–23.

Bryson, L. (1952). Notes on theory of advice. In R. Merton (Ed.), *Reader in bureaucracy*, New York: Free Press.

Coleman, J. (1966, summer). Educational dilemmas: Equal schools or equal students. *The Public Interest*, 70–75.

Coleman, J. (1970, April 5). Message on education: A letter. *The New York Times.*

Coleman, J. (1971). *Equality of educational opportunity: An introduction.* Testimony before the Senate Select Committee on Equal Educational Opportunity, Ninety-first Congress, 2nd Session, Committee Print, 1971, Part 1A, pp. 88ff.

Coleman, J. S. (1975). *Trends in school segregation, 1968–1973.* Washington, DC: Urban Institute.

Coleman, J. S. (1976, summer). Social science: The public disenchantment. *American Scholar,* p. 338.

Coleman, J. S. (1977, May). Population stability and equal rights. *Society,* p. 35.

Coleman, J. S. (1981, April 19). It's how private schools are better than courts. *The New York Times.*

Coleman, J. S., Campbell, E. Q., Hobson, C. J., McPartland, J., Mood, A. M., Weinfeld, F. D., & York, R. L. (1966). *Equality of educational opportunity.* Washington, DC: U.S. Government Printing Office.

Coleman, J. S., Hoffer, T., & Kilgore, S. (1981). *Public and private schools.* Chicago: NORC.

Coleman on the griddle. (1976, April 12). *Time,* p. 79.

The Coleman Report—Again. (1978, September 21). *The Washington Post.*

Conversation with Dr. James S. Coleman. (1979, November). *High School Journal,* p. 49.

Desegregation discounted, scant benefits found for black pupils. (1978, September 18). *The Washington Post.*

Downs, A. (1966). *Inside bureaucracy.* Boston: Little-Brown.

Epstein, N. (1976, February 15). The scholar as confuser. *The Washington Post.*

Epstein, N. (1977, May). The scholar as confuser. *Society,* 36–38.

Fiske, E. B. (1981, April 26). School study said to fail to emphasize main point. *The New York Times.*

Goodman, L. (undated). Memo written at the U.S. Office of Education.

Grant, G. (1966, December 26). An educational time bomb. *The Washington Post.*

Herbers, J. (1966, July 2). *New York Times.*

Jencks, C. S. (1966, October 1). Education: The racial gap. *The New Republic,* October 1, 1966, 21–26.

Memo entitled delayed impact. (1970, April 16). *Newsweek.*

Memo entitled education, why not now? (1970, March 7). *The New York Times.*

Memo entitled the never-never land of education. (1970, March 7). *The Washington Post.*

Marshall, E. (1978, September 30). Coleman recants. *The New Republic,* p. 18.

Moynihan, D. P. (1968). Sources of Resistance to the Coleman Report. *Harvard Educational Review, 38*(1), 23–35.

Nichols, R. C. (1966, December 9). Schools and the disadvantaged. *Science, 154,* 1312–1314.

Office of the White House Press Secretary. (1970, May 21). President's message to Congress accompanying *The Emergency School Aid Act of 1970.*

The president's statement on school desegregation. (1970, March 25). *The New York Times,* p. 26.

Schwartz, R., Pettigrew, T. F., & Smith, M. (1967, September 23). Fake panaceas for ghetto education. *The New Republic.* 16–19.

Semple, R. B., Jr. (1971, April 14). Nixon signs education bill with reluctance. *The New York Times.*

Seppy, T. (1966, July 2). Article written by Associated Press and appeared in *Biloxi [MI] Herald.*

Shanker, A. (1981, April 12). Which Coleman Report do we believe? *The New York Times.*

Sheils, M., & Comper, D. (1975, June 23). Second thoughts. *Newsweek,* p. 56.

Sobovich, R. (1981, April 7). Report backing private schools rekindles controversy. *Columbus Evening Dispatch*.

Stoning the prophet. (1981, May 9). *America*, p. 376.

White House Press Office. (1970, March 3). Memo entitled Message on education reform.

Willie, C. H. (1975, December). *Ebony*, p. 46.

Two

The Obscenity and Pornography Report

PAUL BENDER

Arizona State University College of Law

In 1967 the Congress of the United States established a federal Commission on Obscenity and Pornography "whose purpose shall be, after a thorough study which shall include a study of the causal relationship of [obscenity and pornography] to antisocial behavior, to recommend advisable, appropriate, effective, and constitutional means to deal effectively with [the] traffic in obscenity and pornography" (P.L. 90–100, 81 Stat. 255, 1967). The Commission consisted of 18 members appointed by then President Lyndon Johnson.[1] It began work in July, 1968, and issued its final report and recommendations in September, 1970.

The most prominent—as well as highly controversial—Commission recommendation was that "federal, state and local legislation prohibiting the sale, exhibition, or distribution of sexual materials to consenting adults should be repealed" (Report of the Commission on Obscenity and Pornography, 1970, p. 51, hereafter referred to as "Report"). This recommendation was based in large part on the Commission's finding that "extensive empirical investigation, both by the Commission and by others, provides no evidence that exposure to or use of explicit sexual materials play a significant role in the causation of social and individual harms, such as crime, delinquency, sexual or nonsexual deviancy or severe emotional disturbance" ("Report," p. 52). The Commission also

---

[1]One of Johnson's original appointees, Judge (and former Senator) Kenneth Keating, resigned during the Nixon administration to become U.S. ambassador to India. He was replaced by Nixon's appointment of Charles Keating, the founder of the antipornography group, Citizens for Decent Literature.

affirmatively endorsed legislation prohibiting the distribution of certain explicit sexual materials to children and legislation prohibiting the public display or unsolicited mailing of such materials ("Report," pp. 56, 60). Under the heading of "positive approaches," the Commission recommended that "a massive sex education effort be launched" ("Report," p. 48).

I served (in a part-time capacity) as general counsel to the Obscenity Commission, participated in most of the Commission's deliberations, and assisted in drafting the Commission's final report and recommendations. In what follows, I will try to describe briefly the process by which the Commission arrived at its recommendations and to include some observations about the strengths, weaknesses, and degree of success of the entire endeavor.

Some background in the history and constitutional status of obscenity laws is necessary to understand the questions and the task that faced the Commission at the outset of its work. Standard general obscenity laws in the U.S.—i.e., laws that broadly prohibit the sale, distribution, and in some cases possession of written or pictorial material because of its "obscene" sexual content—mostly date from the second half of the nineteenth century. Prior to that time, obscenity prohibitions were not especially common in the U.S. or elsewhere. In the United States and England, such prohibitions generally applied primarily to antireligious sexual materials; the offense was closely akin to blasphemy and had more to do with that irreverent quality than with sexual eroticism. However, in the latter 1800s Victorian morality, the development of inexpensive methods of printing materials for mass distribution, and the intense efforts of zealots like Anthony Comstock all combined to support the development of laws in the U.S. that sought to ban the distribution of certain written and pictorial materials solely because of their explicit sexual content. By the end of the 1800s, almost every state had enacted such a general obscenity prohibition. So had the U.S. federal government (within areas of federal jurisdiction, such as interstate transportation and the use of the mails). Such legislation continued to exist up to the time of the creation of the Obscenity Commission by Congress in 1967.

On the face of things, standard general obscenity laws might be thought to conflict directly with constitutional principles protecting speech and other forms of expression from governmental censorship. The First Amendment to the U.S. Constitution provides that "Congress shall make no law . . . abridging the freedom of speech, or of the press. . . ." The Supreme Court has held that this protection also limits the activities of state and local governments (through its incorporation into the due process clause of the Constitution's Fourteenth Amendment). The printed word has always been thought to be protected by First Amendment principles, and it has come to be equally clearly recognized that pictorial works—including photographs and films—are constitutionally protected as well. Nor is First Amendment protection restricted to "political" speech (whatever that may mean); the Amendment protects works of fiction, aesthetic works, and entertainments. Since obscenity thus usually takes the form of constitutionally protected speech, laws banning it because of its content (in the case of obscenity because of its sexually explicit content) would appear constitutional questionable, at the very least.

Yet the U.S. Supreme Court, throughout its relatively expansive development of First Amendment principles during the first half of the twentieth century, always appeared to assume that obscenity prohibitions did *not* violate basic free speech doctrines. The Court finally explicitly so decided in 1957 (10 years before the creation of the Obscenity Commission) in a landmark case called *Roth v. United States* (1957). The First Amendment, of course (despite its seemingly unequivocal language), has not generally been regarded as an *absolute* prohibition upon government censorship. Even speech of a type that clearly falls within the protection of the Amendment—advocacy of dissenting political views, for example—can be suppressed or restricted under standard constitutional theory when sufficiently compelling governmental justifications are shown to be present—as, for example, when it is proved that "subversive" advocacy creates a "clear and present danger" of insurrection or revolution.[2] The Supreme Court, however, did not take this "clear and present danger" of harm approach in holding that obscenity laws are consistent with the First Amendment. It did not rest its decision, that is, on a finding that "obscene" materials are likely to be tangibly harmful in their effects. Rather, the Court said that such materials, despite having the *form* of constitutionally protected expression, were simply "not within the area of constitutionally protected speech or press." In the Court's words, such materials were, instead, one of a small number of "well-defined and narrowly limited classes of speech" ("the lewd," "the profane," the "libelous," and the "insulting or fighting words" were the other classes mentioned by the Court) the prevention and punishment of which "have never been thought to raise any constitutional problem." Such utterances, said the Court, "are no essential part of any exposition of ideas, and are of such slight social value as a step to truth that any benefit that may be derived from them is clearly outweighed by the social interest in order and morality." Standard gen-

---

[2]See, for example, the Supreme Court's use of this theory in 1951 to uphold the conviction of high U.S. Communist Party officials in *Dennis v. United States*.

eral obscenity laws were thus held to be constitutionally permissible in the *Roth* case *regardless* of whether there was "proof either that obscene material will perceptibly create a clear and present danger of antisocial conduct, or will probably induce its recipients to such conduct."

The Supreme Court's 1957 *Roth* decision was, however, not by any means a complete victory for then-existing obscenity laws and their proponents. The ultimate practical significance of excluding "obscenity" from the protection of the First Amendment obviously depends upon the definition given, for constitutional purposes, to the term "obscene." The Court in 1957 was clearly *not* prepared to let state and federal legislatures (or the lower courts) define "obscene" in whatever way they wished.

During the period when general obscenity prohibitions were most active in the U.S., courts had used a test for determining what is "obscene" that was adopted from the 1868 English case of *Regina v. Hicklin*. That test potentially permitted an enormously wide range of works dealing with sexual subjects to be considered "obscene." The *Hicklin* definition turned on "whether the tendency of the matter charged as obscenity is to deprave and corrupt those minds are given to such immoral influences, and into whose hands a publication of this sort may fall." The *Hicklin* test thus might deem even the most seriously intended work to be "obscene," if that work bore sexual content that children or others might find titillating. The material involved in the *Hicklin* case itself, for example, was an anti-Roman Catholic tract entitled "The Confessional Unmasked; Showing the Depravity of the Romish Priesthood . . . and Questions Put to Females in Confession." The *Hicklin* court found this pamphlet obscene, not because it was dominantly erotic in intention or effect, but because parts of it might suggest "to the minds of the young of either sex, or even to persons of more advanced years, thoughts of a most impure or libidinous character."

The *Hicklin* obscenity test had been roundly criticized by some of our most eminent and enlightened judges. Federal Judge Learned Hand, for example, openly questioned whether we should be "content to reduce our treatment of sex to the standard of a child's library in the supposed interest of a salacious few" (*U.S. v. Kennerly*, 1913). And U.S. Supreme Court Justice Felix Frankfurter, in reversing a conviction under a *Hicklin*-type statute shortly before the 1957 *Roth* decision, observed that the State there was seeking to "quarantin[e] the general reading public against books not too rugged for grown men and women in order to shield juvenile innocence. . . . Surely, this is to burn the house to roast the pig" (*Butler v. Michigan*, 1957). The *Hicklin* approach in the U.S. had resulted, among other specific applications, in the unsuccessful attempt by the federal government to prevent the importation into the

United States of James Joyce's novel *Ulysses* (*United States v. One Book Entitled Ulysses*, 1934) and in the banning in New York State of Edmund Wilson's highly regarded novel *Memoirs of Hecate County* (*Doubleday v. New York*, 1948) to say nothing of attempts by prosecutors to ban works by William Faulkner, James T. Farrell, and Erskine Caldwell, (e.g., *Commonwealth v. Gordon*, 1949).

In its *Roth* decision, the Supreme Court authoritatively rejected the *Hicklin* obscenity test as "unconstitutionally restrictive of the freedoms of speech and press." Because that definition judged obscenity "by the effect of isolated passages upon the most susceptible persons," it might, said the Court, well "encompass material legitimately treating with sex." The Court remarked, however, that sex and obscenity "are not synonymous," so that the portrayal of sex in literature or art "is not in itself sufficient reason to deny . . . constitutional protection. . . ." The Court substituted for the *Hicklin* test a standard under which a work could constitutionally be considered "obscene" (and thus be censored without a showing of a clear likelihood of harm) only if, to the "average person," applying "contemporary community standards," the "dominant theme" of the material "taken as a whole" appeals to "prurient" interest. Obscenity laws would thus be restricted so as to apply only to materials lacking "even the slightest redeeming social importance."

If the proponents of obscenity restrictions thought that they had won a substantial victory in *Roth* that impression must have been quite short-lived. For in applying its new definition of "obscenity" the Supreme Court, in the decade following the *Roth* decision, held, much more often than not, that the material involved in specific cases before it could not constitutionally be considered to be "obscene." Some of the books and pictures involved in these cases were quite sexually explicit (although graphic photographic depictions of actual sexual intercourse were ordinarily not involved) and probably fell into a category that most people would regard (even today) as constituting "pornography" (perhaps even "hard-core" pornography). In most instances, the Supreme Court did not write opinions in these cases explaining why a finding of obscenity was constitutionally impermissible; the Court ordinarily acted on these cases summarily, merely noting its conclusion that the constitutionally required test had not been satisfied (see, e.g., *Redrup v. New York*, 1967).

By the time of the creation of the Obscenity Commission, it is fair to say that virtually no one with an opinion about obscenity prohibitions was satisfied with the state of the law in that area. Those who applauded the Supreme Court's theoretical validation of obscenity laws in the *Roth* case were dismayed by the fact that convictions relating to what they often regarded as clear "hard-core" pornography were being reversed for failure to establish the existence of constitutional "obscenity" (see, e.g., "Memoirs" v. Massachusetts, (1966), holding the erotic classic Fanny Hill not to be obscene). Those who believed that obscenity should not have been excluded from First Amendment protection in the first place were gratified by the Supreme Court's numerous reversals in particular cases, but they deplored the perpetuation of what they considered an erroneous and dangerous theory of exclusion from constitutional protection—a theory that could be used to justify police harassment, the formal institution of nonmeritorious prosecutions and lower court convictions that, although ultimately subject to reversal (if the litigants had the resources to carry them that far), could still be quite damaging to individuals and to the climate of free expression generally. These people deplored as well the occasional failures of the Court to reverse convictions in specific cases.[3]

The Court's new definition of "obscene" came in for, perhaps, the strongest criticism. Although concededly an improvement upon the Hicklin approach in many respects, the new test was nevertheless almost universally regarded as unsatisfactory by all factions in the debate because of its vagueness and enormous subjectivity. It was never clear, for example, what constituted a "prurient" interest in sex.[4] Nor was it clear how a judge, jury, prosecutor, or police officer could possibly know the quality of the appeal of particular materials to some hypothetical "average person" or whether materials went beyond "contemporary community standards." If, as the Roth opinion suggested (and later cases confirmed), obscene material must also be found to be "utterly without redeeming social importance," similar difficulties were present in making that determination. It often seemed as though "obscene" materials

---

[3]Thus, in 1967 the Court summarily affirmed an obscenity determination regarding the Jean Genêt film, "Un Chant d'Amour," in Landau v. Fording. In 1971, an equally divided Supreme Court summarily affirmed the obscenity of the popular and well-known film, "I am Curious, Yellow" in Grove Press v. Maryland State Bd. of Censors. Another related instance was the Court's 1966 decision in Ginzburg v. United States. There the Court affirmed a conviction on the ground that the defendant had "pandered" sexual materials that were not obscene in themselves. The Court, however, never succeeded in defining "pandering," and the Ginzburg decision was widely regarded as an aberation (albeit an aberation that resulted in a prison term for its unfortunate victim).

[4]If the vagueness of the word "prurient" itself were not bad enough, further confusion was created by the Supreme Court's faltering attempts to define the term. In the Roth case, the Court said that "prurient" material was "material having a tendency to excite lustful thoughts"; but the Court also said (in the same footnote) that a "prurient" interest was "a shameful or morbid interest in nudity, sex, or excretion" (emphasis added). These two seemingly divergent concepts (lust surely does not always entail shame or morbidity) have never been satisfactorily reconciled.

were those sufficiently subjectively distasteful to the particular police officer, prosecutor, judge or juror who encountered them—surely not a sound basis for imposing imprisonment and for banning books and films for the entire population.

When the Roth opinion was written, the Court may justifiably have believed that "obscene" materials were largely self-defining—in the Court's mind they were, perhaps, those materials that were traditionally sold "under the counter" with apparent consciousness of their contraband status in the minds of both buyer and seller.[5] At one time, all or almost all materials with a very high degree of sexual explicitness may perhaps have been so regarded. But that certainly did not remain true in the 1950s and 60s as explicit sexual content more and more frequently found its way into books and films that were taken seriously by critics, that were sold and exhibited openly at "respectable" book stores and theaters, and that sometimes attracted a mass audience. As this development continued the definitional problems connected with obscenity law became truly "intractable."[6]

This, then, was the situation that confronted the Commission as it began its work in 1968. Those who originally proposed the creation of the Commission in Congress undoubtedly thought that obscenity laws should not only continue to exist but also believed that they should be strengthened. They saw the Commission's task as one of formulating advice and recommendations on how to reverse the Supreme Court's apparent trend away from the broad applicability of general obscenity laws. But a clear antipornography Commission bill never obtained the required support in Congress. The legislative compromise that ultimately resulted in the enactment of the law creating the Obscenity Commission was, instead, one that opened all of the basic questions for reconsideration. Most significantly, the legislation that was enacted by Congress placed a great deal of emphasis—as applicable constitutional doctrine had not—on "the effect of obscenity and pornography upon the public, and particularly minors, and its relationship to crime and other antisocial behavior" (P.L. 90–100, §5(a)(3)). The Commission was given the task of studying these questions. The clear implication of this assignment was that, if antisocial effects were not in fact discovered,

---

[5]See Justice Stewart's famous remark in *Jacobellis v. Ohio* (1964), that although "perhaps I could never succeed in intelligently defining 'obscenity' I know it when I see it, and the motion picture in this case, [the well-regarded Jeanne Moreau film, "The Lovers"] is not that."

[6]The characterization is that of Justice Harlan (an immensely thoughtful judge with no firm ideological commitment on the issue) in *Interstate Circuit v. Dallas* (1968).

obscenity law might well justifiably be deemed a questionable enterprise, especially in view of the enormous definitional problems that had arisen and the competing claims on law enforcement resources of clearly dangerous and harmful criminal behavior.

The selection of individuals to serve on the Commission appeared to reinforce the view that the Commission was to take nothing about obscenity for granted. A few Commission members were, it is true, firmly allied with antipornography groups. But others appeared to have strong free-expression orientations (although no one from the pornography "industry" itself was appointed). Most commissioners appeared uncommitted on the basic issues, so far as could be told from their backgrounds and affiliations. There was, moreover, a significant Commission component of social scientists who could be expected to take the relevance of antisocial effects quite seriously. The Commission's chairman, Dean William Lockhart of the University of Minnesota Law School, had co-authored the leading scholarly articles on the constitutional status of obscenity laws. Although these articles (Lockhart & McClure, 1954, 1960) appeared to accept the constitutionality of prohibiting hard-core pornography in some contexts, Dean Lockhart accepted the Commission position only on the understanding that all relevant questions would be examined, and that the direction of the Commission's ultimate recommendations was not to be preordained. He obtained the Commission's agreement to this course at its initial meetings. He also obtained Commission agreement that the fulltime director of the Commission staff should be a behavioral scientist and that the bulk of the Commission's budget should be devoted to gathering information about the alleged harmful effects of sexual materials.

The Commission thus set out to study, as scientifically and objectively as possible, a subject that had not previously been treated in that way by those who made or recommended offical policy. In retrospect, it seems clear that the decision to make the study of effects the central focus of the Commission's attention was the factor that, more than any other, shaped the Commission's main final recommendations. When substantial evidence of antisocial effects was not forthcoming (as it was not), the Commission's recommendation to repeal general obscenity laws became almost inevitable.

One additional preliminary decision related to Commission procedures should be mentioned, as it may also have had a significant impact upon subsequent Commission deliberations. Once Congressional funding for the Commission was secure, Dean Lockhart decided to hold the Commission's initial meetings at Bloomington, IN, the site of the Kinsey Institute of Human Sexuality. Part of these first meetings was spent on organizational matters; another part was devoted to supplying the Commissioners with information about obscenity law (including the relevant constitutional principles) and with information about the then-current state of social and behavioral science research into the effects of sexually explicit materials. By holding the meeting in Bloomington, the Commissioners were, in addition, given the opportunity to become familiar, at first hand, with the subect matter of the Commission's work, for the Kinsey Institute had a comprehensive and well-organized collection of sexual materials of every conceivable kind. The Commissioners were offered the opportunity thoroughly to investigate the collection under the scholarly guidance of Kinsey's professional staff. This exposure reinforced the scientific approach adopted by the Commission. It also tended to demystify the subject, to give every member the experience, to some extent, of being a consumer of a broad range of materials (including explicit materials with aesthetic and educational values), and to make subsequent conversations among Commission members and staff about sexual materials easier and a good deal more informative.

The decision was also made at the outset to divide the Commission members into four panels, each assigned to study one of the four principal delegated areas of Commission concern. Panels were established on Effects, Traffic, Law, and "Positive Approaches." Commissioners were placed on the panels that seemed most suited to their prior experience and interests, and staff members were assigned to work with each Panel. Although the Commission as a whole met thereafter from time to time, most of the Commission's work, up until the time of the formulation and preparation of the final report, took place through these relatively specialized subgroups. The effect was to maximize the attention paid to facts and data and to postpone, until information was gathered, any collective consideration of what recommendations should ultimately flow from that information. If a vote had been taken within the Commission at its first meeting about the advisability of retaining general obscenity provisions in U.S. law, that vote would undoubtedly have been overwhelmingly affirmative. As we have seen, the vote that later occurred, after extensive information gathering and study, went strongly in the opposite direction.

When the Commission met, about 2 years after its work began, to consider what its final recommendations should be, it had before it the findings and reports of its four panels. In essence, those findings were as follows:

> The Traffic Panel reported that the sexual materials industry was neither monolithic nor especially large, as compared with the general traffic in books, films and similar materials in the United States. No hard evidence of connections with "organized crime" was found to exist. Relatively explicit sexual content was found to be present, in varying degrees, in a

broad range of materials from a wide variety of sources with diverse audiences. The market in the most explicit (so-called "hard-core") materials was estimated to be no more than $10 million each year. Most Americans (the Panel found) had at least had some voluntary experience with such very explicit materials—approximately 85% of the men and 70% of U.S. women fell into this category. Ordinarily, the first experience with such materials occurred before the age of 21. The continuing patrons of "adult" bookstores and theaters, however, "may be characterized as predominantly white, middle-class, middled-aged, married males, dressed in a business suit or neat casual attire. Almost no one under 21 was observed in these places, even where it was legal for them to enter." Moreover, the sexual activities most "frowned upon by our society, such as sadomasochism, pedophilia, bestiality, and nonconsensual sex" were "outside the scope of the interests of the average patron of adult bookstores and movie houses." ("Report," 1970, pp. 7–21)

The Effects Panel had undertaken a research program that included a national survey of American adults and young people regarding their experience with sexual materials, quasi-experimental and experimental studies, and studies of the rates and incidence of sex offenses and illegitimacy. It reported that exposure to sexual materials "produces sexual arousal in substantial [numbers] of both males and females"; that some people increase their "masturbatory or coital behavior" when exposed to such materials (most people's behavior, however, does not change), but that such increases are "short-lived and generally disappear within 48 hours"; that established patterns of sexual behavior were "very stable and [are] not altered substantially by exposure to erotica"; that a substantial number of married couples reported "more agreeable and enhanced marital communication" after exposure to erotic stimuli; that "[d]elinquent and nondelinquent youth report generally similar experiences" with explicit sexual materials; that sex offenders "have had less adolescent experience with erotica than other adults"; that the increased availability of explicit sexual materials in Denmark "has been accompanied by a decrease in the evidence of sexual crime"; and that, for America, "the relationship between the availability of erotica and changes in sex crime rates neither proves nor disproves the possibility that the availability of erotica leads to crime." The Panel reported, in sum, that "empirical research designed to clarify the question has found no evidence to date that exposure to explicit sexual materials plays a significant role in the causation of delinquent or criminal behavior among youth or adults." ("Report," 1970, pp. 23–27)

The Positive Approaches Panel reported on sex education, organized "citizen action," groups and industry self-regulation. The Panel found mounting evidence of "dissatisfaction with existing sources of sex information" and concluded that improved sex education "would appear to be potentially powerful in . . . decreasing the possibility of exposure [of young people] to misinformation or information outside its proper context." It found that citizen action groups "can seriously interfere with the availability of legitimate materials in a community by generating an overly repressive atmosphere and by using harassment." Voluntary industry self-regulation (as in the comic book industry, radio and television, and the motion picture industry) was, in the Panel's view, less effective than commercial considerations in shaping the content of materials; such regulation might also "inhibit experimentation with new ideas, dampen response to social change, and limit the sources of cultural variety." ("Report," 1970, pp. 29–35)

The Legal Panel reported "almost universal dissatisfaction with present [obscenity] law" because of its enormous vagueness and subjectivity. With regard to the various elements of the Supreme Court's then current definition of obscenity, the Panel found very little consensus within the U.S. population on judgments about whether particular materials were arousing, offensive or "prurient." In addition, "substantial portions of the population reported effects which might be deemed socially valuable from even the most explicit sexual materials." (Most men, for example, thought that such materials provided both information and entertainment.) In light of these findings, the construction of a clear, objective constitutional definition of what materials could be considered "obscene" for all adults would be "extremely difficult." On the other hand, the Panel found indications of greater receptivity in the U.S. Supreme Court toward legal restrictions directed solely toward distribution of sexual materials to minors or toward unsolicited mailings or open public displays of such materials (The Panel had reference here to cases such as *Ginsberg v. New York* (1968), upholding a statute broadly prohibiting distributions to minors and *Rowan v. Post Office Department* (1970), upholding broad limitations on unsolicited mailings.) Such restrictions would not interfere with consensual distributions among adults and would thus not raise the most difficult constitutional problems. In these limited areas (the Panel believed) specific objective definitions of restricted materials (such as definitions including all graphic depictions of intercourse, however "artistic" or otherwise valuable to a consensual adult audience) were both possible and constitutional. ("Report," 1970, pp. 37–44)

When the Commission met in the spring of 1970 to formulate its final recommendations, there was a remarkable degree of consensus about the main points. Only 3 of the 18 Commission members dissented from the central recommendation urging the repeal of federal, state, and local laws prohibiting the consensual distribution of sexual materials to consenting adults. Two of these 3 dissenters had had close and long-standing affiliations with antipornography groups; the third was a state attorney-general charged with enforcing obscenity laws. As noted above, the Commission's recommendation to repeal standard general obscenity laws seemed to flow almost inevitably from the Commission's original decision to emphasize the centrality of an inquiry into the effects of sexual materials. Once it appeared that solid evidence of antisocial effects was not to be found, a decision, nevertheless, to recommend the continuation of broad obscenity laws would have amounted, in large part, to a seeming repudiation of two years of effort. The Commission's decision was supported, in addition, by the immense difficulties associated with the enforcement of existing obscenity laws and by free speech considerations that struck a responsive chord in most Commission members.

These factors were all discussed openly at the full Commission meeting that preceded the taking of a vote on this issue. The chairman first formulated the main issues as: (a) whether there should be general prohibitions on consensual distributions to adults; (b) if so, what should be prohibited; (c) if not, whether there should be specific prohibitions on nonconsensual distributions and distributions to minors; and (d) if so, what should thus be prohibited. Thereafter, each Commission member in turn stated his or her views on these questions. The formal vote was anticlimactic. After the vote, the staff was asked to prepare a set of recommendations reflecting the discussion.

The Commission was quite aware, in arriving at its final recommendation to repeal existing laws prohibiting consensual distributions to adults, that both Congress and the President would likely find that recommendation to be politically unacceptable. There was open discussion about whether the recommendation should, therefore, be softened, so as to make it more acceptable. To some extent, such softening did take place through the Commission's companion recommendations that legislation be enacted prohibiting the direct distribution of explicit materials to children and prohibiting unsolicited mailings and public displays of such materials. But, in general, the prevailing attitude within the Commission was that the group would not properly discharge its responsibilities if it sought to anticipate the political reaction by modifying recommendations that seemed proper policy from the nonpolitical perspective.

The strength—and indeed the entire justification—of a body like the Commission lay in its ability and willingness to report on the evidence and its ramifications in as objective a way as possible. Everyone present was quite aware that political considerations would surely play the major role in the official decisions regarding whether, how, and to what extent to respond to the Commission's Report. The political process, it was felt, was entitled to the Commission's view of the nonpolitical truth. The Commission thus undoubtedly felt more free to make its recommendations in its role as independent policy *adviser* than it would have felt if it had had final decisional responsibility for the laws that would actually be enacted or retained. A majority of the same Commission members, acting as legislators rather than a citizen advisory panel, might, one suspects, have voted to retain existing general obscenity laws, despite the information obtained through their two years of study.

Although the Commission's failure to find solid evidence of antisocial effects connected with the distribution of sexual materials determined its recommendations regarding general obscenity prohibitions, the same was not true regarding Commission recommendations in the areas of unsolicited mailings, public displays, and distribution to children. Lack of evidence of harmful effects was not deemed to be conclusive in these areas for several reasons:

Most importantly, these limited types of regulations were not seen by most Commissioners as posing strong threats to free expression principles. Even if direct distributions to children, unsolicited mailings, and public displays of certain material were to be prohibited, that would not prevent or significantly hinder those adults who so wished to obtain sexual materials. So long as consensual adult distributions were not to be prevented, the Commission did not take seriously any claim of a constitutional right to "thrust" material upon unwilling recipients. And it was clear (whatever the lack of evidence of *tangible* effects) that a significant minority of Americans found unwanted exposure to some or all explicit sexual materials deeply disturbing.

A stronger case could perhaps be made for the First Amendment rights of children to obtain sexual materials (especially in view of the Commission's findings that such materials were often a valuable source of information to both children and adults), and this issue was discussed to a considerable extent. In the end, however, the large majority of Commission members decided to elevate the rights of parents to attempt to control their children's sex education over whatever First Amendment rights the children themselves might have. The child-distribution legislation recommended by the Commission would, in fact, apply only where distributions to children were made *without* parental consent ("Report," 1970, pp. 56–60). (One can only speculate about whether this recommendation would have been different in substance had the Commission membership included some children.) It is perhaps also relevant to observe in this connection that, despite their unusually great exposure to and experience with sexual materials during the Commission's 2-year life, most Commission members still appeared, at the end of that process, to feel some sense of discomfort when contemplating frank discussion of sexual practices, techniques, and feelings with their children. The Commissioners' stated desire to protect parents' ability to control their children's sex education was thus perhaps influenced to some extent by an unstated desire to protect parents themselves from embarrassment in trying to cope with sexual materials that their children might independently obtain.

Finally, although the Commission had determined not to let the likely public and political reaction to its Report influence the substance of its main findings and recommendations, it certainly hoped that its advice would be given serious consideration. A Report that recommended no affirmative governmental responses whatever to an obscenity "problem" that was considered to be a serious one by many people (however much that view might be influenced by misinformation about effects, law enforcement practices, etc.) was not likely to receive such respect. Recommendations about children, public displays, and unsolicited mailings constituted a positive response in the areas where public concern was strongest and most apparently legitimate, where the law enforcement problems seemed most manageable, and where legislation could do the least harm to basic First Amendment values.

As the Commission expected, its recommendation for repeal of all general obscenity laws was not enthusiastically received in the political arena. President Nixon "categorically" rejected the Commission's "morally bankrupt conclusions and major recommendations"; in his view they displayed "an attitude of permissiveness" that "would contribute to an atmosphere condoning anarchy in every other field" (*The New York Times*, October 25, 1970).[7] The U.S. Senate similarly rejected the Commission findings and recommendations regarding general obscenity prohibitions by a vote of 60 to 5 (U.S. Res. 477, 91st Cong., 2d Sess., 116 Cong. Rec. 36459, 1070). (The Commission was dismayed, I think, by the failure of its affirmative recommendations for child-distribution legislation, and prohibitions on public displays and unsolicited mailings, to blunt this political criticism.) The U.S. Supreme Court also implicitly rejected the Commission's advice in two major obscenity decisions handed down in 1973 (*Miller v. California*, 1973; *Paris Adult Theatre v. Slayton*, 1973). These cases reaffirmed the *Roth* holding that obscenity was not within the area of First Amendment protection (even where consensual distributions to adults were involved) and then broadened the definition of "obscene" somewhat, so as theoretically to permit more materials to be included in that category.[8]

The nation as a whole, however, has in subsequent years followed the Commission's lead more than these immediate official responses would suggest. Since the Commission's Report, about 10 states have, in fact, decided either to repeal or not to enact or reenact legislation prohibiting consensual distributions of sexual materials to adults.[9] And,

---

[7] The President added, somewhat ironically in view of later developments in his own political career, that "American morality" is "not to be trifled with."

[8] The main definitional change was to require a showing of "serious" social value in order to remove explicit materials from the "obscene" category. Under *Roth*, "obscene" materials had to be "utterly" without any sort of value—"serious" or not.

[9] A partial listing (Iowa, Montana, Oregon, South Dakota, Vermont, West Virginia, Alaska, New Mexico) is contained in Dorsen, Bender, & Neuborne, (1976, pp. 546–547).

even where laws continue to exist (as they do in most places), the incidence of prosecutions for consensual adult distributions and exhibitions has been substantially reduced. As a practical matter, even the most explicit materials are now relatively freely available in many parts of the United States, even though such distributions may technically be illegal. Because of the growing acceptance of explicit sexual materials in U.S. society (a trend identified by the Commission and, perhaps, even accelerated by its findings of lack of harm and its forthright recommendations for repeal), antiobscenity crusades based on the supposed evil of sexual explicitness no longer seem to be a source of political strength or appeal. The primary arguments made today for the continued or increased censorship of sexual materials are based on the demeaning characterizations of women that are often contained in or reinforced by such materials. These arguments provide a solid source of criticism of the contents of many sexually explicit books and films; they do not, however, appear to provide a constitutionally acceptable basis for legally enforced censorship.

REFERENCES

Butler v. Michigan, 352 U.S. 380 (1957).
Commission on Obscenity and Pornography, 1970, Report, Washington, DC, Government Printing Office.
Commonwealth v. Gordon, 66 Pa. D. & C. 101 (1949).
Dennis v. United States, 341 U.S. 494 (1951).
Dorsen, Bender & Neuborne, 1976, Political and Civil Rights in the United States, Boston, Ma., Toronto: Little-Brown & Co.
Doubleday & Co. v. New York, 335 U.S. 848 (1948).
Ginsberg v. New York, 390 U.S. 629 (1968).
Ginzburg v. United States, 383 U.S. 463 (1966).
Grove Press v. Maryland State Bd. of Censors, 401 U.S. 480 (1971).
Interstate Circuit v. Dallas, 350 U.S. 676 (1968).
Jacobellis v. Ohio, 378 U.S. 184 (1964).
Landau v. Fording, 388 U.S. 456 (1967).
Lockhart & McClure, The Law of Obscenity and the Constitution, 38 Minn. L. Rev. 295 (1954).
Lockhart & McClure, Censorship of Obscenity, The Developing Constitutional Standard, 45 Minn. L. Rev. 5 (1960).
"Memoirs" v. Massachusetts, 383 U.S. 413 (1966).
Miller v. California, 413 U.S. 15 (1973).
Paris Adult Theatre I v. Slayton, 413 U.S. 49 (1973).
Public Law 90–100, 81 Stat. 255 (1967).
Regina v. Hicklin, L.R. 3 Q. B. 360 (1868).
Redrup v. New York, 386 U.S. 767 (1967).
Roth v. United States, 354 U.S. 476 (1957).
Rowan v. Post Office Department, 397 U.S. 728 (1970).
United States v. Kennerly, 209 Fed. Rep. 119 (S.D.N.Y. 1913).
United States v. One Book Entitled Ulysses, 72 F.2d 705 (2d Cir. 1934).

THREE

THE AMERICAN WAY WITH MENTAL ILLNESS: AN ASSESSMENT OF THE PRESIDENT'S COMMISSION ON MENTAL HEALTH

THOMAS E. BRYANT, ERIK J. MYERS, and KATHRYN E. CADE

The Public Committee on Mental Health, Washington, DC

Over the years, federal health programs have benefited greatly from Congressional and White House support which grew from personal interest in specific health areas. For example, almost all the categorical areas in the National Institutes of Health have strong constituencies in Congress, because individual legislators have had personal or family involvement with the particular illness being treated.

In the mental health field, strong champions with much political power have often influenced and advanced mental health programs because of these family involvements. A prime example is the Mental Retardation Facilities and Community Mental Health Centers Construction Act of 1963 which was of special interest to President Kennedy because he had a mentally retarded sister. The development and passage of that act—and especially the priority, even in the title, given to the mental retardation components—was strongly determined by John F. Kennedy's personal commitment to this legislation.

Thus it was neither new nor unusual when a long personal interest in mental health on the part of Rosalynn Carter resulted in early White House efforts to advance the federal mental health program during the Carter administration.

A few days after the November 4, 1976, presidential election, Rosalynn Carter attended the annual meeting of the National Mental Health Association, as she had done for the previous 3 years. There she announced that the president-elect, her husband, Jimmy Carter, had agreed to set up a national commission on mental health and that, in fact, his staff had already begun planning for the commission.

During that transition period, advisers to President and Mrs. Carter prepared a comprehensive series of recommendations regarding the composition of the proposed commission, the scope of its work, methods of authorizing and funding it, and requirements for staffing it.

Of immediate concern to President and Mrs. Carter was the desire to move quickly to establish the commission following the inauguration. Rapid action would, they thought, demonstrate the depth of the new Administration's commitment to this issue, as well as allow sufficient time to translate the commission's recommendations into specific reforms. This sense of urgency dictated the mechanism used to create the commission. An executive order issued by the President would make it possible for work to begin immediately. It would also provide the statutory base for agency funding and manpower sharing. Ready access to funding sources was crucial, as attempts to obtain Congressional authorization would most certainly delay start-up, a delay that could potentially hinder legislative or administrative follow-up measures.

On February 17, 1977, in a ceremony in the East Room of the White House less than 1 month after he took the presidential oath of office, Jimmy Carter signed Executive Order Number 11973 creating the President's Commission on Mental Health.

The primary focus of the Commission was to be on publicly funded mental health efforts. The Commission was directed to pay particular attention to special segments of the general population broadly defined as the nation's "underserved," those whose mental health needs were still furthest from being met. The stated goal was to improve access, availability, and quality of mental health services for all citizens. To accomplish these ends, the Commission was directed to address a broad range of topics, including research, prevention, improving treatment and care, training and utilization of manpower responsive to present and future needs, and the role and effectiveness of federal and state agencies in carrying out national policy in the mental health field. The Commission would have a lifespan of 1 year, which would allow it to conduct the required analysis and assure sufficient opportunities to affect budgetary and legislative decisions.

The Commission was to identify how America's mentally ill were served and underserved and then to identify:

1. The projected needs for dealing with emotional distress during the next 25 years;

2. The ways the President, Congress, and the federal government might most efficiently support the treatment of the underserved;
3. Methods for coordinating a unified approach to all mental health and support services;
4. The types of research the federal government should support to further the prevention and treatment of mental illness and mental retardation;
5. The roles educational systems, voluntary agencies, and other institutions can perform to help minimize emotional disturbance; and
6. To the extent possible, the cost of mental health programs, how the money should be spent, and how financing should be divided among federal, state and local governments and the private and philanthropic sectors.

At the White House signing ceremony, President Carter announced that Mrs. Carter would serve as the Commission's honorary chairperson and that physician-attorney Thomas E. Bryant would serve as the Commission's chairman and executive director.

The process of selecting the twenty commissioners began immediately. A small ad-hoc committee under the leadership of John Gardner, founding chairman of Common Cause, was convened to make recommendations to the President. This group received nearly 1,000 names for consideration from every conceivable quarter—from members of Congress, governors, mayors, major national professional and voluntary organizations, university officials, and private citizens. The committee also independently sought advice and nominations from leaders in those sectors and related fields.

Following a month of work by the selection committee, President Carter announced his 20 appointments on March 29, 1977. True to the intent of the President and the selection committee, those asked to serve on the Commission represented a wide variety of backgrounds and expertise. Six of the 20 commissioners were mental health professionals; the rest were from other fields. There were 8 women and 12 men, ranging in age from 32 to over 70 and including a former patient, a member of Alcoholics Anonymous, an Episcopalian minister, and a superintendent of schools.

THE COMMISSION BEGINS ITS WORK

The Commission convened for its first working session in Chicago on April 17, 1977. At that time Mrs. Carter emphasized several basic principles that were to guide their subsequent deliberations: the President did not expect the commissioners to "reinvent the wheel"; therefore, every effort should be made to build upon the work that had already been done and to tap all existing sources of data, information, and analysis. It was clear that vast new sums of money for mental health were unlikely, given the economic stringencies of the times. Consequently, the Commission would need to concentrate on areas that offered prospect of more effective use of available resources. Mrs. Carter also advised that, because the President would be involved in a multitude of issues, many of extreme immediacy and importance, to have maximum effect, the Commission's report should be concise and specific.

Having a maximum specific budget of only $100,000 from the discretionary funds of the Executive Office, the Commission would need to rely heavily on supplemental voluntary private and public support. The U.S. Department of Health, Education, and Welfare (HEW) provided a number of staff personnel and substantial other in-kind services to the Commission. Of the Commission's 32 technical and administrative staff members, most were paid by funds raised from foundations and other nonfederal sources. The commissioners and several staff members donated their services for the year-long study.

Beginning in mid-April, the Commission followed a work plan which called for a preliminary report to the President by September 1. The initial task faced by the group was to make an accurate assessment of the nature and scope of the nation's mental health problems and of currently available services.

The process of assessment began with a series of public hearings held during the late spring and early summer. These public hearings took place in Philadelphia, Nashville, Tucson, and San Francisco. More than 400 individuals—psychiatrists, psychologists, social workers, government officials, former patients, parents of the mentally ill, and concerned private citizens—testified. A significant effort had been made to include a wide spectrum of opinion and background among those who would speak at the hearings. Hundreds more submitted written testimony and remarks for the record. The hearings and testimony provided vivid personal and human insights into the issues of service delivery and financing and the stigma of mental illness that the Commission was considering.

In addition, the Commission directed letters of inquiry to all members of Congress, to the governors of the states and territories, and to 250 organizations and associations, both governmental and private, soliciting their views on mental health. Moreover, the Commission received thousands of letters from private citizens offering suggestions and advice. More detailed analyses and statistical material were provided by the Commission's task panels (described in subsequent sections) which met in Washington and around the country, and by a special conference convened in late June to investigate access and barriers to care.

The Commission established separate Task Panels or Liaison Task Panels, eventually numbering 31, to examine key facets of mental health problems or issues. More than 400 individuals served voluntarily on these task panels as they developed their reports to the Commission. The commissioners themselves were divided among the task panels according to their particular interest or area of expertise. They were thereby able to participate more directly and substantively in the overall study effort than when the Commission met as a whole. The Commission did, however, meet monthly as a group throughout the summer of 1977 to review and begin to digest the growing volume of information. In order to cover the maximum amount of material, the commissioners divided themselves into small working groups that met with staff and panel members to study discrete areas of concern in more detail. General discussions of the major themes and content of the task panels' reports proved essential for building consensus among the Commission members' goals and priorities.

The Interim Report

The interim report, due to the President on September 1, was drafted by the staff and circulated to all members of the Commission for comment and approval. It began with a description of the scope and dimensions of the nation's mental health problems and of the country's response to those problems. That description set forth the conceptual framework within which the Commission had worked and within which it would conduct further study as it prepared a final report. It reflected the view of the Commission that America's mental health problem was not limited to those individuals with disabling mental illness or identified psychiatric disorders, and that mental health was more than just the absence of mental illness. It stressed the importance of giving due consideration to those Americans who suffered the mental and emotional effects of poverty and discrimination because of who they were and where they lived, as well as those whose mental health problems did not fit neatly into customary categories of mental disorder.

After reviewing a wide range of community surveys and treatment statistics, the Commission reported there was new evidence suggesting that at any one time as much as 15% of the population needed some form of mental health care, and that the direct cost of providing mental health services amounted $17 billion annually—a figure that referred primarily to costs incurred by people seen by mental health professionals in mental health facilities. Millions more, the Commission found, sought help elsewhere, which pointed up the need for much closer coordination and cooperation between the general medicine and mental health fields. The Commission was also able to document the extent to which particular population subgroups suffered disproportionately from mental and emotional disorders. Achieving a more equitable and responsive allocation of resources and services for these Americans was to become a major priority for the Commission.

The Commission's preliminary recommendations fell into four separate categories: (a) providing needed mental health services; (b) financing such services; (c) expanding the base of knowledge about mental health and mental illness; and (d) identifying strategies that might help to prevent mental disorder and disability. In each area, immediately implementable steps were identified that would help to eliminate unnecessary barriers to care or would provide additional knowledge or information for the planning and provision of appropriate services for those in need. Many of these measures could be implemented by executive action; others were directed at the 1980 fiscal-year budget process. Together, the recommendations presented to the President on September 15, 1977, reflected the Commission's highest priorities for responding to identified needs and its best judgment about actions the President could take immediately.

The Final Report

Having completed the first phase of its task, the Commission immediately began working on its final report ("Report," Vol. 1, 1978). Each commissioner reviewed the reports and policy recommendations prepared by each of the 31 task panels. From the thousands of pages these panels and other special conferences and working groups produced, a central theme and primary goals were to be developed. Competing interests and concerns of the "provider" groups and of the populations to be served had to be balanced. Ways to respond to needs without massive new expenditures of money had to be found. New strategies that would ensure accountability in the delivery of services and better mechanisms for planning and coordinating those services had to be defined in ways that preserved flexibility.

The Commission's letter of transmittal to the President, included in the *Report*, stated, in capsule form, its view of the principal challenges facing public policymakers and mental health professionals:

> The one-year study we undertook at your direction has convinced us that a substantial number of Americans do not have access to mental health

care of high quality at reasonable cost. For many, this is because of where they live; for others, it is because of who they are—their race, age, or sex; for still others, it is because of their particular disability or economic circumstances.

Mental health services in this country are located predominantly in urban areas. For those who live in rural areas, small towns, and many of the poorer sections of the Nation's cities, specialized mental health facilities and personnel are frequently nonexistent, and the services available are rarely comprehensive.

For many members of America's ethnic and racial minority populations, the mental health personnel and services that are available are either inadequate or fail to take into account their different cultural traditions.

Many children, adolescents, and older Americans do not have sufficient access to services or to personnel trained to respond to the special needs which are characteristic of their ages.

While not enough is known about the causes and treatment of chronic mental illness, we do know that thousands who are so disabled receive deplorably inadequate assistance.

Our study has also convinced us that, for the long run, the Nation will need to devote greater human and fiscal resources to mental health. We now devote only 12 percent of general health expenditures to mental health. This is not commensurate with the magnitude of mental health problems and does not address the interdependent nature of physical and mental health. We must begin now to seek a realistic allocation of resources which reflects this interdependence.

Further, since over half the dollars for mental health care are still spent in large State institutions and mental health-related nursing homes, there is an urgent need for a national policy that will alter the current balance of mental health expenditures in order to develop needed community-based services. ("Report to the President," Vol 1, 1978, p. vii–viii)

The Commission went on to outline the steps necessary to bring the country closer to high quality, accessible public and private mental health services for all in need. It recommended that the country:

develop networks of high quality, comprehensive mental health services throughout the country which are sufficiently flexible to respond to changing circumstances and to the diverse racial and cultural backgrounds of individuals. Wherever possible these services should be in local communities.

Adequately finance mental health services with public and private funds so that care is available at reasonable cost.

Assure that appropriately trained mental health personnel will be available where they are needed.

Make available where and when they are needed services and personnel for populations with special needs, such as children, adolescents and the elderly.

Establish a national priority to meet the needs of people with chronic mental illness.

Coordinate mental health services more closely with each other, with general health and human services, and with those personal and social support systems that strengthen our neighborhoods and communities. Broaden the base of knowledge about the nature and treatment of mental disabilities. Undertake a concerted national effort to prevent mental disabilities. Assure that mental health services and programs operate within basic principles protecting human rights and guaranteeing freedom of choice. To achieve these objectives, we cannot rely solely on the Federal government. We must have a strategy developed and implemented by partners—the private sector with the public sector, the Federal government with State and local governments, those working in mental health with those working in general health and related services. In these new arrangements we must define more clearly areas of responsibility and accountability. ("Report," Vol. 1, 1978, p. viii)

After the overview of findings and an assessment of problems and potential solutions came a discussion of the scope of current mental health problems. This was followed by a more detailed exposition of the Commission's recommendations which were organized under eight headings: (a) community supports; (b) a responsive service system; (c) insurance for the future; (d) new directions for personnel; (e) protecting basic rights; (f) expanding the base of knowledge; (g) strategy for prevention; and (h) improving public understanding.

Regarding the service system, the Commission noted that for the previous 15 years one keystone of the federal response to mental health care had been the development of community-based services. To fulfill the national commitment to this concept, the Commission recommended strengthening the existing community mental health centers (CMHC's) and creating a new grant program to replace the current community mental health centers program in order to provide greater flexibility to meet the needs of populations not well served by the centers. It also recommended funding new CMHC's only in areas of greatest need until the new program was in place. The Commission emphasized the importance of establishing as a national priority the pressing needs of the chronically mentally ill. And it urged the development of new partnerships with states, through a mechanism of "performance contracts," to induce the continued phasedown of large state hospitals in preference for more community-based services. Also strongly recommended were changes in federal and state planning mechanisms to facilitate closer coordination with health and related human-service planning to avoid fragmentation and duplication and to promote development of comprehensive networks of care.

To pay for these services, the Commission enunciated a set of principles that would apply in any public or private insurance program (including proposed national health insurance plans) to assure adequate and equitable mental health benefits. The Commission also recommended changes in Medicare to improve outpatient and inpatient coverage for the elderly; changes in Medicaid to improve outpatient benefits; and consideration of a totally new system to finance *non*mental-health support services for the chronically mentally ill.

Other recommendations dealt with redirecting federal training policies for mental health personnel to increase the number of qualified minority personnel and the number of persons trained to deal with the special problems of children, adolescents, and the elderly. To ensure that services would be most effective, the training of mental health personnel should be more clearly focused on the needs of those to be served.

In an historic departure from previous national assessments of mental health policies and programs, the Commission stressed the importance of protecting the basic legal rights of the mentally disabled.

The Commission also strongly urged the President to reverse the decline in federal support for mental health-related scientific research. This decline, which had been especially marked over the previous eight years, had produced deep concern on the part of the American scientific community that promising opportunities for increasing our basic knowledge about the underlying causes of serious mental illnesses would not be supported. While recommending increased research funding, the Commission called for more careful research planning and improved research management to enhance the effectiveness of the recommended increases in dollar support.

Finally, the Commission recognized that underlying the need for these reforms were the stigma and fear associated with mental illness and the mentally ill which were pervasive throughout society. Without carefully conceived and carefully implemented strategies for improving the public's understanding of mental illness and its treatment, and the need for more research, the necessary degree of public support for the proposed reforms would not be forthcoming. Conversely, the commissioners felt that if the public could better understand the manifestations of the various types of mental illness and the proven potential of certain therapeutic approaches, sufficient public support would be generated to assure the reforms they were recommending.

On April 27, 1978, the commissioners presented their final report to the President. Carter, saying that the group's efforts, as supplemented by the work of thousands of lay and professional volunteers across the country, would "have a profound beneficial effect on our country in years to come," pledged to move swiftly to implement the recommendations.

WHAT WE KNOW AND WHAT WE DO:
IMPLEMENTING THE COMMISSION'S REPORT

In assessing mental health care (in the United States) . . . we have been struck by the inconsistencies that exist between what we know should be done and what we do. We know that services should be tailored to the needs of people in different communities and circumstances, but we do not provide the choices that make this possible. We know that people should seek care when they need it, but we do little to change the public attitudes that often keep people from seeking help. We know that people are usually better off when care is provided in settings that are near families, friends and supportive social networks, yet we still channel the bulk of our mental health dollars to nursing and state mental hospitals. ("Report," Vol. 1, 1978, p. 12)

A dispassionate assessment of the 117 recommendations contained in the Commission's *Report to the President* reveals little that is radical, controversial, or startlingly new. No bold new national approach to mental health is prescribed, nor is there a call for greatly increased federal or state spending. In truth, it appears that the commissioners took their own words to heart and recommended, in most instances, that the nation simply move closer to doing what we know should be done.

Given the moderate tone of the Report, the apparent agreement over what needed to be done, the support of the White House, and the acknowledged interest of some leading members of Congress, it seemed to some that implementation would be relatively easy. The substantial involvement of Mrs. Carter and President Carter's personal pledge to see that the recommendations were carried out boded well for quick action.

The many, diverse constituent groups that had worked with the Commission had achieved a marked degree of consensus on the next steps to take legislatively and administratively. Moreover, the 1980 expiration of the Community Mental Health Centers Act would provide a timely opportunity for thorough Congressional consideration and action of the Commission's findings and recommendations.

In spite of these advantages, the process of implementing the recommendations turned out to be inordinately lengthy and full of unforeseen obstacles. The process of public policy change is, however, in constant if sometimes subtle motion, and while this report is primarily concerned with what has happened between 1978 and 1981, it is evident that policy in this area has been thrown into a state of uncertainty and flux that will conceivably last for several years. To understand why the reforms recommended by the Commission could not be quickly enacted, even in a political climate that at first seemed highly favorable, one must examine the legislative process.

THE ADMINISTRATION ACTS

It has become axiomatic in Washington that visible, forceful White House leadership is essential to maintaining the momentum of any major executive branch initiative. Since mental health has traditionally been an issue with little political appeal, such visible, forceful White House leadership was seen as especially essential, if the Commission's recommendations were to be rapidly implemented. Unfortunately, many senior Carter White House officials and Cabinet officers perceived the Administration's interest in mental health to be a sort of "pet project" of the President's wife and not a major domestic program priority. The first order of business for advocates of the Commission's report was, therefore, to get the attention of the President's senior staff and to enlist their aid in the implementation process.

The President assigned primary responsibility for coordination and follow-up to Special Assistant for Health Issues Peter Bourne, M.D. Dr. Bourne had been a close friend and associate of President and Mrs. Carter for years and had led the effort to create the Commission. He was also a long-time friend and associate of Dr. Bryant, the Commission's chairman, who had kept him informed of the Commission's progress during the previous year. The two of them, working with Mrs. Carter and her staff, developed a strategy for lifting the proposed mental health initiative from the "pet project" status to that of a major new Carter Adminisstration effort. Dr. Bourne and his staff prepared an analysis of the recommendations and then convened a working group of representatives of the federal agencies involved. While the majority of the recommendations directly affected the Department of Health, Education, and Welfare, other departments, such as Justice, Housing, and Urban Development, and especially the Office of Management and Budget, had crucial roles to play in the implementation process.

During the summer of 1978, Dr. Bourne performed the crucial advocacy function within the Executive Office. However, Dr. Bourne left his White House post in August, and no senior-level advocate or coordinator was designated to replace him within the ranks of the President's domestic policy advisers. Although Mrs. Carter did carry on a highly visible advocacy campaign for the specific reforms recommended by the Report, she was not a government official or employee. Consequently, after Peter Bourne's departure, responsibility for implementing the Report rested primarily with HEW Secretary Joseph Califano and was not shared by any member of the senior White House staff. Despite the myriad demands for his attention, Secretary Califano established a departmental task force to identify the HEW program implications in the Report and to propose legislative, budgetary, administrative and programmatic responses to the recommendations.

This HEW Task Force was a major, time-consuming undertaking. After six months of further study and analysis, using personnel assigned to it from within the department, the Task Force produced its own report ("Report of the HEW Task Force," 1979). That report contained the outlines of a new "community program that was to be the cornerstone of the mental health legislative reforms initiated by the Administration in response to the Commission recommendations."

The first opportunity for significant federal actions, however, came with the preparation of the fiscal-year 1980 federal budget. The Commission had recommended various reforms which were estimated to require a $400 million increase in mental health expenditures for fiscal-year (FY) 1980 over FY 1979. The increases were recommended for four general areas: research, manpower training, services, and financing of care.

When HEW Secretary Califano met to brief Mrs. Carter in late October, 1978, on the HEW Task Force work and the Department's other legislative and budgetary plans for FY 1980 (which would begin October 1, 1979), he stated his belief, based on staff judgments, that HEW could justify requesting an additional $250 million for mental health in FY 1980. Despite this projection, the Department's later submission to the Office of Management and Budget (OMB) for FY 1980 requested only an additional $83 million for mental health. While it may not have been realistic to think of full funding for all Commission-proposed reforms, Mrs. Carter, Dr. Bryant, and others felt that it was important that a clear signal be sent to the public and the mental health community that the federal government was serious about undertaking major mental health reform.

Mrs. Carter and the others let Secretary Califano and the director of the Office of Management and Budget know of their concern, and the Administration's final mental health budget requests for FY 1980 reflected the impact of those concerns: the total of $633 million sought for mental health included a $30 million increase in research funds, a $99 million increase to begin the implementation of the new legislation the Administration intended to send to Congress, and a $40 million change in Medicare and Medicaid programs to improve coverage and services.

To most impartial observers it seemed that the Carter Administration did make good its pledge of increased financial support for federal mental health efforts. Between 1976 and 1981, funds for research increased nearly 65%, having decreased steadily during the previous seven years. Although an Administration-wide policy cut funds for health professional training, the National Institute of Mental Health's manpower training program was protected in order to respond to the critical needs identified by the Commission. Dollars available for direct services—primarily community-based services—also increased from approximately $236 million in 1976 to $367 million in Carter's final FY 1981 budget request.

REGULATORY REFORMS

The impact of the Commission was quickly felt in the executive agencies charged with key mental health responsibilities. Within HEW, the most dramatic changes occurred at the National Institute of Mental Health (NIMH), one of three research and federal service coordinating institutes of the Alcohol, Drug Abuse, and Mental Health Administration (ADAMHA) of the U.S. Public Health Service. For NIMH, the increased research support reversed a decline in support that had begun i 1969. The new dollars enabled the Institute to undertake studies in childhood and adolescent psychopathology, hyperkinetic and learning disorder syndromes, and on the comparative efficacy of various types of mental health services.

An Office of Prevention was established within NIMH, the first in its history. The program of this office was focused initially on research directed toward identifying strategies for intervention in early life and with high-risk populations. More recent studies undertaken by this office include the effects on children and families of marital disruption and of the occurrence of alcohol and drug abuse and mental disorders among parents. The emphasis on prevention studies relating to children was in direct response to the Commission's belief that, "Although effective programs to reduce distress and emotional disorder can and should be developed for the entire life span . . . helping children must be the nation's first priority in preventing mental disability" ("Report," Vol 1, 1978, p. 51). The very existence of the Office answered the need for a structured, focused, and visible effort to demonstrate the importance of prevention as an integral part of national policy.

In addition, the Institute's entire training program was reorganized to address personnel shortages identified by the Commission. To stem the demonstrable decline in the number of clinical psychiatrists, NIMH enlisted the assistance of HEW's Health Resources Administration to recruit more psychiatrists for the National Health Service Corps. The support policy for the broad clinical training program was redirected to encourage larger numbers of minorities to pursue careers in mental health and to increase the numbers of people trained to deal with the special problems of children, adolescents and the elderly. Furthermore, activities were initiated to link academic centers with public service settings to help relieve the severe shortage of personnel there.

In response to a major Commission recommendation, and intraagency steering committee was established by the new Health and Human Services (HHS) Secretary Patrica R. Harris in August, 1979, to develop a national plan for the care of the chronically mentally ill. The steering committee, under the leadership of Surgeon General Julius B. Richmond, established two work groups: one on program policy and one on financing. All major HHS bureaus and principal operating units participated in the committee's work and figured in the development of its report.

By December, 1980, the steering committee had concluded its study and issued a proposed plan of action that was to be implemented in phases as financing permitted. The report, entitled *Toward a National Plan for the Chronically Mentally Ill*, (DHHS, 1980) contains a series of specific programmatic, regulatory and fiscal recommendations designed to:

> function as an integrated strategy for federal action with the following objectives: to minimize the need for institutional care for persons with chronic mental illness, to assure high quality care for those who must be institutionalized, to provide for the development and financing of appropriate aftercare services and community alternatives to hospitalization, and to assist states and communities in making the most appropriate use of facilities and resources which currently serve this population. (DHHS, 1980, p. 1)

Of particular importance was the recommendation relating to how key fiscal policies of HHS could and should be revised to assure short- and long-range resource allocations to support an adequate, appropriate service capacity at the community level. But because of the far-reaching implications of this part of the report, the Department was unwilling to endorse it without further analysis and study. Consequently, it was published as a discussion document, with the advisory that it was "intended to stimulate further public dialogue and comment" and did "not reflect a final Departmental position."

Action on the "national plan" was deferred, primarily because of the political sensitivity of launching such a major program on the eve of a new Administration, headed by a President of a different political party. But it would be difficult to refute the charge that the chronically mentally ill had been studied repeatedly, and in large measure neglected, for the previous 20 years, and that taking no action on the National Plan continued this neglect.

The national plan exists now as a comprehensive set of governmental actions that, if taken, could ameliorate the current situation faced by the chronically mentally ill in local communities. It remains for the new leaders in the White House, the Congress, and in state capitals and city halls to address this vulnerable, overlooked group of citizens.

LEGISLATIVE REFORMS

The Mental Health Systems Act

By far the most comprehensive mental health initiative undertaken by the Carter Administration in response to the President's Commission was the development and introduction of the Community Mental Health Systems Act. The effort leading to enactment of this major legislative reform measure mere hours before Congress recessed for the year in September, 1980, and only a few weeks before the presidential election, stretched over two years and was fraught with delays, confusion, failures of leadership, and frequent compromises. What began as an Administration initiative ended as a Congressionally crafted program. The consensus developed in 1978 among the various mental-health constituency organizations in support of the Commission's recommendations came apart in the Congressional deliberations and had to be redeveloped along different lines. Lack of leadership from senior White House officials—with the exception of Mrs. Carter's continuing participation—contributed substantially to the delays and confusion.

The delays began at the Department of Health, Education, and Welfare. There, as stated earlier, Secretary Califano's Task Force took six months to analyze the Commission's report and recommendations. The Task Force's own Report contained detailed specifications for a new community mental-health systems act based on a revision of the existing Community Mental Health Centers Act. When the Report was made available to private mental health organizations, many objected strongly to some of the specifications, finding them to be chiefly a restatement of the existing law, with few of the innovative provisions suggested by the Commission. The HEW draft legislation met similar reservations at the White House from Mrs. Carter's staff and from Dr. Bryant, who was called in for consultation during the OMB review of the proposal. There were seven rewrites of the proposed legislation before President Carter submitted the bill to Congress on May 15, 1979—13½ months after the Commission had presented its report. The bill submitted by the President contained many of the recommendations and concepts developed by the Commission in its attempt to design a responsive service system, but several of its more ambitious suggestions had been dropped.

These delays within the Administration seriously complicated the budget process. The Administration, hopeful that its proposals would be rapidly enacted, sought funding to begin the new initiatives. But the Congressional appropriations committees were unable to earmark funds for what were, as yet, unauthorized programs.

Perhaps the greatest price paid for the delays was the gradual disintegration of the coalition of mental health organizations that had formed behind the Commission's work. With the passage of time came the loss of momentum necessary to keep the legislative proposals moving through Congress. As time passed, it became easier for different interest groups to raise objections to certain aspects of the proposed bill that seemed incompatible with their individual priorities. The absence of high-level staff attention from the White House was a continuing factor in the delay. National health insurance and the health planning laws were preoccupying the White House domestic policy staff and the secretary and the legislative draftsmen at HEW. It was not until Mrs. Carter and Secretary Califano traveled together to Geneva, Switzerland, to attend the annual meeting of the World Health Organization that a sense of resolve seized the Department and the White House staff on the need to submit a Mental Health Systems Act. And, even after the bill was introduced in Congress, another 18 months passed before it became law.

The Process in Congress

In the summer of 1979 there were several days of hearings in both the Senate and the House of Representatives on the Administration's proposed "Community Mental Health Systems Act." Testimony came from a broad array of "interest groups": the National Association of State Mental Health Program Directors, the National Mental Health Association, the National Council of Community Mental Health Centers, the American Federation of State, County and Municipal Employees, the Mental Health Law Project, the American Psychiatric Association, and other groups. Testimony was also submitted by HHS and by other Administration officials. While there was general agreement on the need for new mental health legislation, there was disagreement on which

Commission recommendations to emphasize and on the scope of the legislation.

To the mental health groups it was clear that a strong outside coalition was needed to press for passage by both Houses of Congress. To forge this coalition, it was necessary to resolve some major differences, especially regarding the role state agencies should play in the provision of mental health services financed by federal dollars and delivered in local settings. To what extent were the state agencies to have control over the distribution of funds and to be accountable for their expenditure?

The original Carter bill proposed a "State Program" for services for the chronically mentally ill and for severely disturbed children (traditionally a state responsibility); for prevention; and for improved data collection procedures, with the bulk of funds going to local communities. It also proposed a "Pilot Program" for a few states that would allow them to manage all funds coming into the state under the Act, but did not specify the criteria to be used for selecting the states or even the number of states that might qualify.

This approach was attacked from two sides: The states felt that it did not go far enough in allowing them to manage federal mental health funds; and advocates for community programs felt that there were too few safeguards to protect federal funds. The community groups also wanted to be eligible to receive direct support from the federal government for program areas reserved for states under provisions of the Administration bill.

To reforge the coalition, hundreds of hours were invested by the leadership of three major constituency groups—the Mental Health Association, the National Association of State Mental Health Program Directors, and the National Council of Community Mental Health Centers—to work out compromise positions in concert with the Senate Subcommittee staff who encouraged this intensive interaction. What emerged as the full Senate Committee bill (S. 1177) in April, 1980, represented not only a statement of agreement but, of equal significance, a strong coalition for passage of a new "mental health systems act."

The Senate version of the bill passed on July 24, 1980, with a wide bipartisan margin. House and Senate conferees then met to resolve the differences between the two versions, a step that involved rearguing and reworking many of the same issues once again. The Conference Report was filed on September 22, 1980, just before midnight and just in time for passage before Congress recessed. P.L. 96-398, the Mental Health Systems Act of 1980, was signed into law by President Carter on October 7, 1980, in a short ceremony held at the Woodburn Community Mental Health Center in Fairfax, VA.

The Final Act

The Mental Health Systems Act (P.L. 96-398) was the first major reform of federal publicly funded mental-health programs since the 1963 Community Mental Health Centers Act, and it reflected the many changes that had occurred since the 1963 Act became law. The concept of community-based services was retained, but was more sharply defined. States, long the primary source of funding and management for publicly funded mental health programs, gained recognition of their pivotal role, as well as incentives to undertake responsibility for coordinating the federal mental-health efforts within an electing state's boundaries. Moving away from traditional federal grant concepts, the new Act emphasized "performance contracts," as recommended by the Commission. This innovative funding scheme was designed to provide incentives to perform, and accountability, according to plans which were negotiated in advance.

Priority populations. The Systems Act concentrated the limited federal funds on groups within the general population that had been ignored or were distressingly underserved by the existing system. Mindful of the Commission's Report, the Act identified as priorities services for the chronically mentally ill, severely disturbed children and adolescents, the elderly, and racial and ethnic minority populations. Existing community mental health centers or new nonprofit entities could receive grants for providing certain services to these groups without the immediate requirement of providing comprehensive services to the entire geographic catchment area.

State incentives. Under the Act, a state could apply to become the manager of federal mental-health services within its boundaries in coordination with its own programs. Many states had developed the capacity to promote community-based services as well as institutional programs.

Grants were also to be made available to assist states in improving the administration and planning of mental health services. While the funding levels authorized for these purposes were relatively low, this provision was clearly intended to promote a unified federal, state and local partnership in providing services for the mentally ill.

Performance contracts. Many groups had pressed for increased accountability, particularly those representing populations neglected by the existing system. The Systems Act established the concept of a negotiated "performance contract," whereby federal state, and local entities would enter into mutually agreed-upon contracts that specified expected performance, timetables, evaluation procedures and criteria, and penalties for noncompliance. The Act provided funds for evaluation and monitoring by either HHS or state authorities on contract to HHS.

Other changes. Funds were to be made available to support the nonrevenue-producing activities—evaluation, consultation, and education—of community mental-health centers that had used up the maximum of eight years of federal funding allowed under the old Act. Such grants could be made for an additional 2 years to buttress the efforts of no longer-eligible centers to become independent of federal support.

An Office of Prevention within NIMH was statutorily authorized, the first recognition by Congress of the importance of prevention activities and the promotion of mental health.

A model bill of rights for state consideration and grant funds for advocacy programs on behalf of the mentally ill were the result of compromises in the House and Senate over how to deal with the protection of patients' rights. The result struck a middle course by setting out, but not requiring states to adopt, a "bill of rights" for the mentally ill, with some override authority given to the states during the initial year of the program.

Additional Legislative Reforms

One major set of recommendations of the President's Commission concerned the protection of the basic rights of those receiving mental health services, particularly in an inpatient setting. To ensure adequate protection, the Commission made a series of far-ranging recommendations, including the development of an advocacy system for the representation of mentally disabled individuals and the enforcement of existing federal laws and regulations prohibiting discrimination against mentally disabled persons seeking to equalize opportunities for them. The Commission also advocated that each person have the maximum opportunity to choose services and objectives appropriate to his or her needs and preferences.

One legislative measure that was enacted enabled the U.S. Attorney General to bring suit against state authorities for a pattern of denial of the basic constitutional rights of institutionalized patients. Federal court decisions had ruled that the Justice Department could not initiate suits of this nature absent specific statutory authorization. The new statute clarified the authority of the Civil Rights Division of the Justice Department to bring suit.

HHS and other federal agencies did not favor a mandatory patients' bill of rights at either the federal or the state level. Nor was there strong support for the creation of a separate advocacy system. Although the early Senate version of the Mental Health Systems Act contained a mandatory bill of rights applicable to states opting to receive federal funds, and a greater level of support for advocacy, these components of the Senate bill were extensively modified in the process of conference and compromise on the bill. The final draft of the Act included only a *suggested* model of patients' rights for states to consider enacting and a modestly funded advocacy demonstration program.

Related Activities

In addition to influencing governmental regulatory reforms and legislative actions, the Commission's Report stimulated change across a broad front of the private and public sectors, not only at the national level but at the regional, state and local levels as well. No complete survey of these activities has been conducted, but several deserve mention as indicative of the response to the Commission's work.

A variety of statewide conferences were held to assess the implications of the Report from a state perspective. In Texas, for example, the Hogg Foundation for Mental Health sponsored a 2-day meeting attended by providers, consumers, and policymakers. In North Carolina, the governor convened an invitational conference involving more than a thousand people from around the state to determine what actions should be taken there. Similar efforts were launched in other states and at the county and city levels around the country. In addition, the major mental health organizations—professional associations and voluntary groups—conducted educational campaigns.

Special populations were particularly interested in the Commission's work. The Washington Heights–West Harlem Community Mental Health Center held a round-table discussion on the impact of the Report for New York City. The Texas Department of Mental Health and Mental Retardation collaborated with the Urban Resources Center at Texas Southern University to examine issues related to services for blacks. And the National Coalition of Hispanic Mental Health and Human Services Organizations set up a task force to ensure that the recommendations, as they pertained to Hispanic communities, were implemented at local and regional levels.

The problems of the chronically mentally ill were addressed in a documentary report on deinstitutionalization produced by WNET-TV, the public broadcasting television station in New York City. This program was shown nationally, and in many communities local programs were prepared to examine the issue from the local perspective. Some of these local programs included a call-in component, with experts providing information and referrals to the viewing audience.

For the first time, a coalition of community foundations collaborated on a project to increase foundation involvement in the mental health field. The project's staff provided materials on mental health to the participating foundations, identified means by which the foundations could become more active in this field, established mechanisms for information exchange among the participants, and provided some funding opportunities that otherwise would not have existed. This project has significant long-range implications. A study conducted in 1976 found that foundations allocated only 4% of their total health expenditures to mental health, mental retardation, child abuse, and drug and alcohol abuse activities. The conclusion reached by the Community Foundation project was that the philanthropic sector should become much more involved in these areas.

Both Rosalynn Carter and Commission Chairman Bryant traveled extensively to present the Commission's findings. They urged groups as diverse as the Washington Business Group on Health and leaders in the movie and entertainment industry to think about ways they might address the nation's mental health problems.

In addition, Mrs. Carter recognized the unique opportunity she had to influence public attitudes by virtue of the attention and respect naturally given a First Lady. She often stated her belief that when public figures spoke honestly and openly about mental health-related issues, it made it easier for other people to do so. In numerous articles, speeches, and other public appearances, she appealed for greater understanding and sympathy for those afflicted by mental and emotional disorders. In her February, 1979, testimony before the Senate Subcommittee on Health and Scientific Research, she noted:

> The challenges involved in promoting better mental health for all Americans are many and complex, but none demand more of our attention than that of society's attitudes toward the mentally ill. There is no issue that touched me more personally during my work with the Commission than stigma. . . . Until we break the self-feeding cycle of fear, discrimination, and lack of understanding, our efforts to improve the quality of care for all who need it will be in vain. This means rethinking our own attitudes about mental illness and emotional problems. It means raising our children so that if they are confronted with mental illness in themselves, their families, or friends and neighbors, they aren't afraid or ashamed to seek help. It means speaking out on behalf of the mentally ill and working for their rights as citizens.

Unfinished Agenda

The Commission Report set out an agenda that its members believed would take a decade or more to implement fully. Half a decade later, it is clear that more remains to be done than has been done. Some of the advances just discussed have been delayed or reversed. For example, the Mental Health Systems Act, the capstone of the Commission's work, was largely repealed by the Alcohol, Drug Abuse, and Mental Health Block Grant portion of the Omnibus Budget Reconciliation Act of 1981 (P.L. 97-35). While some of the elements of the Systems Act's approach to service remain, the block grant scheme for mental health services has substantially removed the federal government from an active partnership with state and local authorities. How this approach will work is conjecture at this time; it is, however, a definite setback to the true partnership among federal, state, and local governments recommended by the Commission and established by the Systems Act legislation. The reasons for the reversal do not, for the most part, have anything specifically to do with mental health. The changes result from the desire of the new Administration and the new Congress to curtail federal expenditures in most areas other than defense spending. And while the Mental Health Systems Act had the benefit of 18 months of public comment and careful adjustment, no separate vote on the mental health provisions of the Omnibus Budget Reconciliation Act was ever recorded.

Some policy initiatives recommended by the Commission never emerged from the talking stage. Medicaid and Medicare financing reforms never advanced significantly in Congress, nor were they forcefully pursued by HHS or the White House.

Perhaps most important, fewer dollars will be available. This is true particularly for publicly funded mental-health services and clinical mental health manpower training. It is true in both an absolute dollar amount and in adjusted purchasing power after inflation.

THE NEW ADMINISTRATION ACTS

Before the effective date of the Mental Health Systems Act (October 1, 1981), a hastily created Alcohol, Drug Abuse, and Mental Health Block Grant, one portion of the Omnibus Budget Reconciliation Act of 1981 (P.L. 97-35) canceled the Systems Act and with it the chance for major reform. The Budget Act was a triumph for President Ronald Reagan, who sought to achieve two goals: reduced federal expenditures for social programs and reformation of the federal–state relationship. "Block granting" of federal funds was the means chosen to reduce expenditures and to consolidate previously "categorical" (individually authorized) federal programs and turn their management over to the states, with minimal federal control.

The block grant provisions of the Budget Act provide that existing federally funded community mental-health centers (CMHC's) must get *some* funding, although no percentage of current funding or minimum amount is set. The number of CMHC-mandated services is reduced to five. A center may also provide services to the chronically mentally ill, to severely disturbed children and adolescents, to the elderly, and to other underserved population groups, or for coordinating purposes with general health care centers; however, the authorized funding levels were cut approximately 25% from 1980 spending.

The public hearings conducted by the President's Commission and its Task Panels and the Congressional hearings on the Mental Health Systems Act pointed out that states by themselves lacked sufficient resources to develop effective programs and services for the deinstitutionalized population. States were already hard pressed to find the funds to upgrade the care offered at state hospitals. The new block grant and the federal funding cuts will make these goals even more difficult to achieve.

The suggested patients' bill of rights section of the Mental Health Systems Act is retained in the Budget Act, but no funds are authorized for advocacy. Moreover, the U.S. Supreme Court recently ruled in the Pennhurst case that a similar bill of rights contained in the Developmentally Disabled Assistance and Bill of Rights Act of 1975 was *not* mandatory. Rather, the Court found it to be an expression of Congress's wishes. The effect of these developments will be to show the movement toward national legal standards for the mentally disabled.

Support for research on the causes and treatment of mental illness is another area of concern. For the past 30 years the federal government has been the primary source of support of investigators involved in biological, psychological, and epidemiological research in mental health. In 1978, the President's Commission reported that almost 88% of all monies invested in these activities came from the federal government. The Commission also noted that most important advances in treatment of serious depression, schizophrenia, and behavior and learning disorders could be traced to the financial investment the United States had made earlier. That investment has paid off handsomely: New knowledge about the functioning of the brain and about human behavior has vastly improved our ability to control, remediate, or even prevent many mental and emotional disorders and has shifted the emphasis in mental health care from purely custodial concerns to specific medical, social, behavioral, and rehabilitative therapies.

Federal support for mental health research did increase during the 1977–1980 period as a direct result of the Commission's strong recommendation that the national research effort be restored to its pre-1969 levels. In absolute terms, funds increased approximately 65% during this period, yet expressed in inflation-adjusted dollars, NIMH had by 1980 regained a purchasing power of only 75% of the 1969 level.

During the spring and summer of 1981, as the new Congress and Administration sought to reduce the size of the federal budget, research for mental health was targeted for substantial cuts. As a result of persuasive arguments advanced by those within NIMH and HHS, by the nongovernment research community, and by mental health professional and voluntary groups, the proposed cuts were largely restored. Nonetheless, the Commission's recommendation that the research investment in the United States be commensurate with the magnitude of the problems associated with mental health is far from being realized. Without predictable, sustained funding, talented researchers will be discouraged from pursuing careers in mental health.

Many of these setbacks are the result of a continued lack of public understanding of mental illness and of those with mental or emotional problems. In its *Report*, the Commission pointed out that, despite some improvement in removing the fears and misunderstandings that surround mental illness, "many who need help do not seek it, and many who have received help do not admit it" ("Report," Vol. 1, 1978, p. 55). The stigma that is associated with mental illness continues to frustrate efforts to develop support in the legislative and executive branches of government for improving the availability and quality of care, removing unduly restrictive reimbursement rules for mental health services, and other aspects of capital investment that would improve the nation's capability to deal with increasing occurrence of emotional and mental health problems.

A FINAL NOTE

Most Americans tend to think of serious mental illness as a rarity, as something that strikes a few unfortunate people. Yet the truth is that it is not that rare. The best estimates indicate that from 10% to 15% of the American population need some form of mental health services at any one time.

In addition to the widespread misperception about the extent of mental illness in this country, the variety and complexity of mental illness with its multiple underlying causes, some known, many not, are poorly appreciated outside a relatively small circle of trained professionals, scientists, well-informed patients and their family members and people who work with them.

Underlying the gap between knowledge about mental illness and wide public appreciation and understanding of that knowledge is the stigma long associated with mental illness and the mentally ill. This stigma had its origins in ignorance in times past when little was known about how the brain functions—when "demons" and myths were invoked to explain aberrational thoughts and bizarre behavior.

This stigma was reinforced, even in more recent times, when those with serious mental illness were "put away" in institutions where they could not be observed by the general public. Long before the advances in modern therapeutic methods that were made possible by scientific discoveries which enabled greater understanding about how the brain functions, stigma was thoroughly ingrained.

Stigma of this sort leads to discrimination in a very raw form: The most distasteful characteristics of a tiny portion of the mentally ill—particularly aggression and violence—are, in the minds of many, the characteristics of all.

The impact of stigma can be measured in many ways. One is to look at where people seek help. While 21% of identifiably disordered individuals seek specialized mental health services, 54% are seen only in outpatient general health-care settings, another 3% only in nursing homes, and 20% receive *no* recognized health or mental health care at all.

Another way to measure the impact of stigma is to look at the consequences of seeking professional help. In 1978, the President's Commission on Mental Health reported that:

> Few disagree with the principle that no individual who needs assistance should feel ashamed or embarrassed to seek help. Yet people who have mental health problems or who have had them in the past are often discriminated against when they seek housing or employment, when they are involved in divorce or custody proceedings, when they are asked to serve on juries, or even when they attempt to vote. ("Report," Vol. 1, p. 55)

The suffering exacted by society on the individual following or during treatment for mental illness may be the equal of that imposed by the condition itself. The National Institute of Mental Health estimates nearly 150,000 individuals with insurance for psychotherapy never file a claim for their treatment for fear of disclosure to fellow workers or their employer. Many more insured employees decide to forego treatment entirely, because they cannot pay on their own.

This consequence of stigma is of particular importance to business and industry. Studies conducted by Kaiser Permanente and the Kennecott Corporation show definite increases in employee productivity and decreases in the utilization of general health-care services when psychotherapy coverage is utilized. Clearly, if prevailing public attitudes and peer pressure keep many employees from seeking appropriate care, even when covered by their employer, these gains will be only partially realized, and the effective cost of obtaining insurance coverage will, as a consequence, be greater.

These few data, selected from the many available, graphically set out both the lack of public understanding of mental illness and the widespread negative attitudes toward those affected by it. The realization that this twin problem of lack of understanding and negative attitudes was severely undercutting the efforts of mental health volunteers and professionals alike led in 1983 to the formation of a coalition of the major national mental health organizations. Each of the participants already conducted an information and public education program of its own but saw the need for a larger, concerted effort aimed at modifying negative perceptions about mental illness and those affected by it. Each of the organizations also saw the need for this new joint undertaking to be broadly based and independent of parochial concerns to maximize its appeal.

The new coalition has been named the *Council on Understanding Mental Illnesses (CUMI)*. Discussions to date have produced a working statement of purpose, and the group has begun planning a major national public education campaign, with an initial focus on the special problems encountered by seriously ill children, youth, and young adults and their families and on the problems of the aging.

Planning for this public information campaign has been undertaken at a time of considerable turmoil and uncertainty in the mental health field as various levels of government seek to determine what is their appropriate role in providing mental health services to those in need. Unfortunately, these discussions are themselves taking place in times of economic uncertainty, and proposals are being voiced in the Congress and in state legislatures to cut back on levels of publicly funded care and to save public dollars by increasing the responsibilities of the private sector.

In the coming debates on these and related issues, the various organizations which have formed CUMI will no doubt often take opposing positions. Despite these differences, the members are united on one front—the need to furnish the public more accurate information about mental illnesses and emotional disorders.

Such a public information campaign is long overdue in the mental health field. Similar campaigns have been launched with success in the areas of cancer detection and treatment, diabetes, and epilepsy, to name but three.

In order for a public education campaign addressing the problems of severe mental illness and emotional disorders to enjoy similar success, it will have to be carefully conceived and implemented. This will require the attention and talents of individuals and organizations heretofore not extensively involved in the mental health field, such as communications and media experts, people who understand how best to change public attitudes through educational efforts.

The organizations which have banded together to form CUMI understand that the proposed campaign must of necessity be a multiyear, ongoing effort. The stigma associated with mental illness and the resulting discrimination against the mentally ill, much like racial discrimination, will not yield to short-term fixes.

Securing sufficient resources to mount an effective educational campaign will itself be difficult in these times of increased demands on traditional philanthropic funding sources.

Nevertheless, the effort must be made, because we are convinced that without a better informed public, support for research, training, and publicly funded services will continue to erode. The result of that erosion will be continued suffering and anguish on the part of fellow citizens, suffering and anguish that should concern us all.

REFERENCES

Department of Health and Human Services Steering Committee on the Chronically Mentally Ill. (1980). Toward a National Plan for the Chronically Mentally Ill. Public Health Service, DHHS. Washington, DC.

Report to the HEW Task Force on Implementation of the Report to the President from the President's Commission on Mental Health. DHEW Publication No. (ADM) Washington, DC, U.S. Government Printing Office.

Report to the President from the President's Commission on Mental Health (Vol. 1) (1978). Washington, DC: U.S. Government Printing Office.

Report to the President of the President's Commission on Mental Health (Vol. 2) (1978). Washington, DC: U.S. Government Printing Office.

FOUR

FROM THE SOCIAL POLICY PERSPECTIVE: COMMENT AND CRITIQUE

RON HASKINS
University of North Carolina at Chapel Hill

As the three studies in this section amply demonstrate, there are no easy generalizations to be drawn from case studies. In truth, there are nearly as many routes between social policy idea and social policy enactment as there are pieces of social policy. There are major social policies, such as the guaranteed income for families with disabled children in the Supplemental Security Income program, that received virtually no attention from professionals, from policymakers, or from the media (Breen, 1979). There are also potential federal social policies, such as the guaranteed annual income and universal health insurance, that have received great media attention, have been the object of millions of dollars of research by social scientists, have been the subject of countless articles, books, and Congressional hearings, and yet have never been enacted into official social policy.

The three case studies in this section illustrate both the interplay between social science, the media, and policymakers and the varying degrees of success that are enjoyed by large-scale efforts, such as social science studies and commissions, to inform and formulate American social policy.

By way of introduction, I would first call attention to the very different policy problems addressed by these three case studies. The fundamental problem addressed by the Coleman Reports (1966b, 1975) is poor school achievement by minority students. Poor school performance by minority students and students from low-income families is a perennial social problem that has long held the attention of social scientists and policymakers, particularly since President Johnson's War on Poverty in the mid-1960s. Insofar as there has been scientific progress on this problem, it has been to show that short-term interventions, such as preschool and compensatory programs, do not have a lasting influence on achievement and that family background is by far the most powerful predictor of school achievement. Unfortunately, it is also now clear that there is no single solution to the problem—no magic bullet. This, of course, makes for an interesting scientific and public policy issue.

The pornography problem, by contrast, does not have anything like the long-term implications of school achievement by minority or low-income students. It is largely an emotional issue that surfaces from time to time, primarily through the efforts of bombastic politicians and fringe groups. Indeed, the most remarkable thing about the Commission on Obscenity and Pornography (1970) is that it concluded that pornography did not have a major influence on the behavior of adults, and that pornography was therefore not a policy problem.

The problems addressed by the President's Commission on Mental Health (1978) were, and are, of undoubted validity. Indeed, perhaps the major difficulty facing an individual or group trying to assess the status of mental health in the U.S. is the breadth, depth, and importance of the problems that fall under the rubric of "mental health." To cite a few examples at random, as a society we have major problems with depression, alcoholism, and domestic violence. These conditions cut across color and class lines, though demographic information shows that some groups suffer disproportionately from specific conditions.

There are, moreover, three major difficulties that interfere with our attempts to deal with mental health problems. First, we have little reliable information about the specific developmental conditions that determine personality development. What conditions produce an alcoholic, a child abuser, or a schizophrenic? Perhaps the only answer consistent with current knowledge is that a variety of genetic and environmental conditions interact in exceedingly complex ways to produce these and other disorders. In short—like school achievement by minority and low-income students—this policy problem is extremely complex, and our current knowledge does not allow us to make confident statements about causality.

Second, our treatments for mental health problems are not very powerful. Some, such as institutional treatment, have fallen into disfavor and are immensely expensive as well. Others, such as community-based programs, are relatively new and have not yet proven very effective. These first two problems are not unrelated. Though it is not necessary to understand the cause of a behavioral problem to design successful treatments, it certainly is helpful to understand causes in developing treatments. Thus, since causes of mental health problems are but dimly apprehended, it is not surprising that treatments are only moderately successful. Nor is there yet solid evidence that the recent emphasis on prevention will substantially alter the rates, or consequences, of specific mental health problems.

Finally, as the Mental Health Commission showed quite convincingly, the American system of delivering and financing mental health services presents some rather interesting difficulties. To name just two, there are not enough facilities or trained personnel to meet the needs of seriously disturbed people—let alone your run-of-the-mill depressed executive, and health care financing favors physical over mental health and discriminates against the poor and unemployed.

Keeping in mind this brief overview of the social policy problems addressed by the three case studies, let us deal with each of the studies in more detail. More specifically, I would like to draw several practical conclusions about the formulation or enactment of social policy from each of these case studies.

THE COLEMAN REPORTS

The original Coleman (1966b) Report has exercised a continuing influence on the academic community and the complex nexus of social scientists, the media, interest groups, and policymakers and their staffs that influence federal social policy. And for good reason. Section 2 of the Report summarized differences in the schools attended by students of various ethnic backgrounds, but especially blacks and whites. The objective characteristics of the schools attended by these groups—such as per-student expenditures, age of school buildings, and number of books in the library—proved to be quite similar. Thus, despite the conventional wisdom prevailing in 1966, the Coleman Report constituted a large-scale, authoritative source of data showing that educational inputs to black and white students were not all that different. This conclusion was strongly resisted by academicians and the media as the chapter by Grant and Murray shows.

Section 2 of the Report also showed, however, that there were impressive differences in the social environments of the schools attended by whites and blacks. Since most whites and blacks attended segregated schools, and since color is strongly associated with social and academic characteristics, the student environments experienced by whites and blacks were very different. Indeed, this was the greatest difference found in between-school characteristics.

In Section 3 of the Report, Coleman focused on standardized achievement measures, attempting to relate the differences in school inputs described in Section 2 to differences in achievement. Simplifying somewhat, these analyses demonstrated that the most important factor associated with achievement was students' family background; next most important was the social characteristics of the student body; next was teacher characteristics; and least important was objective school characteristics such as per-pupil expenditures, age of buildings, and books in the library.

With some help from hindsight, two conclusions from these findings seem especially important and controversial. First, the school inputs about which public policy had been most concerned, namely, those directly affected by per-pupil expenditures, turned out to be relatively unimportant in accounting for variance in student achievement. This finding, as the quote from *The Washington Post* cited by Grant and Murray trenchantly put it, was an educational "time bomb." Because it was a basic challenge to a fundamental premise of American education—that expenditures on school facilities and equipment would have a substantial impact on learning—the conclusion could have been expected to provoke strong reaction. It did—and still does.

Second, Coleman himself believed that the finding that student social environment was associated with achievement provided a strong justification for integration. The most efficient way to improve the social environment experienced by black and other minority students, who as a group lacked precisely the background characteristics associated with achievement, was to put them in schools with white students, who by and large possessed the background characteristics associated with achievement by their fellow students.

If Coleman's findings were as straightforward as I have suggested, and if they provided a solid rationale for integration—which is what the administration and the Congress were looking for when the study was commissioned—then why all the sound and fury? And what can this case study tell us about the tangled relations among academic research, the media, and public policy? Grant and Murray do a fine job of providing us with answers to these questions. Let me briefly summarize the two I consider most important.

First, it is nearly an axiom of media reporting that complex social science reports can befuddle, intimidate, and even alienate all but the most dogged journalists. Anyone interested in using the electronic and print media to inform the public and create mass sentiment favoring a particular policy position can never count on accurate reporting if the press receives only a jargon-filled, 700-page behemoth packed with tables and appendixes. The blind eye in this case is not that of the beholder. Grant and Murray's rendition of the July 1, 1966, press conference announcing the Coleman findings demonstrates this principle quite clearly.

Aides to Education Commissioner Howe wrote a press release that, if not inaccurate, was certainly misleading. Evidently they did so with full confidence that the Washington press corps would rely on the press release and not the text of the Coleman Report itself.

Nonetheless, the saga of the Coleman Report shows that you can't fool all the press all the time. Thus, Coleman's (1966a) own review of his findings and their policy implications in the September, 1966, issue of *The Public Interest* effectively and succinctly conveyed his views to the social science community and the few reporters who read such journals. Jencks's October article in the *New Republic* (1966) reached an even wider audience, and Nichols's (1966) superb and provocative article in *Science* forcefully brought the Coleman message to a wider audience still. By December, *The Washington Post* was bringing its "educational time bomb" thesis to the American public.

This case study brings me to the following set of suggestions regarding social science reports and the media. Academicians have three responsibilities in communicating policy-relevant findings. First, they must make available a short and vivid document summarizing their findings in plain English. Second, they must draw the policy implications that seem most appropriate and express these in a similarly unadorned fashion. Third, if necessary, they must make themselves available to the media to answer questions about the results and conclusions.

Though Grant and Murray are not as bold as I have been in making these recommendations, their story of the Coleman Report shows what can happen to good and important social science work if its authors do not effectively communicate their results to audiences other than the dozen or so graduate students who will read the journal version of their work. Most of our work, of course, deserves to be read by graduate students. But it isn't only the Coleman Reports, Moynihan Reports (1965), and Jensen reviews (1969) that deserve attention from the American public. A small but not insubstantial portion of empirical work by social scientists has direct implications for public policy. The public pays the bill, and they do not do so to insure that the *Journal of Abstract Research* has something to fill its pages.

What I am arguing is that social scientists have a responsibility to draw and publicize the practical implications of their work. If they don't, somebody else will—or what's worse, their work will be ignored. In this regard, the final sections of Grant and Murray's chapter, which might be aptly titled "The Education of James Coleman," is quite instructive.

A second generalization that might be drawn from the story of Coleman's well-publicized Reports is at once more complex and less certain. That social scientists must draw the practical implications of their work and be ready to defend their judgments I take as axiomatic. The problem is that findings are one thing, policy recommendations are another. Social science is conservative, cautious, cumulative; policy recommendations are bold, innovative, argumentative, even provocative. Further, not many people care whether correlation is causation, or whether and under what circumstances causal arguments—for policy judgments are inherently causal—based on social science research can be considered valid. By contrast, journalists, policymakers, and concerned citizens care very much whether the school achievement of minority youngsters can be improved by changing the social environment provided by the public schools.

Based on his 1966 study, Coleman concluded that the achievement of minority students could indeed be improved if they went to schools populated by middle-class students. Since so few blacks were middle class, Coleman concluded that integration held some promise of increasing black achievement, because integration would increase the proportion of middle-class students with whom blacks went to school. In 1966, then, Coleman supported integration.

By 1975, however, with the publication of *Trends in School Desegregation, 1968–1973*, Coleman was disappointing many of those who supported integration. In fact, as Grant and Murray point out, he came in for some rather strong criticism from members of the academic and civil rights communities. On inspection, however, Coleman's basic position had not changed at all. He originally favored integration on the grounds that empirical data suggested that appropriate mixes of students would improve the achievement of black students. Now new data was available showing that the busing that was necessary to bring together the appropriate mix of students in urban areas had the perverse effect of resegregating students by causing white families to move to the suburbs. Thus, busing defeated the very purpose for which it was designed. In short, the conditions that Coleman concluded in 1966 would increase achievement among minority students had not been achieved by busing.

The problem, of course, is that such a conclusion is easy enough to misinterpret. As Grant and Murray demonstrate, Coleman's conclusions were in fact misinterpreted, not only by the media but by members of the academic community as well. Since complex conclusions are always subject to misinterpretation, especially by people who don't like the conclusions, I am led to argue that such misrepresentations and acrimony as Coleman generated with his 1975 report are an inevitable part of taking a public position on controversial issues. Public figures, including social scientists, need thick skin.

THE COMMISSION ON OBSCENITY AND PORNOGRAPHY

Commissions are to empirical studies as meetings are to lucubration. The general idea is to assemble a group of people representing every known group that has anything to do with the topic at hand and to have them produce a report containing: (a) an assessment of the problem; (b) an explanation of the problem; and (c) a recommended solution to the problem. As I have argued elsewhere (Haskins, 1983), commissions are a superb way to buy time, to evade an issue, or to draw attention away from a president or a Congress, but often not a very good way to make policy.

Paul Bender, a lawyer who was general counsel to the Pornography Commission, provides us with an excellent survey of this Commission, its activities, its recommendations, and the rather pathetic fate of its primary recommendation. The story can be quickly summarized.

The Commission was established by Congress in 1967 to study the "causal relationship" of obscenity and pornography to "antisocial behavior" and to recommend means to deal with traffic in obscenity and pornography. At the time, there was little doubt in the minds of policymakers that pornography contributed to antisocial behavior—as the above-quoted wording of the charge to the Commission suggests. Nonetheless, after completing its work, which included several empirical studies, the Commission concluded that pornography did not have a major influence on antisocial behavior such as crime, delinquency, or sexual deviancy. Logically enough, the Commission used this finding as justification for its major and most controversial recommendation; namely, that "federal, state and local legislation prohibiting the sale, exhibition, or distribution of sexual materials to consenting adults should be repealed." Like the recommendations of many commissions, this recommendation did not produce its intended effect. Indeed, as Bender points out, President Nixon categorically rejected the Commission's "bankrupt conclusions and major recommendations" as overly permissive and likely to contribute to "an atmosphere condoning anarchy." The Senate reacted even more sharply. In an action that opened a new chapter in the history of epistemology, the Senate passed a bill rejecting the Commission's findings. This episode bestowed upon the Pornography Commission the dubious distinction of causing the U.S. Senate to declare as null and void the results of social science research.

The story of the Pornography Commission demonstrates several of the strengths and weaknesses of commissions as a tool of public policy. A general examination of Presidential and Congressional commissions (Haskins, 1983) suggests that most commissions are remarkably independent. The idea of a commission is to appoint informed and reasonable people to study a problem and make recommendations free of the political constraints that are an inevitable part of the legislative process. Thus, it should come as no surprise that several commissions—notably the Kerner Commission (National Advisory Commission, 1968) on civil disorders in the U.S., the Surgeon General's 1972 committee on TV and violence, and the Commission on Population Growth (1972)—have produced recommendations that were bold and, to say the least, devoid of political feasibility. This I take to be a great strength of commissions, and the Pornography Commission was unsurpassed in this respect. To the extent that commissions should examine the evidence and make recommendations, letting the chips fall where they may, the Pornography Commission was eminently successful.

A second generalization suggested by the Pornography Commission is that commissions which experience a change of administrations during their tenure are likely to see their recommendations receive a frosty reception. This generalization applies with special force when the administrations in question represent different political parties. In the case at hand, the Pornography Commission was appointed by President Johnson but reported to President Nixon. One can hardly imagine two Presidents with more diverse political philosophies and priorities. Even so, given the touchiness of the pornography issue and the riskiness of appearing to support smut, one might doubt whether the substance of President Johnson's response to the Pornography Commission would have been any different than that of President Nixon.

As Bender indicates in his last paragraph, however, the immediate response to a Commission's recommendations should not be confused with the Commission's ultimate impact. Although the Pornography Commission recommendations were rejected by President Nixon and the U.S. Senate in 1970, since that time several states have either repealed or refused to strengthen their pornography laws, and prosecutions for legal violations of pornography offenses—and particularly for cases involving distribution of materials among consenting adults—have declined sharply in recent years. Moreover, as Bender points out, "antiobscenity crusades" have lost a great deal of their political appeal. This trend may well represent a change in American mores—a trend that may have been accelerated by the Commission's "no harm" finding and its recommendations for repeal of most pornography laws.

THE MENTAL HEALTH COMMISSION

Like several recent commissions, and most notably the Select Panel for the Promotion of Child Health (1981), the President's Commission on Mental Health (1978) produced a massive, thorough, and competent report. Briefly, the Commission Report summarized the major mental health problems faced by America in the late 1970s, reviewed several potential solutions to these problems, and presented detailed discussion of eight general areas in which improvements in the nation's mental health system would be effective and timely. In all, the Commission presented 117 specific recommendations to President Carter.

The chapter by Bryant (who chaired the Mental Health Commission), Meyers, and Cade is an excellent summary, not simply of the Mental Health Commission and its Report, but of the fate of the Commission's major recommendations. This latter part of their story is especially instructive and illuminates several of the points made earlier.

Unlike the Coleman Report and the Pornography Commission, the Mental Health Commission reported under extremely propitious circumstances. Rosalynn Carter had served as honorary chairperson of the Commission, President Carter was seriously interested in mental health and committed to doing something about the problem, there was substantial consensus among commission members about the generally incremental approaches recommended by the Commission, and the Commission recommendations were quite moderate in tone and scope. Further, the President enjoyed a majority in both houses of the Congress, and the administrative branch of the federal government was favorably disposed to taking action on Commission recommendations. Few commissions have delivered their recommendations into such a favorable political setting.

Despite these favorable conditions, the Commission recommendations led to only minor reform in mental health services. Perhaps the clearest example of this generalization was the Mental Health Systems Act of 1980.

Slippage in attempts to implement Commission recommendations began when Dr. Peter Bourne, the President's close friend and special assistant for health issues, left the administration in late 1978. Until that time, Dr. Bourne had played the critical role in responding to Commission recommendations by serving as a top-level force in the White House to produce bureaucratic action. After the Commission Report was delivered to the President, Bourne worked closely with Commission Chairman Bryant and a group of federal agency representatives to produce an action plan. After he left the Administration, his pivotal duties fell to Secretary Califano who proceeded to study the Commission recommendations to death. Consequently, it was not until May, 1979—after several time-consuming rewrites of the Carter legislation—that the legislation was introduced in Congress. There followed several months of Congressional testimony and legislative revision. The final legislation, watered down and underfunded at that, was not passed by the Congress until September, 1980. Within 5 months, the nation had a new President who was, to say the least, hostile to mental health initiatives. Indeed, Reagan's Omnibus Budget Reconciliation Act of 1981 in effect ended several of the most innovative features of the Mental Health Systems Act, and especially the financial partnership between federal, state, and local governments.

Several points can be made about the fate of the Mental Health Commission recommendations. First, as was the case with the Pornography Commission, a change in presidential administrations spelled doom for Commission recommendations. Despite this similarity between the two commissions, however, we should attend to a major difference in timing between the respective commission reports. Whereas the Mental Health Commission reported to the President who had initiated the Commission, the Pornography Commission reported to a newly elected President. Thus, the findings and recommendations of the Pornography Commission were rejected out of hand by the new administration, while the findings and recommendations of the Mental Health Commission were actively pursued by the Carter Administration. Indeed, the Carter Administration was actually successful in shepherding legislation through the Congress that embodied several of the Commission's primary recommendations. Thus, it can fairly be said that the immediate impact of the Mental Health Commission was much greater than that of the Pornography Commission.

In fact, the reasons for the substantial immediate impact of the Mental Health Commission bear emphasis. Unlike the Pornography Commission, the Mental Health Commission made recommendations that were quite feasible. Although fewer recommendations probably would have been advisable, the major recommendations concerning mental health financing and federal–state–local partnership were incremental in nature and based on years of experience in federal–state relations. Thus, the recommendations were not difficult to translate into legislation, and undoubtedly seemed reasonable to Senators and Representatives who in fact later approved the legislation.

Moreover, after the Commission Report had been officially received by the President and the fanfare had died down, a structure was put in place to produce action on Commission recommendations. This structure was notable in several respects. First, a well-placed White House bureaucrat—Dr. Bourne—was responsible for organizing the Administration's implementation of Commission recommendations. Dr. Bourne was not only in a strong bureaucratic position to act with authority, but also had a long-standing personal relationship with the President which ensured access to Mr. Carter and gave his actions added authority. Second, Dr. Bourne involved the major departments of government that would implement the legislation, thereby bringing them in for suggestions and negotiations early in the legislative process. Finally, Dr. Bryant, the Commission chairman, worked closely with Dr. Bourne in drafting the original legislation. All in all, these procedures could serve as a model for insuring timely and direct action on the recommendations of any commission. To the extent that commissions wish to effect action and not simply discussion, these several characteristics of Mental Health Commission follow-up deserve repetition.

CONCLUSIONS

The chapters in this section, and the foregoing review of the case studies described in these chapters, do not constitute a neat package of algorithms for designing social policy and insuring its enactment and implementation. Nonetheless, they do accurately depict the complexity of relations among social science research, policy deliberation bodies such as commissions, the media, and policymakers. I conclude, then, as I began—with the dictum that there are not simple and infallible rules for the construction and enactment of social policy.

On the other hand, as I have tried to show, each of these case studies offers several generalizations that can serve as rough guidelines for those who would either create or apply social science knowledge to the design of social policy.

REFERENCES

Breen, P. (1979). *Participation of disabled children in the supplemental security income program.* Unpublished manuscript, University of North Carolina, Bush Institute for Child and Family Policy, Chapel Hill.

Coleman, J. S. (1966a). Educational dilemmas: Equal schools or equal students. *Public Interest, 4,* 70–75.

Coleman, J. S. (1966b). *Equality of educational opportunity.* Washington, DC: U.S. Government Printing Office.

Coleman, J. S. (1975). *Trends in social desegregation, 1968–1973.* Washington, DC: Urban Institute.

Commission on Obscenity and Pornography. (1970). *The report of the commission on obscenity and pornography.* Washington, DC: U.S. Government Printing Office.

Commission on Population Growth and the American Future. (1972). *Population and the American future.* Washington, DC: U.S. Government Printing Office.

Haskins, R. (Ed.). (1983). *Child health policy in an age of fiscal austerity: Critiques of the Select Panel Report.* Norwood, NJ: Ablex.

Jencks, C. S. (1966). Education: The racial gap. *New Republic, 155,* 21–26.

Jensen, A. R. (1969). How much can we boost IQ and scholastic achievement? *Harvard Educational Review, 39,* 1–123.

Moynihan, D. P. (1965). *The Negro family: The case for national action.* Washington, DC: Office of Policy Planning and Research, U.S. Department of Labor.

National Advisory Commission on Civil Disorders. (1968). *Report of the national advisory commission on civil disorders.* Washington, DC: U.S. Government Printing Office.

Nichols, R. C. (1966). Schools and the disadvantaged. *Science, 154,* 1312–1314.

President's Commission on Mental Health. (1978). *Report to the President* (3 Vols.). Washington, DC: U.S. Government Printing Office.

Select Panel for the Promotion of Child Health. (1981). *Better health for our children: A national strategy* (4 Vols.). Washington, DC: U.S. Government Printing Office.

Surgeon General's Scientific Advisory Committee on Television and Social Behavior. (1972). *Television and social behavior: Reports and papers* (6 Vols.). Washington, DC: U.S. Government Printing Office.

PART TWO

FROM THE SOCIAL SCIENCE PERSPECTIVE

FIVE

TELEVISION AND CHILDREN: A PUBLIC POLICY DILEMMA

ELI A. RUBINSTEIN and JANE D. BROWN
University of North Carolina at Chapel Hill

TV Violence Held Unharmful to Youth. (Gould, 1972)
Report Links TV Violence to Aggression. (Russell, 1982)

Those two front page headlines, the first in *The New York Times* and the latter in *The Washington Post*, mark the difference over time in print media response to a complex scientific inquiry. That difference is partly due to the accumulation of hundreds of studies published in the intervening years and, concurrently, a greater familiarity by the news media with this scientific issue. As might be expected, the television industry's corporate reaction was somewhat different. That contrast provides an intriguing example of how scientific information is interpreted by the media, especially when such findings directly effect one branch of the communications industry.

In order to understand this sequence in which television is itself both the object of scrutiny and then a judge of the validity of that scientific inquiry, it is important first to review the findings and then see how they were reacted to, both by the television industry and in the media generally. And, finally, it is necessary to see how social policy has been influenced by this special circumstance of the industry reaction to an outside examination of itself.

THE 1972 SURGEON GENERAL'S REPORT

A number of publications have reviewed the major research program on the effects of television on children initiated in 1969 and concluded in 1972, which resulted in five volumes of technical studies plus an overall evaluation and separate report to the Surgeon General by a prestigious scientific advisory committee. In addition to extended articles (Bogart, 1972; Rubinstein, 1976), the entire effort was analyzed in depth by Cater and Strickland (1975) to evaluate its impact on public policy.

As most individuals who have looked at 'the history of American television know, public concern about violence on television has been active, at varying levels of intensity, for more than 30 years. Until 1969, however, no government attention had gone beyond Congressional inquiries at which various expert opinions were expressed. Network officials had been called in to testify and invariably stated that televised violence was not excessive and that there was no scientific evidence that it was harmful. In any case, these officials contended, violence was being reduced. No government action was forthcoming until the next round of hearings two to five years later, which repeated the scenario of expert opinion and industry rebuttal.

In March 1969, Senator John Pastore, then chairman of the Senate Subcommittee on Communications, in a letter to Secretary Robert Finch of the Department of Health, Education, and Welfare (DHEW), asked that the Surgeon General be directed to appoint a committee of distinguished scientists and "conduct a study" to "establish scientifically" whether televised violence is harmful to children. Senator Pastore had long been concerned about this question and wanted a definitive scientific answer. It was that request and the expenditure of $1 million which resulted, three years later, in producing 43 new studies.

For the first time, major new research was brought to bear on the issue. Furthermore, the work in the Surgeon General's program had been accomplished under the direction of the National Institute of Mental Health (NIMH), which had a reputation for sponsoring and supporting much of the innovative research being done by the most competent social scientists in the country. The technical reports included a wide range of studies from laboratory experiments to field studies involving hundreds of children. Sociological studies of how the industry produces children's programs and a survey of how the public and television critics perceive televised violence were also included. An extensive survey was done of how violence on television was seen from the broadcast industry's point of view. And, finally, a periodic content analysis of the level of televised violence was established (Gerbner, 1972) which has continued ever since to monitor annual changes in levels of violence on prime-time commercial television.

The total body of scientific findings produced in this research program provided important new evidence by which to determine the answer to Senator Pastore's question. The advisory committee came to a unanimous conclusion that the "convergence . . . of evidence constitutes some preliminary indication of a causal relationship" between televised violence and later aggressive behavior in children (Surgeon General's Scientific Advisory Committee, 1972, p. 10, hereafter referred to as the Surgeon General's Committee).

At this point, the media became involved in their role as information disseminators. Soon after the Scientific Advisory Committee had written its report to the Surgeon General, but before the technical reports had been physically put into publishable form, plans were developed for a press conference by the Surgeon General on January 19, 1972. He was to give a brief summary of the findings and the committee's conclusion that there was preliminary evidence of a causal relationship between televised violence and later aggressive behavior in children. In preparation for this public release the "findings and conclusions" summary chapter was printed as a separate document to be distributed the day of the press conference as a background to the Surgeon General's remarks. The full report was then to be made available to the public.

At least one writer, Jack Gould, television editor of *The New York Times*, received not one, but four leaked copies of that summary chapter on January 10 (Cater & Strickland, 1975). *The New York Times* front-page story appeared the following day. In addition to this premature disclosure of the story, the headline was a misinterpretation of the findings. Gould never quoted the key Committee conclusion that preliminary evidence of a causal relationship had been found, but instead noted in his lead sentence that the "Surgeon General has found that violence in television programming does not have an adverse effect on the majority of the nation's youth, but may influence small groups of youngsters predisposed by many factors to aggressive behavior" (Gould, 1972).

That *New York Times* story, and especially the unequivocal headline, produced a flurry of public and political reaction. The effect of that story on further press coverage by other newspapers reveals how influential the headline was in adding confusion to the interpretation of the findings. An analysis by Tankard and Showalter (1977) documents that the misinterpretation was never fully corrected. More importantly, the government study itself had been under an earlier cloud because it had been revealed in an earlier magazine article (*Science*, May 22, 1970) that some members of the Scientific Advisory Committee had had direct or indirect affiliation with the television industry. Thus, *The New York Times* headline, in the absence of the published report, fueled Congressional and public suspicion that there had been a "whitewash." Some of the researchers whose work had lead to the Committee conclusion of the causal relationship were especially irate. Since these scientists also had not seen the published committee Report, they were incensed at the presumed misreading of their findings. Some of the scientists lost no time in complaining both to Congress and to the press. The controversy stimulated additional articles in newspapers and national news weeklies.

Despite an after-the-fact news briefing held by the Surgeon General on January 17, 1972, in which he clarified the findings and denied the whitewash, there was sufficient public concern and confusion that Senator Pastore decided to hold public hearings to reassess the report and, more importantly, to address the question of policy recommendations to Congress and the networks—a step that the Surgeon General and his Advisory Committee had specifically been enjoined by the Secretary of DHEW from taking in their original scientific inquiry because DHEW had no regulatory responsibility in this area.

On March 21–23, 1972, hearings by the Senate Subcommittee on Communications heard testimony from Jesse Steinfeld, the Surgeon General, Eli A. Rubinstein, the vice chairman of the Advisory Committee and coordinator of the research program, and 7 of the 12 members of the Committee. Various researchers who had contributed to the Report, the chairman and members of the Federal Communications Commission, the presidents of all three networks and the president of the National Association of Broadcasters also testified (U.S. Congress, 1972).

Under questioning from Senator Pastore, the Surgeon General unequivocally asserted that the evidence was sufficient to warrant action to reduce violence on television. The Surgeon General stressed that the Committee had come to a unanimous conclusion in its Report. No members of the Committee at the hearing disagreed with the assertion that action was warranted and all agreed there was too much violence on television. Agreement came specifically from Joseph Klapper, who was the director of social research at CBS and from Thomas Coffin, in a comparable position at NBC. Furthermore, all three network presidents agreed that the time for action had come and they pledged to redouble past efforts to reduce televised violence in the future (U.S. Congress, 1972).

At the conclusion of the hearings Senator Pastore declared that a "scientific and cultural breakthrough" had been achieved. Certainly those who had participated in this research effort believed that significant changes would follow from the conclusions of the Surgeon General's program. Those expectations were not to be fulfilled, at least in the decade that followed.

AFTER THE SURGEON GENERAL'S PROGRAM

In a scholarly overview of the trends in violent content in television, Comstock (1982) calls the period immediately following the Surgeon General's Report (1972–1974) one of "controversy and apathy." As he notes, debate began to develop on the value and accuracy of measuring televised violence. The networks began to question the validity of the violence index developed by Gerbner and his colleagues. At the same time, the NIMH commissioned the Social Science Research Council (S.S.R.C.) to evaluate measures of violence and to recommend methods of measurement. The Council, after two years of deliberations, essentially endorsed the Gerbner approach, with some modifications (S.S.R.C., 1975).

More importantly, no clear plan of policy action was developed from the Surgeon General's efforts. Various policy recommendations were voiced at the hearings held by Senator Pastore in March, 1972, but none included plans for implementation. Senator Pastore himself called for an annual violence index, to be published by the Secretary of the DHEW. No formal steps were initiated to develop such a formal survey. Instead Gerbner and his colleagues have accomplished annual monitoring with funds solicited from various federal and private sources (Signorielli, Gross, & Morgan, 1982).

Ironically, one of the most specific sets of policy recommendations appeared in an article in the *Reader's Digest* in 1973 by the Surgeon General. (The article was actually ghost written by a senior editor of the magazine, but attributed to the Surgeon General, with his agreement, because magazine policy at that time precluded staff-written articles.) In that article the Surgeon General reaffirmed his conviction that immediate action was needed and recommended that: (a) television stations air public service messages that "Too much TV can be hazardous to your child's mental health"; (b) the FCC require stations to publicize the results of scientific evaluations to be made of the merits and demerits of programs children watch; (c) the FCC formally adopt a "family television time" for broadcasting between 7:30 and 9 p.m.; and that (d) parents "demand" better television for their children by joining citizens' action groups and petitioning the FCC to require quality programming for television (Steinfeld, 1973). Of these four recommendations, only the "family television time" was adopted and that was on a voluntary rather than required basis.

The "apathy" that Comstock refers to is perhaps better called a brief dormant period, because by 1975 a number of circumstances rekindled the concern about televised violence and its effects. Probably the most influential event was a fortuitous involvement of the American Medical Association (AMA) with this issue of televised violence.

In the December 8, 1975, edition of the *Journal of the American Medical Association* (JAMA), a cover story highlighted the scientific evidence on the effect of televised violence. The author called for a "major, organized cry of protest from the medical profession in relation to what, in political terms, I consider a national scandal" (Rothenberg, 1975). The author, a psychiatrist and pediatrician, with no prior formal involvement in television research, wrote the article out of a personal interest in the topic and sent it to JAMA, even though he was not a member of the AMA. The journal editor decided to feature the article as a cover story, which immediately brought it to the direct attention of 250,000 readers in the medical profession.

Within the year, the prestigious *New England Journal of Medicine* had articles and editorials calling for an end to televised violence. In a special analysis, Feingold and Johnson (1977) surveyed the responses from more than 15,000 readers of the *Journal* denouncing the violence on television. They also noted that both advertisers and network executives had been contacted and had shown some qualified concern about the problem. Stating that the burden of responsibility ws on the industry to prove that televised violence was not harmful, Feingold and Johnson called for continued public pressure through boycott of products advertised on violent shows and through written complaints to the networks.

At the same time, in June, 1976, the AMA House of Delegates officially adopted a policy identifying televised violence as an "environmental hazard" threatening the health and welfare of young Americans. The president of the AMA wrote to a number of major advertisers requesting that they not sponsor programs with excessive violence. The national PTA also pressed for reduction of televised violence. The networks responded by acknowledging the public outcry and promised to reduce the violence level.

In 1977, for the first time since the Surgeon General's report in 1972, the annual content analysis by Gerbner showed a decrease from levels of the previous year (Signorielli et al., 1982).

Furthermore, the Congress and the FCC were getting into the act again. In 1974, the FCC had issued a report and policy statement on children's television (U.S. FCC, 1974) calling for increased educational and informational television, but no formal rules were adopted, making the statement of little threat to the industry. Also in late 1974, the concept of "family viewing" was developed for early evening viewing time. In 1975, the plan was voluntarily adopted as part of the industry self-regulatory code. (Ironically, various writers' and directors' guilds complained that the family viewing hour was an infringement of First Amendment rights and the Federal District Court in Los Angeles declared the rule unconstitutional. It had been, nevertheless, continued as an informal procedure.)

Congress, through the House Committee on Interstate and Foreign Commerce, held public hearings in 1976 and 1977 on televised violence. By a narrow vote of 8 to 7, the Committee indicated its concern about such violence, but concluded that parental supervision and industry self-regulation were the most effective controls. The minority of 7 were more firmly convinced by the scientific evidence of televised violence's harmful effects and argued that the FCC had effective ways to influence programming change and should use those methods (Comstock, 1982).

Thus, no tangible government intervention followed the considerable visibility of the question produced by the normally influential medical profession.

By 1978, the AMA decided to move to other public issues and discontinued its campaign against televised violence. The PTA continued its efforts, but at a much reduced level. In 1978, despite the earlier protestations of the networks that change was taking place, the Gerbner index showed a rise in violence (Signorielli et al., 1982).

BEYOND VIOLENCE: NEW RESEARCH DIRECTIONS

While little progress was being made on policy issues, research on television and children was flourishing. At the time of the Surgeon General's report in 1972, about 500 publications on television and youth had been published. By 1975, that number had doubled, and by 1980 almost 3000 such publications had been produced (Pearl, Bouthilet, & Lazar, 1982).

More importantly, violent content on television was no longer the central focus of attention. In an overview of television and social behavior (Withey & Abeles, 1980) the clear extension of research interest beyond violence is documented in chapters ranging from psychological effects of black portrayals on television to an examination of organizational and economic influences on the structure and operation of American television. Only one chapter (Bogart, 1980) directly discusses the violence question in an historical account of research and policy developments in the five years after the 1972 Surgeon General's Report.

In another and even more comprehensive review of research developments through the mid-1970s (Comstock, Chaffee, Katzman, McCombs and Roberts, 1978) it becomes evident that scientists had turned their attention to so many questions beyond violence that the title of this review, "Television and Human Behavior" was an apt description of the range of topics under examination.

A number of major new topics were beginning to emerge that had only been initial forays in the Surgeon General's program: the effects of advertising on children; the converse of the violence question, i.e. how does "prosocial" programming affect positive behavior?; and developmental changes in children's responses to television. One topic already being researched, but not addressed at all in the Surgeon General's program, since it was not related to the issue of violence, was that of television news and television's impact on the political process. By 1977, a considerable research literature had accumulated on this topic. Also, the impact of television on special populations, such as women, the blacks, the poor and the elderly was beginning to be examined.

In the broadest context, the approach of all this new research examines "television as a teacher." That rubric, in fact, was the title of a research monograph published by NIMH (1981). A group of researchers contributed chapters in which television's role as a teacher was documented from various perspectives. This informal instruction by television goes well beyond the more obvious approaches such as those demonstrated by "Sesame Street" and the "Electric Company." By the later part of the 1970s, research had clearly shown that television influences social learning in multiple ways. Even cognitive development has been shown to be affected, not just as a function of time spent watching television, but as a result of the influence of learning the structural codes of television on the development of information processing (Salomon, 1979).

Siegel (NIMH, 1981) raises a critical question that derives from television's role as a teacher: How competent and conscientious are the television writers and producers in providing this informal education? Siegel makes the intriguing observation that, unlike doctors or teachers, the television professionals get no direct feedback on how they affect children. This absence of direct knowledge about response only reinforces the television writers and producers' sense of security that they have no responsibility for the children's welfare. What is needed, Siegel argues, is the same professional linkage between practice and research that exists in fields like health, education, and agriculture.

A TEN-YEAR REEVALUATION

By this time, in the late 1970s, despite an ever enlarging body of research, a public policy stalemate was in effect. Public reaction had waxed and waned during that decade. Even though some public groups, especially those with a religious affiliation, were expressing concern about both sex and violence on television, no major government interest seemed apparent.

In October, 1979, the FCC did issue an extensive report on television programming for children. In that report, a long delayed follow-up to its 1974 report, the FCC examined the amount, quality, and scheduling of children's programs. The Commission noted that its 1974 policy statement had put broadcasters on notice that they had a responsibility to treat children as a special audience with special needs.

The FCC found that characteristics of "the advertiser-supported broadcasting system, result in the failure of the market to provide a socially optimal level and type of television programming for children" (U.S. FCC, 1979, pp. 42–43). The staff report recommended a rule requiring 5 hours per week of educational or instructional programming for preschoolers and 2½ hours per week for school-age children. Unfortunately, by the time the FCC got around to considering a formal implementation, the political climate had cooled toward all manner of government regulation, and no action was taken by the FCC.

In the meanwhile, the research findings continued to accumulate. In early 1979, a group of researchers in the field suggested to the Surgeon General, Dr. Julius Richmond, that a comprehensive review be published on this body of literature as an update to the original Surgeon General's Report. Initially it was intended that this 10-year update be issued as a Surgeon General's Report, in much the same way as the Surgeon General had been issuing periodic reports on smoking and health. However, by the time the comprehensive review had been completed in 1982, Dr. Richmond was no longer Surgeon General, and it was decided to issue the Report as a responsibility of the National Institute of Mental Health, with the aid of a group of seven senior advisers.

The Report was issued in two volumes. The first was a summary report. The second was comprised of a series of 24 review articles by experts commissioned to prepare integrative analyses of specific topics selected by the advisory group to represent areas of importance. Again, as in the original 1972 Report, where the emphasis was on entertainment programming, research on political socialization and on news programs were omitted. The coverage, however, was specifically intended to reflect a research agenda which had long since removed the violence question from the focus of scientific attention, even though it still held center stage in the public arena.

If any single statement epitomizes what was found it might be the following: "Television can no longer be considered as a casual part of daily life, as an electronic toy. Research findings have long since destroyed the illusion that television is merely innocuous entertainment. While the learning it provides is mainly incidental, rather than direct and formal, it is a significant part of the total acculturation process" (Pearl et al., 1982, vol. 1, p. 87).

What are the major research findings that document the conclusion that television is now a significant influence on child development? The ten-year update of the 1972 Report to the Surgeon General divides the research output of the past decade into five major categories: cognitive and affective aspects of television; violence and aggression; social beliefs and social behavior; television and social relations; and television and health. In addition, the update looks at the role of television in American society.

Violence and Aggression

The most widely publicized conclusion of the 1982 NIMH Report was on televised violence. The press and the network news all had stories in early May, 1982, which highlighted the finding that violence on television leads to aggressive behavior by children. That conclusion was not universally accepted. As might be expected, the television industry was especially critical. Nor is it likely that the criticism will soon disappear.

Granted that the data are complex and that no single study unequivocally documents the connection between televised violence and later aggressive behavior, the convergence of evidence from many studies is overwhelming and was so interpreted in the NIMH Report.

In the simplest terms, only three possibilities exist in this equation: (a) television has no significant relationship to aggressive behavior: (b) television reduces aggressive behavior; or (c) television increases aggressive behavior. Almost all the studies reviewed in the past decade support the third possibility. Both in the original Report to the Surgeon General and in the 10-year update, the so-called "catharsis" theory (that TV reduces aggressiveness) was repudiated.

What remains as a troubling question comes from the handful of studies which conclude that television has no significant relationship to aggressive behavior. Indeed, the most recent and most comprehensive study supporting the "no relationship" finding is included in the NIMH Report (Milavsky, Kessler, Stipp, & Rubens, 1982). Based on a panel survey of more than 3,000 children over a 3-year period, these researchers concluded that no evidence emerged which "causally implicated" televised violence in the development of aggressive behavior. That conclusion and the original data probably will be reexamined by other researchers. Controversial interpretations are likely.

What is self-evident in this situation, as with other complicated scientific questions, is that research is almost never unequivocal in its interpretation. Nevertheless, this major research finding of the NIMH Report regarding the linkage of televised violence to later aggressive behavior clearly represents the psition of the great majority of scientists working in this field. The burden of proof to contradict this conclusion is yet to be met.

Cognitive and Affective Aspects of Television

Another area of research that has received much scientific attention over the past decade involves how the cognitive and emotional development in children modifies or influences their response to television. It has long been recognized that children do not see or understand what is viewed on the television screen in the same way an adult does. Much recent research has been devoted to analyzing what changes in attention and comprehension occur as the age of the viewer increases from that of preschooler through adolescence.

The research reviewed in the NIMH Report clearly documents that first- and second-grade children are not yet able to follow a complex plot line through the entire sequence of discrete scenes. An important corollary of this finding is that young children are often unable to relate a series of complex actions to their final consequence. Thus, when industry spokespersons claim that their programs are fundamentally prosocial because good ultimately triumphs over bad, they ignore this important finding. The young child is much less likely to make the interpretive connection and, therefore, less likely to learn the moral lesson.

The entire process of growing up with television means that not only do children perceive differently at different stages of development, those stages of development are themselves influenced by extensive television viewing. For example, in what ways do the structural forms of television influence the way children process information? And in what ways do aspects of form influence how content is perceived? Research on these and other questions is still in its early stages, but already reveals important findings. Children's attention is heightened by lively music, sound effects, special visual effects, high levels of physical activity or action, and rapid changes in scene.

What is important in these and other findings about the effects of structural form is that it adds a new dimension to the understanding of television effects. It may be, as some research suggests, that aggression can be stimulated by high levels of action even without high violent content. Or it could be that children, already associating high action with high violence, respond to the former even when the latter is not present (Pearl et al., 1982).

Another area of research in which content itself is not the focus of concern involves the concept of arousal. Findings suggest that some television viewing can heighten a state of general arousal. This increased level of excitement may then be channeled into various behaviors, including aggression, depending on the existing circumstances. Thus, exciting television programming, regardless of specific content, may induce certain behaviors. While we have no evidence of any long-term effects of high arousal, it is not inappropriate to ask if the excitatory influence of television viewing has any effect on the child's response to other stimuli in the child's environment that are less stimulating. Are the child's expectations of excitement, enhanced by television, unmet in the classroom? And, if so, that are the consequences?

Research on the influence of television on emotional development is still in its early stages. It is clear that television viewing can produce emotional response. Does a continued arousal of emotions ultimately lead to decreased emotional response? Data are scarce, but it is an important question. Indeed, one of the most intriguing questions—for which no answer is presently available—involves the long-term effects of vicarious emotional experiences through television. The combined visual and auditory messages on television allow the young child to become involved in events not only long before any similar real-life experiences, but in a range and diversity far beyond the ordinary realities. The effects of such vicarious experiences may or may not be cumulative and may or may not be significant. They are, however, different in quality and quantity and from those experienced by children growing up in pretelevision times.

The effects of television viewing on educational achievement and aspiration have also received some attention. Findings are more suggestive than definitive. It does seem likely that heavy viewing relates inversely to school achievement. At the same time, heavy viewers with low IQ's and/or from family settings where intellectual stimulation is low may actually be learning more from television relevant to school subjects than they would without that input from television. High-IQ students who are heavy viewers may show less school aspirations. However, all these relationships are complex and subject to other concurrent influences (Pearl et al., 1982).

All these findings on cognitive and emotional development as they relate to television viewing suggest a need for increased emphasis on teaching children critical television viewing skills. Research is only in its early stages in trying to educate both parents and children on how best to cope with this "anonymous teacher" in the home. Learning how television works may provide the best safeguard against its potentially negative effects and the best reinforcer for its potentially positive influence.

Social Beliefs and Social Behavior

Among the potentially damaging influences of television is the way it may shape viewers' perceptions of the real world. Much concern has been raised about the racial and sexual stereotypes shown on television. Indeed, stereotypes of all kinds are common, including those of age and occupational role. To the extent that television shows minority groups in demeaning roles, or women in excessively passive and subordinate positions, or older people as senile and burdensome, or an overrepresentation of doctors, lawyers, policemen, or other professionals, to that extent, the young viewer—especially the heavy viewer—is seeing a distorted image of the real world.

Even before the research began to show that stereotyping can influence the viewers' perceptions, efforts by coalitions among these various groups began to pressure for change. Ethnic groups, women's groups, and senior citizen's groups have all had some modest success in reducing the level of stereotyping.

A more subtle and perhaps pervasive research finding centers on how watching television affects the viewers' perception of the "real" world. A major area of research suggests that heavy viewers see the world as a mean and scary place, precisely because so many more mean and scary incidents take place on television than in the everyday experiences of most of us. Indeed, if many children identify with victims rather than aggressors on television, then the frightened feelings admitted by child viewers should be of more general concern than the violence-aggression linkage.

On area of research to which the television industry has paid some attention concerns the concept of prosocial behavior. Over the past decade, considerable research has investigated the obverse of the televised violence–aggression linkage. It is of significance to the aggression effect that programming which provides high levels of prosocial behavior can induce helping behavior in the viewer. These studies further document the strength of the general finding that observational learning takes place from television viewing.

Both laboratory studies as well as field studies have consistently shown that such behavior as cooperation, friendliness, delay of gratification, and generosity can be enhanced by appropriate television programming. Furthermore, films and television can be used to help viewers cope with fears, whether those fears involve strange animals or fear of surgical procedures (Pearl et al., 1982).

Finally, it comes as no surprise that academic research is now documenting what advertisers have long known; television advertising socializes children toward active consumer roles.

Television and Social Relations

What do we know about the family as portrayed on television? More importantly, what, if anything, does television viewing do to family interactions?

These questions are partially answered by recent research. As might be suspected, family life on television is marked by much stereotypic portrayal of families. Whether it is a bumbling and inept father, or precocious children, or the marked contrast between working-class and middle-class families, family life on television is either predominantly funny and simplistic or excessively tragic. More subtle themes reveal a strong effort toward upward mobility by children in the working-class families. None of this is inherently bad, of course, but it adds further to the conclusion that children watching television are being subjected to a variety of cultural stereotypes.

What is of greater importance may well be how families respond to and deal with this attention-getting member of the household. One body of research indicates that parents do not usually watch television with their children. Furthermore, while parents have often expressed concern about the levels of violence and sex on television, there is relatively little parental control or supervision of their children's viewing.

The relative lack of parental attention or interaction is doubly unfortunate, because recent research reveals that parental intervention, through discussion, can mitigate against negative effects of viewing and also enhance positive effects. In this connection, it is encouraging that television programming now often includes public service announcements urging parents to watch with their children and to talk about what they see on television.

Television and Health

One area of recent attention that offers some interesting possibilities for a more constructive use of television viewing involves health-related television research.

Content analysis of television programming suggests that many subtle health messages are conveyed which are only beginning to be recognized as influential on the viewer. Relatively little smoking occurs on today's programs. In contrast, alcoholic use, both casual and heavy, is shown twice as often as drinking coffee or tea, and many more times than the consumption of soft drinks (Pearl et al., 1982). What do children learn from this beverage-drinking pattern, which is the inverse of real-life practice? What messages are conveyed when very few television characters buckle up their seat belts and when drivers are often exceeding the speed limits or otherwise demonstrating reckless driving?

In a more direct fashion, television has been used to mount health campaigns. To date, these campaigns have had mixed success. However, as research continues and better understanding develops as to the designing of health messages, future campaigns should prove more effective.

One recent research activity attempting to extend the uses of television in health matters relates to the problem of mental illness. The mentally ill, not incidentally, are often shown as dangerous and violent and rarely depicted in a sympathetic light. What about the uses of television by the mentally ill? Surveys of television viewing in mental institutions show such viewing to be an important dayroom activity. Based on that finding, research has been initiated to see if television viewing by disturbed children under full-time care in a psychiatric setting can serve as a modest therapeutic intervention. A one-year pilot field study suggests that a diet of prosocial programming not only can hold the children's attention, but tends to reduce aggressive behavior (Pearl et al., 1982).

These findings on institutionalized children carry some promise that other institutionalized individuals, such as those in homes for the aged, hospitals, and penal institutions, might also benefit from a more planned and tailored diet of television programming. Research in that direction may be one more constructive approach to a more productive use of this leisure time activity.

The Role of Television in American Society

What is still missing in all the research on television and behavior over the past decade is a broad theoretical framework within which to conceptualize this body of knowledge. Obviously, many of these investigations can be subsumed under social learning theory. And yet, the fact that television markedly influences not just social learning, but our social institutions—including the family, law, politics, and religion—suggests that it plays a unique role in American society and should be so viewed conceptually.

Lacking such a theoretical framework, scientists will still continue busily to examine the various phenomena which demarcate television's role in how we behave as individuals within which we function. Eventually, we may be able to develop the broader constructs within which these various areas of investigation can become a more integrated set of findings.

What is also needed is a clearer understanding of the structural pressures and constraints within the television industry that have produced the programming that now exists. An examination of how the system works reveals a number of self-evident factors. Ratings and audience response strongly influence the quality and character of programs. Competition among the three networks, and now cable systems, puts great pressure on the production system. Furthermore, because all of this is part of a large bureaucratic enterprise, no individual or small group of individuals has full control over the development of programs. Neither the directors, producers, writers, nor television executives independently determine what appears on the television screen. Thus, when outside groups call for change, it becomes hard for the system to respond. And, finally, it is of no small significance that some of the groups calling for change may not be reflecting the tastes of the so-called "mass audience" of television.

MEDIA COVERAGE AND RESPONSE TO THE TEN-YEAR UPDATE

By a curious coincidence, the 10-year update, like the original Surgeon General's Report, was initially reported as a front-page exclusive story, because a reporter got the story before an official government release was prepared.

For the 10-year update, *The Washington Post* story set the tone for subsequent coverage. Although the Report itself deliberately relegated the violence issue to a minor role in the research picture, it was clearly the major media focus. However, unlike the earlier *New York Times* story in 1972, this article was an accurate account of the report. The headline "Report Links TV Violence to Aggression" reflected the story correctly (Russell, 1982).

The 10-year update coverage has been reviewed in an extensive scholarly paper (Hobbs, 1983). It is clear from that review that there was little subsequent misinterpretation of the Report, although few of the later newspaper pieces went beyond the violence issue.

What was different this time was the reaction by the television industry itself. The immediate response was to claim that the Report was "inaccurate" and that most of the members of the scientific advisory group were individuals who had "publicly identified positions on the role of television in society." What is ironic about the latter comment is that it was a reaction identical in kind but opposite in implication from the public complaint 10 years earlier about the presumed prejudice of the members of the Surgeon General's Scientific Advisory Committee, five of whom had been directly or indirectly affiliated with the industry.

It is of further significance that, in 1972, the industry not only did not call the Surgeon General's Report inaccurate, but rather the initial response was "conspicuous silence" (Cater & Strickland, 1975, p. 113). At the Pastore hearings 2 months later, all three network presidents acknowledged that the findings warranted serious consideration. The president of the ABC, in the most forthright response, stated that the Report would influence changes in ABC's fall scheduling, as it related to programming for children. He further declared that ABC would spend $1 million on relevant research in the next four years.

Many months after the 10-year update, in 1983, ABC issued a 32-page brochure (Wurtzel & Lometti, 1983) which attempted to refute the conclusions of the ten-year update on televised violence. Since that ABC statement makes no reference to the larger body of research reviewed in the update, nothing in the argument undermines the major NIMH conclusion that television teaches. In attempting to contradict the research findings on violence—and by calling the evidence "correlational"—the ABC statement sounded remarkably like that of the tobacco industry in its position on the scientific evidence about smoking and health. Obviously, the disagreement on the evidence by the networks will continue.

Perhaps the potential for differences in media analysis of the scientific findings is most dramatically illustrated by looking at two contrasting magazine articles. In the January, 1983, issue of the *Reader's Digest*, Eugene Methvin (the same journalist who wrote the Surgeon General's article in 1973) wrote an article "TV Violence: The Shocking New Evidence." In the January–February issue of the *Washington Journalism Review*, Eric Mink, a radio and television critic of the *St. Louis Post-Dispatch*, wrote an article, "Bum Rap for the Box." Two more dissimilar interpretations of the same research findings would be hard to find.

Methvin (1983) begins by citing individual cases of serious antisocial copycat behavior and then points out that TV violence has not decreased in the past 14 years. He cites various studies and conclusions that TV violence is harmful. He concludes that parents must be more firm in controlling and guiding their children's viewing. Simultaneously, he urges more careful attention to which companies carry advertising during violent programs, so that viewers can complain to those advertisers. The article is dedicated to alerting the public to a problem and suggesting how best to cope with it.

Mink (1983), on the other hand, begins by making an analogy to a courtroom case in which the defendants are "the mediocrity mongers of commercial television" and the plaintiffs are government agencies, social scientists, and others "spouting realpolitik and psycho-babble in defense of society." The charge is that television is turning us into a "nation of rampaging maniacs." Mink's verdict is "Not guilty, by reason of common sense." Obviously, Mink's "charge" is a considerable distortion of the research findings.

The rest of Mink's article is a quick and casual review of research findings and a dismissal of the strength of converging evidence, by noting that even a large number of "flawed studies" cannot be presumed to be significant. He then describes the only decisive study, which he simultaneously points out is impossible to do. Namely select two large samples of infants, matched for hereditary factors. Then subject both groups to identical environments and comparable life experiences, except that one group watches TV violence and the other does not. Having thus relegated significant research to an unachievable standard of perfection, Mink concludes, "Twenty years of flimflam is enough. Let's move on."

It is of some significance that public opinion polls for years have shown that the public believes there is a linkage between TV violence and crime. A Gallup poll in May, 1982, found that 66% of the public endorse a ban on televised violence until 10 p.m. That opinion had not changed much in 5 years of previous polling.

THE PUBLIC POLICY DILEMMA

While the scientific facts will probably continue to be debated, and the public will have no unchallenged authority to trust, the policy question still remains. Are the data on television and children conclusive enough to warrant some form of action and, if so, what action is most appropriate? In this connection, it is important to go beyond the violence issue. It is also important to distinguish television from earlier forms of entertainment media.

Two circumstances nullify the old argument that television is no more harmful (or influential) than older sources, such as books, radio, and the movies. First, none of these earlier modes came even close to occupying the sheer amount of time and attention that television does. Second, we now have sufficient hard evidence that television influences the viewer, with both positive as well as negative effects.

What is perhaps even more indefensible in the television industry's position is that, unlike the tobacco industry, the research findings are actually more a guide toward improvement than a threat toward extinction. It is in this context that the media's emphasis on violence masks the real issue: television is a powerful teacher whose potential benefits are not being realizd. The blame for this tunnel vision is a shared one. The television industry is too concerned with defending itself to see beyond the violence question. Parents are too willing to use television as a baby sitter to give it the careful attention it deserves. And the government has recently been too engrossed in its efforts toward deregulation to recognize its responsibilities toward children in this matter.

Having thus emphasized the need for change, it would be gratifying to be able to describe precisely what needs to be done. Unfortunately, no clear plan emerges, either from the body of research or from an examination of previous policy efforts. Indeed, perhaps the most compelling lesson to be learned from past efforts is that there is no single objective to be pursued. There is, however, a clear design for failure. Any time-limited effort, no matter how well developed or how successful, will not have any enduring results.

Examples of this problem are numerous. One recent instance is illuminating. In a thorough analysis of the development and production of an excellent program series for children, Johnston and Ettema (1982) point out that the series was produced as an experimental effort to educate children against stereotypic attitudes about sex roles. As an experiment it was successful. Unfortunately, its impact has been short-lived, because it was not continued. The authors stress the need for a continuing process in order to build on past experience and develop an organizational memory which fosters continued progress toward an ultimate goal.

Perhaps an equally important lesson to be learned from this experiment, and from the longer experience in the production of "Sesame Street," is the invaluable benefit that accrues from a continuing and close collaboration between research and production personnel. The complementary advantages of marrying these two sets of expertise has been a major source of the success of such programs.

Complex Imponderables

At the same time that there are lessons to be learned from past efforts to improve television for children, there are problems for which satisfactory solutions are not readily apparent. One is related to the distinction between "television children watch" and "children's television." The latter is rather easily identifiable, but not automatically so. Saturday morning cartoons are clearly children's television, despite their questionable value. But only about 15% of children's viewing time is devoted to Saturday morning programming. The rest of the time is spent well into evening prime time. Indeed, 4% of the audience watching television during prime time is less than 6 years old, and 9% is between 6 and 11 years of age (Comstock et al., 1978). Thus, 13% of the audience is 11 years or younger. How does the industry respond to this portion of the audience? More importantly, what obligation does the industry have in those instances, such as late afternoon, when the audience is largely children? Local affiliate stations, who control that time, will often put violent programs, in reruns, in that time slot. The determination as to when children's interests should be protected in this audience age mix is not easily reached.

An even more difficult matter is inherent in the bureaucratic structure of the television industry. As noted earlier, efforts toward change, even with the best of intentions, are not easily achieved. Like other large institutions, television has become a ponderous structure where control is a shared responsibility. Even if a network president called for dramatic change, the system itself would tend to resist. This is not to excuse the status quo, but to explain its seeming permanence.

In this regard, despite seeming discontent on the part of the audience, the ratings serve as the most tangible guide toward audience taste. It is not altogether an excuse on the part of industry executives to state that the audience gets what the audience wants.

And, finally, what neither the researchers nor the industry have successfully achieved is a clear guide to the effective use of research findings. It is all very well for those of us in the academic community to talk about the implications of the research findings. What is missing is the clear translation from the theoretical not just to the applied, but to the practical.

The more subtle and complex translation of research findings into program use is much less easily attainable. In each instance, whether it is teaching cognitive skills such as on "Sesame Street" or prosocial lessons such as on "Fat Albert," what is required is the continuing active collaboration of child development specialists and production personnel. When less sophisticated and informed procedures are used periodically under external pressure to reduce the levels of violence, the results have sometimes been counterproductive. The response has been to show "sanitized violence" in which the gory consequences are not shown. This sanitized violence may only stimulate imitation, because the violent act carries with it no moral deterrent.

It is precisely because there is an urgent need to know how best to translate all this knowledge that the present unwillingness of the television industry to address this need energetically is so short-sighted and self-defeating.

Multiple Approaches

There are, of course, a variety of approaches toward inducing change in how television serves its young viewers. One recurring theme has been in reference to the health of these viewers. The original Surgeon General's Report was concerned about the mental health of children. The involvement of the AMA was similarly justified. The 10-year update discussed health promoting possibilities. And, more recently, an edited volume (Sprafkin, Swift, & Hess, 1982) was devoted to exploring prevention and control measures around the concept of enhancing the preventive-health impact of television.

Another approach has centered on the activities of various public action groups. Four of the most well-known of these groups deserve mention. Each has a somewhat different philosophy in its mode of operation.

Action for Children's Television (ACT) is one of the oldest and largest such citizen's groups. It began in 1968, with a focus on televised violence. Later, it concerned itself with television advertising to children. ACT has been most effective in the political arena, mobilizing its members nationwide to write to Congress as well as the networks in defense of better programming and advertising practices for children. It has petitioned the FCC to make the Commission a more effective regulatory agency working for the welfare of children. In addition, ACT holds annual symposia, publishes research reports, and distributes a periodic newsletter with information on relevant developments. It also gives national awards for good children's programs.

Media Action Research Center (MARC), a church-affiliated group, has been active since 1972 in developing a program of community workshops to make parents more aware of how television affects the viewer. A handbook to use as a guide in "Television Awareness Training" is now in its second edition (Logan & Moody, 1979). It is used widely both in the United States and internationally. This kind of awareness training is one part of a larger effort to teach critical viewing skills, now being provided in a number of centers in the United States.

The National Council for Children and Television (NCCT) is a coalition of concerned citizens and representatives from the television industry. The Council holds periodic meetings and publishes a quarterly, "Television and Children," which provides a forum for information, research, and opinion on children and television. Through collaboration with industry personnel, NCCT holds periodic workshops to promote a better collaboration among researchers, industry personnel, civic leaders, and corporate executives.

The National Coalition on Television Violence (NCTV) concentrates its efforts on reducing televised violence. It monitors programs to determine levels of violence and to identify which advertisers appear on high violence programs. NCTV has encouraged its members to write these advertisers to put pressure on them to discontinue sponsoring such programs. In early 1983, the coalition moved close to, but has not actually recommended, a formal boycott. NCTV publishes a periodic newsletter in which it publicizes its latest ratings as well as recent relevant research findings.

All of these efforts, plus others, serve to keep the issue of television and children in the public awareness. While this awareness is necessary, it is not sufficient to induce extensive change. Indeed, as all these organizations have been saying with increasing insistence in recent years, commercial television is not being responsive to the needs of the young viewer.

Perhaps the most difficult stumbling block to change is the inability or unwillingness of the television industry to address its responsibilities to the young viewer, except as an integral part of its corporate profit and loss decision-making process. If a program for children gets the ratings, it stays. If the audience is less than the competition for that time slot, it goes. Until the industry is willing to modify that approach, or until the government offers some tax incentives or other inducements to compensate for lost revenue, commercial television will probably not change in its programming for the young viewer.

CONCLUDING REMARKS

If the above account seems to suggest there is no clear path to change, it is both correct and not unique among issues of social policy for children. We have attempted to show that the research findings, especially those of recent years, do document a need for change.

What is unusual in this instance is that when television is itself an object of scrutiny, its role as a source of information conflicts with an understandable corporate self-defensiveness. Thus, what industry executives say or do about research on television directly affects television's coverage on this topic. Television's investigative attention, which makes everyone from politicians to major corporations sensitive to such scrutiny, does not extend with equal vigor to self-examination. Indeed, this is one area in which television does not compete with the print media in coverage of a story.

A combination of developments must emerge before real change will take place. First, a larger proportion of the public must become actively concerned about the effects of television on children. Second, the government must find an appropriate posture, short of regulation, that indicates its intention to safeguard the welfare of children in this area. Third, the industry must abandon its corporate defensiveness and more constructively use its resources to more adequately meet the needs of its young viewers.

The path to any of these objectives, let alone all three, is not clear. And yet, there is some hope. As we have shown, some efforts have been made in all three directions. Unfortunately, as of this writing, the government's movement toward deregulation minimizes the likelihood of meaningful government involvement. That government stance also allows the industry to continue the status quo with no fear of any strong public pressure for change. Simultaneously, public concern is limited to a fairly small group of activists. Whie polls continue to show that at least two thirds of the public is concerned about televised violence and excessive commercials, few of those polled are sufficiently aroused to take any action.

As for television itself, despite its defensiveness, some good will toward better television for children is expressed by industry representatives. It is of interest to note that in a recent survey which was part of a larger study of policy options for improving television for preschool children, Gaddy (1983) found that 93% of a sample of industry executives agreed that television could be made more educationally effective. More importantly, 63% of the industry respondents said television *should* be made more educationally effective.

At the same time, one indicator of a low potential for change is that efforts to produce some new form of special national forum for children and television have never succeeded. In an examination of the many proposals made over the past 20 years to develop an operating national center for children and television, Rubinstein (1981) concludes that there is no strong support for such a continuing institution. It seems paradoxical that such a mechanism which should, and could, serve all the parties concerned—the public, the industry, and the government—has insufficient support from any one of the three to bring it to fruition.

All the above circumstances define the public policy dilemma relating to better television for children. At this time, the best hope is that some improvement will come from a growing public awareness that television is indeed teaching our children and that the young viewer can and should be served better. As in so many other areas of social policy, if and when a critical mass of public concern develops, changes will begin to take place.

REFERENCES

Bogart, L. (1972). Warning: The surgeon general has determined that TV violence is moderately dangerous to your child's mental health. *Public Opinion Quarterly, 36*, 491–521.

Bogart, L. (1980). After the Surgeon General's Report: Another look backward. In S. B. Withey & R. P. Abeles (Eds.), *Television and social behavior: Beyond violence and children.* Hillsdale, NJ: Erlbaum.

Cater, D., & Strickland, S. (1975). *TV violence and the child: The evolution and fate of the surgeon general's report.* New York: Russell Sage Foundation.

Comstock, G. A. (1982). Violence in television content: An overview. In D. Pearl, L. Bouthilet, & J. Lazar (Eds.), *Television and behavior: Ten years of scientific progress and implications for the eighties.* Washington, DC: U.S. Government Printing Office.

Comstock, G., Chaffee, S., Katzman, N., McCombs, M., & Roberts, D. (1978). *Television and human behavior.* New York: Columbia University Press.

Feingold, M., & Johnson, G. T. (1977). Television violence—reactions from physicians, advertisers, and the networks. *The New England Journal of Medicine, 296* (8), 424–427.

Gaddy, G. (1983). *Television as an instrument in the informal education of preschool children: An analysis of national options.* Unpublished paper, University of North Carolina.

Gerbner, G. (1972). Violence in television drama: Trends and symbolic functions. In G. A. Comstock & E. A. Rubinstein (Eds.), *Television and social behavior (Vol. 1); Media content and control.* Washington, DC: U.S. Government Printing Office.

Gould, J. (1972, January 11). TV violence. *New York Times,* p. 1.

Hobbs, R. (1983). coverage of the 1982 NIMH report on television and behavior. Unpublished paper, Harvard University.

Johnston, J., & Ettema, J. (1982). *Positive images: Breaking stereotypes with children's television.* Beverly Hills: Sage.

Logan, B., & Moody, K. (Eds.). (1979). *Television Awareness Training: The viewer's guide for family and community.* New York: Media Action Research Center.

Methvin, E. (1983, January). TV violence: The shocking new evidence. *Reader's Digest,* 49–53.

Milavsky, J. R., Kessler, R., Stipp, H. H., & Rubens, W. S. (1982). Television and aggression: Results of a panel study. In D. Pearl, L. Bouthilet, & J. Lazar (Eds.), *Television and behavior: Ten years of scientific progress and implications for the eighties.* Washington, DC: U.S. Government Printing Office.

Mink, E. (1983, January–February). Bum rap for the box. *Washington Journalism Review,* 35–37.

National Institute of Mental Health. (1981). *Television as a teacher: A research monograph.* Rockville, MD: Author.

Pearl, D., Bouthilet, L., & Lazar, J. (Eds.). (1982). *Television and behavior: Ten years of scientific progress and implications for the eighties.* Washington, DC: U.S. Government Printing Office.

Rothenberg, M. B. (1955). Effect of television violence on children and youth. *Journal of American Medical Association, 234*(10), 1043–1046.

Rubinstein, E. A. (1976). Warning: The Surgeon General's research program may be dangerous to preconceived notions. *Journal of Social Issues, 32*(4), 18–34.

Rubinstein, E. (1981). A brief history of proposals for national communications centers. In Neuman, W. R., *The social impact of television: A research agenda for the 1980's.* New York: Aspen Institute.

Russell, C. (1982, May 5). Report links TV violence. *Washington Post,* p. 1.

Salomon, G. (1979). *Interaction of media, cognition, and learning.* San Francisco, CA: Jossey-Bass.

Siegel, A. (1981). The properties of television and its effects on children. In National Institute of Mental Health (Ed.), *Television as a teacher: A research monograph.* Rockville, MD: Author.

Signorielli, N., Gross, L., & Morgan, M. (1982). Violence in television programs: Ten years later. In D. Pearl, L. Bouthilet, & J. Lazar (Eds.), *Television and behavior: Ten years of scientific progress and implications for the eighties.* Washington, DC: U.S. Government Printing Office.

Social Sciences Research Council. (1975). *A profile of televised violence. Report submitted by the committee on television and social behavior.* New York: Author.

Sprafkin, J., Swift, C., & Hess, R. (1982). *Rx television: Enhancing the preventive impact of TV.* New York: Haworth Press.

Steinfeld, J. L. (1973, April). TV violence is harmful. *Reader's Digest, 102,* 37–45.

Surgeon General's Scientific Advisory Committee on Television and Social Behavior. (1972). *Television and growing up: The impact of televised violence.* Washington, DC: U.S. Government Printing Office.

Tankard, J. W., & Showalter, S. W. (1977). Press coverage of the 1972 report on television and social behavior. *Journalism Quarterly, 54,* 293–298.

United States Congress. (1972, March 21–24). Senate Committee on Commerce. Subcommittee on Communications. *Surgeon General's report by the scientific advisory committee on television and social behavior.* Hearings, 92nd Congress, 2nd Session. Washington, DC: U.S. Government Printing Office.

United States Federal Communications Commission. (1974, November 6). Children's television programs: Report and policy statement. *Federal Register, 39,* No. 215, Part 2, 39396–39409.

United States Federal Communications Commission. (1979). *Television programming for children: A report of the Children's Television Task Force (Vol. 1). Overview.* Washington, DC: Federal Communications Commission.

Withey, S. B., & Abeles, R. P. (Eds.). (1980). *Television and social behavior: Beyond violence and children.* Hillsdale, NJ: Erlbaum.

Wurtzel, A., & Lometti, G. (1983). *A research perspective on television and violence.* New York: American Broadcasting Companies.

Six

Health Education = Health Instruction + Health News: Media Experiences in the United States, Finland, Australia, and England

NANCY MILIO

University of North Carolina at Chapel Hill

The mass media inform, persuade, and entertain. While pursuing these general purposes along with the goal of holding a minimum share of the audience, the particular messages that audiences receive may be different than the ones intended. Recently, a prize-winning television advertising campaign designed by a public relations firm for England's national Health Education Council was intended to show parents how their smoking habits influenced their children. What was originally hoped to discourage parents from smoking in order to prevent their children from taking up the habit turned out to encourage children to mimic the adults they saw smoking on TV; and so the commercial was canceled (Budd, 1981).

As this experience illustrates, the effects of efforts to harness the possibilities of the mass media for health-related messages are vulnerable to all the uncertainties of mass communication: Not only may unintended effects occur, but when the intended results occur, they may emerge by unexpected paths and not by a simple, direct influence on individuals' behavior, as later examples will show. Furthermore, as I will argue, the most important effects of health messages may not only occur indirectly but may result when health education is not even the intention of the communication.

This chapter will focus primarily on the intentional use of the mass media by health professionals to inform or persuade audiences and the direct as well as the unexpected ways this influence works. This use will be called "health instruction." Also to be considered is the more complex, less explored area, "health news," which is the use of the media to report health-related information having no persuasive intent, but which nonetheless may have profound, long-term effects on health, personal health behavior, and health policy.

My view is that both *health instruction* and *health news*, whether the intent is educational or entrepreneurial, are health education. They are teaching people about what health is and how to improve it by sifting information from selected sources, packaging it in a time–place–depth context, and by advocating, reporting or implying selected ways of solving health problems (Milio, 1983). The result is an almost universally typical message emphasizing personal responsibility for health problems and, if noted, short-term causes and consequences; preferred solutions are seen to be treatment for people as individuals, rendered by specialists with advanced technologies, or, where prevention is espoused, it is put forward, again, as what individuals can do for themselves. If a flaw in this approach is acknowledged, it is shown as either a scandal, a bottleneck in the delivery of health services, or a lack of knowledge or resistance to advice among the public. This health message exists in health news and in health instruction.

The 1980s will see rare media efforts to fundamentally alter its health message even as more widespread, media "innovation" will bring the public little more than old wine in new wineskins—the typical message packaged in new information technologies.

MEDIA EXPERIMENTS IN HEALTH INSTRUCTION

One of the most sophisticated and lauded demonstrations of the intentional use of television to influence personal health behavior was done in Finland in 1978. A series of 7 prime-time programs monitored the experiences and progress of a group of volunteer smokers who met with a leading physician in the television studio during a 3-month period. About 100,000 smokers watched the series and 10% of them quit for at least 6 to 12 months; these 10,000 quitters were 1% of the 1 million Finns who smoke. In the province of North Karelia, small groups were organized to view the programs together in homes. The groups were difficult to form and maintain, but where they persisted, the effectiveness of the TV series doubled: 20% of the smokers quit permanently (Puska & Koskela, 1979).

Another careful experiment in the use of mass media for health instruction, also regarded as successful and (misleadingly) compared with the Finnish effort, was the Three-Community Study near Stanford, CA (Mayer, 1981). Here, two small rural towns were exposed to information intended to decrease people's risk of cardiovascular disease, including advice to avoid smoking. As in Finland, both newspapers and television were used. One town, the control, received no special messages; a second town received only media messages; and the third had special group sessions, in addition to media advice, for people who were at high risk of heart disease. The beneficial reductions in risk after three years resulting from changed eating habits are questionable on methodological grounds (Leventhal & Win, 1980). However, among smokers there was a drop of 11% in the media-only town, and even more (15%) in the control town (Meyer & Schultz, 1980). Among those in the small, high-risk sample, 50% of the smokers quit. Some critics have questioned whether this large drop, which included only those who continued in the group and could be followed up (about half the total), might have occurred without any media antismoking advice. Similar large quit-rates occur among smokers who know they are at high risk of illness, but not among smokers who think they are healthy (Milio, 1981).

Thus, the effectiveness of the special mass media messages in reducing the prevalence of smoking in this demonstration is questionable, even among high-risk people, and seems unimportant in explaining the similar reductions of 15% and 11%, respectively, for the populations in both the no-media (control) and media-only towns.

Finally, a third mass media project, modeled after the California study, was the 1979 "Quit for Life" campaign in New South Wales, Australia. Using a similar three-town design, the preliminary findings showed (a) after 15 months, a 6% larger drop in smokers in the two test towns than in the control down, but (b) small group efforts did not make a significant difference. The conclusion, similar to the Stanford conclusion, was that small groups add little to the *total* reduction in smoking and cardiovascular risk in a community population, compared with what can be achieved through a policy of media information alone at a far lower cost. High-risk individuals, the most highly motivated, are as likely to benefit from their health care practitioners' advice as from a small support group.

Pathways to Success and Failure

How might some of the variations in overall results from these three planned mass media experiments in health instruction be explained? Based on a wide range of literature and contacts with the experimenters, the following speculations are proposed.

The overall decline in the prevalence of smoking was 10% in Finland, 6 to 12 months afterward, and for comparable measures, 6% between the media and control towns in Australia, 3 months afterward, and no significant difference between towns in California after 3 years. The formats of the media messages are not likely explanations for these differences in effectiveness. The Finns' messages were more intense and of short duration. The others' messages lasted several months but were primarily public service announcements or paid advertisements on television. All three included fliers and columns in the local press.

The main difference in these situations, one that goes far in explaining media effects, is the historical and social context in which the experiments occurred. The Finns, after several years of debate, wide publicity, and strong public, professional, and news media (which are under public control) support, implemented in 1978 the world's most stringent antismoking measures, including a total ban on advertising, an increase in cigarette taxes, and restrictions on smoking in public places (Leppo, 1978). Thus the social climate favored people's efforts to avoid smoking and, to help sustain that motivation, reduced their options to smoke conveniently or economically.

The Finns concluded that their small groups (in which members were *not* especially high risk) doubled the effectiveness of the TV message; the Australian and California investigators did not think this component could add significantly to benefits for the general average-risk population. The difference in Finland, however, was what preceded the TV program and small groups: 5 years of a community-wide, multifaceted program to reduce heart disease, organized by, and implemented through, North Karelia's community associations. They, in other words, had a fund of experience on which to draw, one in which local people were leaders; this was quite unlike the health professionals who came "from outside" to lead the groups in New South Wales and California. In all three cases, however, groups had difficulty sustaining regular attendance (for time and weather reasons in North Karelia), thus making this mode of health instruction for feasible as a mass public-health policy in most communities.

In Australia, no restrictions were in force, other than a newly agreed nationwide code by which cigarette manufacturers were voluntarily to avoid appealing to youth in their promotion efforts. A unique situation developed in the experimental towns, however, in which the cigarette industry complained to publishers about the "Quit for Life" newsprint campaign, succeeding temporarily in ending the antismoking messages. The controversy, won by the campaign after public hearings, ironically produced far more publicity than the campaign itself could have in the media towns. This extra publicity may then help account for the apparent effectiveness of the campaign messages in the media towns as compared with the control town and puts the Australian experience on a par with the California experiment where there was no difference in smoking cessation between the health-message towns and the no-message town.

Although there were no differences in the California towns' rates of smoking prevalence, the 11–15% reductions (resulting more from fewer, younger people not starting rather than from smokers quitting) are important signals of changes in patterns of behavior. If special health messages don't account for them, what may?

A study of national smoking trends over the past two decades suggests that the news reports of the definitive 1964 U.S. Surgeon General's report on the health effects of cigarette smoking triggered several chains of social response that have led to the current continuing drop in the cigarette habit (Warner, 1977).

The most direct effect of this health news moved many individual smokers to attempt to quit, just as the antismoking commercials did at the end of the 1960s. But these tend to show up on graphs as troughs which are only temporary dips in a long-term slowly declining curve of smokers.

The long-term decline is more likely the result of the indirect effects of the widespread publicity on health damage from cigarettes initiated in 1964. A change in public awareness and opinion created a social climate which mobilized groups of nonsmokers and former smokers to make a political issue of cigarette control. This was not as successful nationally as what had occurred in Finland, but was sufficient to get a Congressionally mandated yearly health report on progress toward reducing smoking and a national survey to monitor smoking habits. This in itself ensures at least annual health news reminding the public and policymakers of the effects of smoking More important were the local and state successes of organized health action which resulted in a large increase in tobacco tax laws and ordinances banning smoking in public places. These restrictions then supported smokers who wanted to quit and helped deter those who might otherwise have started. Such measures would have a similar effect on the localities in the three northern California towns.

In Finland, Australia, and the U.S., it was the long-term effect of health news punctuating the public mind and placing the smoking-health issue on the agenda of public discourse that defined it as a public problem about which people formed opinions. This then provided a social climate in which health instruction, intended to affect personal habits, was carried out. The news reports were not intended to lead to social changes or engender political action, but they did nonetheless tap and strengthen previously submerged antismoking sentiments and efforts. The resulting changes in law, regulation, and public opinion then made the difference in how effective health instruction could be in each of the countries.

HEALTH AIMS AND THE MESSAGE IN THE MEDIA

If this hypothesis is generally correct, then the drop in Finns' smoking will be sustained and will accelerate downward, whereas the impact of the antismoking campaign in Australia's experimental towns will diminish; and the California towns will continue to parallel the national slow decline until more stringent public health measures in taxation, regulation, and education are taken to counter-balance the cigarette industry's promotional efforts.

The mass communications balance between the industry and health instruction in the U.S. continues to favor tobacco, although this may change somewhat during the 1980s (Milio, 1982). For example, since the major path for reducing smoking prevalence is by decreasing the rate of new smokers (mainly young people), the target for both antismoking persuasion and cigarette advertising is young people. Youth, as others, do what they do depending on what is possible for them—ranging from teeth brushing or eating to buying products. As a practical matter, these activities are "choices"—conscious decisions among alternatives—only initially, when new circumstances or opportunities present themselves. Otherwise, they become unconscious habits (Milio, 1981). As they mature, children have many new opportunities because of their rapidly increasing capacities. Adults have new opportunities as, for example, their real income increases. Those who wish to persuade people to change their behavior—whether by commercial advertising or health instruction—aim to place their message before the age–income groups who are experiencing new opportunities: children and youth and "upscale" adults. And, as shown earlier, those who do not seek to change behavior (as in health news reporting) may nonetheless also influence behavior, especially among these ready-for-change groups.

Federal funds for health instruction about smoking, used to develop TV and radio public-service announcements, were $350,000 in 1980–81, roughly one tenth of federal health-information broadcast campaign funds. By comparison, cigarette manufacturers spent 16% of their sales, $1 billion for advertising in 1980, $400 million going to the leading magazines for the 18 to 24-year-old "upscale" market ("Report on the National Conferences," 1982). A recent Federal Trade Commission investigation documented that their advertising strategies are intended to persuade young people to start smoking, although advertisers claim their intention is only to retain or increase their market share among current smokers (Subcommittee on Oversight, 1981).

Health educators' standards of their persuasive success differ from that of advertisers, and their job is inherently harder. Advertisers merely try to persuade people to do more of, or modify, what they already do (whether eating cereal or smoking), promising immediate rewards with certainty, and offering images of prestige or glamour that are constantly reinforced by the commercial world. Health educators not only want more than a small-percentage shift in behavior, they must also face the harder task of persuading people to change old habits and take on new ones, offering only the probability of better health in an uncertain future. These values are not readily supported in a consumer-oriented economy (McCron & Budd, 1979).

Health educators thus want more. But most studies show, as illustrated earlier, that the intentional use of the mass media to directly affect behavior is either negligible or not sustainable without a supporting architecture of environmental changes to permanently make the doing of healthful things easier (Gatherer, 1979; Rose, 1980; Wallach, 1981).

Paradoxically, the individual-oriented message that health instruction sends, just as the one implicit in most health news, deemphasizes the kinds of social and environmental changes that could make health instruction more effective.

There is general agreement by broadcast media observers of news, advertising, and entertainment programs (Gerbner, Gross, Morgan, & Signorielli, 1981), although little systematic analysis to date, that the health message projected by the mass media, intentional or not, is a declaration of dramatic diseases, how to treat them, especially with new high technology medicine, and how to make the systems delivering this new technology work more efficiently or more honestly. The focus is usually an individual, whether a patient or medical expert, regardless of whether either is representative of a large group. Moreover, when, through intentional efforts by special interest groups or government agencies, information on the *prevention* of illness is reported, the emphasis continues to be on the individual and what he or she can do to avoid a specific health problem.

The Press

This message of individual responsibility is repeated in the national print media, according to a systematic review of the health news stories in *The New York Times* Information Bank (Levin, 1979). This computerized service abstracted and categorized all health issues and events for 1978 in over 60 newspapers and periodicals. The categories themselves suggest a view of health. For example, "preventive medicine" is separate from "occupational and environmental issues"; "mental health" and "drug abuse, tobacco, and alcoholism" are also separated, and health services is categorized as an economic or supply problem, but not in terms of impact on people's health. These groupings are clearly topical and event-oriented and do not allow for a framework that could focus on the interconnections among the groupings that might lend a different meaning to the causes, consequences, and solutions of health problems; for example, how economic or environmental conditions and policies affect life style.

Altogether, about 1,800 health stories were printed in 1978, of which by far the largest share (half) appeared in *The New York Times*. Of the almost 900 stories, the *Times* gave almost equal weight to each major topic, except "preventive medicine" which had only half the number of stories as most other topics. By contrast, the *Wall Street Journal* carried only 7% of the 1,800 items and focused heavily on occupational and environmental issues; it gave a similar emphasis as the *Times* to medical research and the costs and political issues in health care but provided much less attention to mental health, drug abuse, or disadvantaged groups.

A comparison of *Newsweek* and *Time* with *Science* and *Scientific American* offers further illustration. Each of these pairs of periodicals ran only 40 of the total health-news items. Of the science journals' 40, the overwhelming share (44%) were on biomedical research, followed by preventive medicine (20%) and mental health (15%), with almost no attention to disadvantaged groups or to the political issues involved in health care (2%). The health news profile in the two weekly news magazines shows emphasis on biomedical research (25%) and family health problems (24%), secondary attention to preventive medicine (15%), drug abuse (15%) and mental health (10%), and least to environmental or occupational health issues, or to disadvantaged groups, or political issues (3% each).

Given the topical groupings made by the Information Bank, it is clear that the health message presented throughout the year by each publication is not a random one, however unintended it might be. The variation in health news profiles of each suggests how health-related stories are selected to match the presumed interests, both intellectual and monetary, of the readership. The reader of *Scientific American*, for example, is the most professional and best educated of the leading popular health and science magazines, according to 1981 marketing research. The health news profile presented to readers must, over time, also help shape their understanding of the existence and nature of health issues and what to do about them, as has been found to be true for other news on public issues (Asp & Miller, 1980; Gray, 1977).

Although the local press may sometimes give more attention to local health issues, it, like the national press, treats problems topically, separating disease from health, mental from physical, and personal from environmental and occupational health issues; nor does it compare biomedical therapy with other means or question the effectiveness of health service policies in comparison with other social policies (Burd, 1981). The picture thus presented, which mirrors traditional medical thinking and the bureaucratic division of responsibility in governmental and other health agencies, tends to reinforce traditional perceptions among the public.

In sum, the health message of the mass media is that the answer to modern disease is to be found in the world of medical expertise, or, as the alternative, or perhaps complement, in individuals' personal lives through their own habits or life style, disciplining themselves to follow the latest advice about diet, exercise, relaxation, drinking, smoking, sex, and childbearing. Some of the major (and unfounded) assumptions behind these messages are that cures for modern chronic disease are possible and can revive people's health; that improved medical care will improve health; that individuals will act differently if they have the right information and do what is necessary to avoid health problems; and finally, that the main ways to improve health are either medical treatment or personal prevention.

CHANGING THE HEALTH MESSAGE

Although rare, attempts are being made to change the typical broadcast media health message to one that might more effectively alter people's behavior in ways health educators want but which their personal advice approach is not able to effect or sustain. The two British examples that follow may be revolutionary; the new U.S. Cable Health Network may present a lot more of the same.

Although British people, like Americans, place high value on health, according to public opinion polls, the British Broadcasting Corporation (BBC) audience research showed they are not personally very worried about heart disease as compared with inflation, unemployment, or cancer. People are interested in dramatic, eventful "medical breakthroughs" recall such events, and place them together with other such reports presented by the mass media in past decades.

But since people cannot seek information about issues of which they are not aware and cannot learn or retain information unless it has some connection to what they already know (Bateson, 1980), a journalist, or any would-be educator, is risking failure by offering an audience new material, or old information from a new point of view. By definition, a "new point of view" challenges long-held ideas and requires effort for a listener to compare, evaluate, accept, or discard. And effort is just the opposite of the general expectation to be entertained by the mass media. Further, for the journalist (or more accurately his or her mass media employer) to offer new ways of thinking to an audience is contrary to the media formula of holding audiences by giving them what they want, which means, in effect, drawing on what they are already familiar with. So spins a self-enforcing cycle of "more of the same" type of adult learning for large sections of the public served by the mass media.

The Process at BBC

Faced with this social reality, there nevertheless seems to be an attempt to break this cycle in the creation of the health message at BBC. Its program production process illustrates both how—through its structure anchored in law, organizational makeup, and operations—the agenda-setting effect of television begins and how opening the process can alter the agenda. Closely tied to the decision of what shall be put on the public information agenda is the question of how a topic or issue will be treated, that is, how the problem will be framed. If, for example, the prevention of heart disease is to be the topic, will it be defined as a personal or societal problem, with what range of cause(s), effect(s), and solution(s), and from what points of view will these be considered? Together, these decisions frame the issue; they define the nature of the problem and its significance and suggest what could or ought to be done about it. In other words, the issue, constructed from information coming to both broadcasters and public, will depend on who the observers (scientists, politicians, manufacturers, consumers) are that supply it, and the context, both in terms of programmatic style and format and scope and depth of material, in which it is presented.

Briefly, BBC is, in structure, supported by license fees paid by owners of television sets and governed by a board which monitors its activities according to the Parliamentary law which chartered the system. Its purpose is to disseminate information, education, and entertainment to the entire population.[1] The unit charged with "adult education," or

---

[1]British TV consists of two publicly financed channels, BBC 1 and 2, and a commercially sponsored independent system transmitting on a third channel, joined by a new fourth commercial channel (TV 4) in 1982. The independent network has the same general purposes as BBC, but these are broadly interpreted by network owners and are less directly accountable to the public.

BBC's educational tasks are carried on through three organizations: the School Broadcasting Council, which produces televised programs for the school

nonschool, nonuniversity programming, conducts its work through regular television program schedules. It regards such BBC productions as "Ascent of Man," which was widely used in American college courses as well as in a Public Broadcasting System TV series, as "entertainment," not "education."

For the first time in its history, and possibly in the life of national television anywhere, BBC planned in 1982 a series of six 25-minute programs on the prevention of heart disease from a new point of view. It had, as have many other television networks worldwide, dealt with health promotion and disease prevention in the past, ranging from child safety to nutrition, exercise, and quit-smoking skills. Always, however, it implicitly followed the point of view of the British Health Education Council (HEC), a quasi-governmental body financed by the Department of Health and Social Security. The HEC, a tacitly independent agency, was in substantial accord with the government's view that prevention is a personal responsibility. HEC has used almost two thirds of its annual $8- to 9-million budget to conduct paid advertising campaigns in the

---

system; the Open University, which has its own production facilities for its exclusively noncampus degrees and higher education credits; and BBC Continuing Education (CE). BBC-CE is to promote "adult education" in a nonformal way through the regular television program schedules. All BBC 1 and 2 programming time is ultimately allocated by the BBC controllers. BBC-CE slots are usually Saturday and Sunday mornings until 1 or 2 p.m. and slots of 10 or 25 minutes at 6:30 on Sunday evenings as well as late night slots at 11 p.m.

Within the CE department of BBC are 12 "strands" or thematic programming units headed by a producer. These units evolved over the department's life of 17 years and include public affairs, science, leisure, languages, consumer affairs, and health. Until it became a separate strand in the mid-1970s, health-related programs appeared under any of the other thematic units.

Each spring "strand meetings" are held in which the department's 60 producers begin to chart the program agenda for the following year. They discuss program topics which seem to have had little treatment in depth or variety of point of view and negotiate any possible overlap among the strands. Ideas come from individual BBC producers, generated by their contacts with expert groups or consultants that are a prime source of information. Another source of input is from "education officers" who are contact and liaison people in public and private organizations such as local sports councils or health officials. These individuals suggest program ideas and also promote upcoming productions in local areas, so that community activities can be, and often are, planned to coincide with the broadcast schedule.

One or two program series are selected by each BBC strand and are then refined in "offer meetings" in early summer. These "offers" are short program proposals, usually drawn up by producers who outline the background, aim, audience, form, content, and collaboration desired for a series. The "offer" that the strand producer accepts then guides the more-or-less open-ended research and production process of the succeeding months, work done by about two or three people for each series.

mass media, mainly television, designed mainly by the advertising agency that also conducts the political campaigns of the Conservative party in power (St. George, 1981).

BBC television, whose communication strategy has long been at an opposite pole from the 30-second ad, short-term campaign strategy of the Health Education Council, chose in 1982 to also define the problem of heart disease not only as a matter for prevention (rather than treatment) but more uniquely as a political and socioeconomic issue, rather than a personal, individual affair. It intended to show the limits of what individuals can do to help themselves when government policies encourage corporations and agriculture to produce items, such as cigarettes, and subsidize commodities, such as high fat, high salt foods, which individuals are at the same time advised to avoid.

How BBC producers arrived at this sociopolitical perspective is a less clear-cut process than the formal agenda-setting stages charted by its legal mandate and organizational routine. However, the general shape of the process becomes apparent from reports of people who were directly involved both inside and outside BBC TV.

Acting within its charge to inform and educate the *general* population (and therefore hold 50% of the national audience)—and knowing that "to program in the public interest, you have to interest the public"—the BBC "health strand" programming unit sought a new angle on topics it had presented since its inception. A further factor giving, perhaps, new impetus to this yearly planning task might have been its awareness that the upcoming independent TV-4 network was planning a new approach to health issues.

As one source of new ideas, BBC producers researched their own experience and that of other countries and found BBC production techniques had not only improved over the mid-1970s but also were at least as effective as elsewhere. BBC's health programs were able to retain prime-time audiences of 8 million (of a total population of 56 million); to elicit appreciative recollections from half the viewing audience several months later; to induce about 1% to write in for free material which two thirds of them claimed to be using up to 6 months later; and to pave the way for public acceptance of the Health Education Council's health-selling advertisements.

In spite of BBC's relative success in reaching a responsive target audience, the health strand producers were also aware that the major health problems were not declining. They were informed too of (mainly U.S.) research of the limitations of TV health education critically summarized for them by the British Centre for Mass Communication Research.

Having posed a challenge to themselves to think in new ways, the health strand executive convened six outsiders to assist in this process. The choice of experts would obviously point the way toward the advice BBC would receive. The six were "top people" in their fields, "nonconformists" who had become known to BBC directly or by reputation over recent years. All were men who took a public health view of health issues and worked actively in community health, one with deprived groups, another as health-policy analyst and advocate, and one who was the new, but soon-to-resign, director of the Health Education Council, who had tried to reorganize and redirect the Council's efforts along less conventional lines.

The conclusions of these discussions, which essentially were to center around the issue of why heart disease continues as a major problem taken from a political–economic vantage point, were then fed into the health strand planning meetings along with the other types of information about past productions, media research, program gaps, the expected efforts and approaches of others such as the HEC and alternate media, and so on. The decision to emphasize the policy influences on behavior and social conditions that contribute to heart disease was then refined to include the more typical individual, personal perspective as well, in order to attract and hold the target audience. The audience for the six 25-minute weekly programs was identified both from audience-viewing statistics and epidemiological health data: all adults, but especially men over age 25.

Following these decisions, program proposals were made at the yearly June "offers" meeting. The proposal selected included investigative reporting and filmed interviews with health scientists, commercial producers, and agricultural and government officials; analysis of the effects of farm policies in the European Common Market to which Britain belongs; the intention to work with the HEC and other groups, as well as develop an accompanying free booklet for viewers on request; and to attempt longer-term coordination with local groups and develop a national campaign as ways to sustain and deepen incipient interest by the public.

Evolution at TV 4

Meanwhile, BBC's rival, the new commercial Channel 4, was gearing up for its first year, scheduled for late 1982. Aiming at innovation, the health-program planning process moved within months from a conventional proposal: "Eat better—look better—feel better," the "curious, wide-eyed" exploration of a "food-loving, weight-watching, medically trained housewife," and "celebbrity" to get people to change their eating habits, to an 8-program series designed around interwoven, recurrent themes, exposing the audience to a new point of view. This was to give them "insight into the range of choices available for better nutrition and health at the individual, social, and political level." TV 4 shifted, in other words, from a victim-blaming point of view: "Why do people choose to eat the wrong food?" to "What is responsible for the eating patterns of the nation, and what is needed for healthful changes?" It reversed typical prime-time "entertainment with information" to prime-time education, that is, taking-people-from-here-to-there.

To understand this shift in the framing of a health issue, one particularly unexpected for a commercial station, a look at TV 4's organizational underpinnings and informal processes is helpful.

Channel 4 was set up by Parliamentary law in 1980 in accordance with the Conservative government's intent to promote competition generally and between the private and public sectors in particular. In this case, TV 4 became a second commercial channel in the Independent Television Network (ITV) under the quasi-governmental Independent Broadcasting Authority (IBA), competing with the two channels of the public BBC. TV 4 is charged with being innovative in form and content; providing alternate programming for interests not satisfied by ITV, including a significant share of "adult educational" programming; and obtaining many programs from independent producers, those not franchised to supply ITV.

TV 4 is owned by IBA, and its initial funds were shares bought by IBA's constituent 15 ITV companies. TV 4 projects self-supporting revenues and an eventual profit from advertising, if it can hold 10% of the British viewing audience. Its board of directors is appointed by IBA and includes the station's two top executives.

In one sense, BBC influence may be felt through the initial staffing of TV 4. Four of its top program chiefs and 5 of its 13 commissioning editors (who, apart from management personnel, *are* TV 4) have worked for BBC.

The weekly programming schedule reflects both TV 4's competitive relation to BBC and its complementary link to ITV. For example, it schedules 22% of its 60-hour broadcast week to news, single documentaries, and public affairs compared with BBC's 25% and ITV's 21%; but in addition, TV 4 plans 13% for "nonlabeled" educational programming, including documentary series. This compares with about 3% of such programming each for BBC and ITV, although they also have additional, formal educational programming for schools, the off-campus Open University, as well as other segments for children and religious affairs. Finally, where BBC and ITV offer 11 to 14% of their week in sports, TV 4 will provide only 2%, and this will cover non-British activities. Most programming begins at 5 p.m. daily.

Within this framework, the production process at TV 4 is carried forward by commissioning editors, each in charge of a programming area such as youth, the arts, music, single documentaries, multicultural programs, and education-documentary series. Health falls under this last adult information–education rubric and has a late and early prime-time slot at least twice weekly.

It is up to the editors to develop an approach to their program areas, in consultation with three senior editors (for actuality, fiction, and education), in conformity with the channel's legal mandate, fiscal limits, and long-term profit requirements. Within these limits, they are free to innovate. For example, the editor's intention for health programming is to reverse the thematic emphasis of current media presentations, noted earlier, such as medical technology, health care scandals, individualistic-behavior change, and the physical-dramatic aspects of illness, all customarily done as short or single-topic programs. In contrast, she wants to develop the nonmedical causes and nonindividualistic solutions to health problems, emphasizing prevention over treatment and the emotional, social, and mundane aspects of illness, portraying these themes as series with as much audience interaction, follow-up, and local coordination as possible.

How effective such editorial policy can be depends on contacts, communication, and negotiation with large numbers of producers who offer program proposals.

Thus the initial health-program proposal to TV 4 by an independent producer for a food and nutrition series went through three drafts, all unacceptable, over a 6-month period before a major reversal in approach was made by the producer. This turnabout occurred when the commissioning editor, after several private talks with interested parties, reassembled the production team in a day-long session which included potential outside funders (the national Health Education Council) to supplement TV 4's budget. They were joined by several print journalists and health professionals known to hold nontraditional views about health improvement and to be generally supportive of new ways to frame and program health issues.

It was during this brainstorming, undirected discussion that recurrent themes emerged that would be woven into a series of eight topical programs, themes that would begin with individual facets of an issue such as "Sunshine Breakfast" and move viewers toward economic and political aspects. The themes included comparative perspectives (international, regional, class, historical); psychosocial (sex, age); biological; holistic (family, work, community contexts); political–economic (agriculture, commerce, and government policy), information–communication (credibility, probability, risk, scientific knowledge, fads).

A range of formats, production techniques, related program materials, activities, and other uses were also discussed to guide the prospective producer's next steps.

Why the shift in viewpoint at Channel 4 and BBC?

The impetus for the turnaround in framing the health message at TV 4, like BBC, was built into its mandate and structure. It was to reach those unserved by ITV with innovative programming; BBC was to retain its audience share as TV 4 entered into direct competition. Both networks require only a stable audience, unlike U.S. commercial channels which seek ever larger shares to enlarge profits and cover the evergrowing costs of entertainment programming.

The formal production process at BBC and TV 4 is similar to all information-related programming—information gathering, construction, presentation, and feedback. The extra effort or risk of seeking new information sources, forms of construction, and formats for presentation was partly balanced in 1982—unlike previous years—by the risk of losing in competition or thwarting their mandates to educate and to hold minimum audience shares. The risk was feasible, because both BBC and TV 4, being assured of operating funds, have time to test, to fail, and to try again over a period of years, unlike the quick program response to audience shifts built into the fiscal arrangements of commercial U.S. TV networks.

Innovation on Cable TV

The coming of U.S. cable television, with its dozens of new channels and potential variations in financing and public access, promised new opportunities for health and other information and entertainment programming. The Cable Health Network (CHN), launched in 1982, makes this claim. Its aims are, according to its marketing manual, to "not only educate and entertain" but also to "transform" the lives of viewers and to "present a credible environment" for advertisers. This commercial objective is based on marketing research which shows that advertising associated with highly regarded TV programs is better recalled by consumers. CHN expects to be highly regarded because of the high visibility of the medical profession in its programming. To build its audience, it also both advertises and uses material related to such "upscale" publications as *Health, Science, Omni*, and *Psychology Today*, enhancing its "narrowcasting," aimed at well-educated, affluent adults.

Telecasting 24 hours daily via satellite, CHN expected to have a beginning audience of about 4.5 million which would increase tenfold by 1985. Its all (but 2) male management team of 15 has backgrounds in network and cable television, advertising and marketing, and is

chaired by a physician–talk-show personality. The 50 "support organizations" from which CHN may draw some expertise and to which it
offers to send its speakers, are mainly biomedical and disease-oriented
groups; only a school health group may be possibly regarded as a public
health-focused organization.

The initial program menu consists of 10 series, in mainly half-hour
segments, each screened from 3 to 10 times within 24 hours over a week.
The series include medical breakthroughs ("What's New in Science and
Health"); exercise and food ("Keeping Fit"; "Diet, Nutrition, and Eating
Well"); mental health ("Thinking and Feeling"; "Healthy Relationships"); overcoming dramatic, real-life health problems ("Human Interest and Lifestyles"); and "Self-Help" and "Medical Care." Each series
is to emphasize the usefulness of the information to viewers and is
presented by professional experts, individuals who reflect the audience,
and celebrities.

Judging from these program plans the health message implicit on
CHN is, again, that modern health problems are mainly a private, individual affair rather than a public, collective responsibility; that mind
and body are separate; that the causes of health problems are mainly
biomedical and interpersonal rather than environmental and interor-
ganizational; that the most important consequences of the problems are
short-term and personal, not long-term and societal; and that solutions
lie in a person's coping with his or her problem or in being treated with
ever-advancing medical technology, rather than seeking preventive action through organized efforts to change social policies.

The emphasis of CHN's health message, though it is not likely to
be the exclusive one in every program, is not surprising, considering its
principal sources of information (biomedical experts) and its format,
which is geared to attract a specific consuming public for its prospective
advertisers.

CONCLUSION

Health instruction in the mass media "works" when people's social and
political environments allow them to give up old habits easily and make
new choices. But the health professionals' message is largely directed
at individuals, who, as such, cannot do much to change their environments. When health instruction or health news has reinforced organized
efforts to alter environments through policy changes, patterns of living
have changed and been sustained.

If the aim of health professionals is to create more healthful personal
and societal ways of living, the unintended, implicit, and pervasive

health message in mass media news (as well as the intended message in health instruction) should be framed to educate the public to a new view of today's health problem and of how to deal with it. Such an effort is risky, however, for the media and perhaps for health professionals, because it is contrary to mainstream practices. But as experiences elsewhere show, it can be done.

REFERENCES

Information not otherwise cited is based on interviews with individuals directly involved in the issue at hand in the respective countries and on unpublished documents obtained from them: in England at BBC Education in London; the Centre for Mass Communications Research, Leicester, July, 1982; in Australia, the State Department of Health, Sydney; the Commonwealth Department of Health, Canberra, June and July, 1981; in Finland, the National Board of Health, Health Education Unit, and the National Epidemiological Laboratories, Helsinki; the North Karelia Project, Kuopio, July, 1980.

Asp, K., & Miller, A. (1980, August 28–31). *Learning about politics from the media in Sweden and the United States.* Paper presented at the American Political Science Association annual meeting, Washington, DC.

Bateson, G. (1980). *Mind and nature: A necessary unity.* New York: Bantam.

Budd, J. (1981, March 24). *The mass media campaign.* Paper presented at the Health Education Council Seminar, University of York, England.

Burd, G. (1981, August). *Press responsibility for health news.* Paper presented to the Association for Education in Journalism annual meeting, East Lansing, MI.

Cable Health Network. (1982). *Informational compendium.* New York: Author.

Gatherer, H. (1979). *Is health education effective?* London: Health Education Council.

Gerbner, G., Gross, L., Morgan, M., & Signorielli, N. (1981). Health and medicine on television. *New England Journal of Medicine, 305*(15), 901–904.

Gray, P. (1977). *Communication and community final report to UNESCO of the English section of an international research study.* Leicester, England: Centre for Mass Communication Research.

Leppo, K. (1978). Smoking control policy and legislation. *British Medical Journal, 1,* 345–47.

Leventhal, H., & Win, A. (1980). Cardiovascular risk modification by community-based programs for life-style change: Comments on the Stanford study. *Journal of Consulting and Clinical Psychology, 48*(2), 129–142.

Levin, A. (Ed.). (1979). *Focus on health: Issues and events of 1978 from the New York Times Information Bank.* New York: Arno Press.

Mayer, M. (Ed.). (1981). *Health education by television and radio. Contributions to an international conference with a selected bibliography.* Munich, Germany: K. G. Saur.

McCron, R., & Budd, J. (1979). Mass communication and health education. In I. Sutherland (Ed.), *Health education: Perspectives and choices,* pp. 199–216. London: Allen & Unwin.

Meyer, A., & Schultz, A. (1980). Skills training in a cardiovascular health education campaign. *Journal of Consulting and Clinical Psychology, 48*(2), 129–142.

Milio, N. (1983). *Primary care and the public's health: Judging impacts, goals, and policies.* Lexington, MA: Heath.

Milio, N. (1982). Progress in primary prevention: The smoking-health issue. *American Journal of Public Health, 72*(5), 428–429.

Milio, N. (1981). *Promoting health through public policy.* Philadelphia, PA: F. A. Davis.

Puska, P., & Koskela, K. (1979). A Comprehensive TV smoking-cessation program in Finland. *International Journal of Health Education, 22*(4), supplement.

Report of the national Conference on Smoking on Health: Developing a blueprint for action. (1982). New York: American Cancer Society, 252–256.

Rose, G. (1980, March 15). Heart disease prevention project. *British Medical Journal.*

St. George, D. (1981, November 28). Who pulls the strings at the HEC? *World Medicine* (London), 51–53.

Subcommittee on Oversight and Investigations, House Committee on Energy and Commerce. (1981, June 25). *Cigarette advertising and the HHS antismoking campaign.* Washington, DC: U.S. Government Printing Office.

Wallach, L. (1981). Mass media campaigns: The odds against finding behavior change. *Health Education Quarterly, 8*(3), 209–260.

Warner, K. (1977). Effects of the antismoking campaign on cigarette consumption. *American Journal of Public Health, 67*, 645–650.

Seven

A Visitor's Guide to Recent Child Mental Health Research and Policy Development*

JON E. ROLF and JEANNETTE L. JOHNSON
National Institute of Mental Health

INTRODUCTION

The purpose of this chapter is to explore the cross-fertilization of research and policy decisions in the area of child and adolescent mental health. This task should seem like a rather simple and somewhat mundane task to a typical American with an interest in child health and welfare. To thousands of researchers in academic and clinical settings, the task must also seem a logical social validation of their efforts. But for the relatively small proportion of researchers who have actually attempted to have their data-based opinions influence policy development, the task is actually a complex constellation of interactive organizational and political checks and balances against change. These few researchers might claim that shifting the inertial movement of child mental health policy with new research findings is about as likely to produce measurable and lasting effects as does the change of seasons on the advance and retreat of glaciers.

Yet significant changes in policy have occurred in the past several years. Children in residential treatment have been deinstitutionalized. Disturbed and handicapped students are educated in regular (mainstream) classrooms. Victims of child abuse and family violence are given legal and restorative services. The effects of divorce on children and parents have become legitimate fields of scientific inquiry and have come to provide substance for legal precedents. Fathers now attend their wives

*The opinions expressed by the authors in this chapter are not necessarily those of NIMH.

in the previously off-limits obstetrical suites. Parents of premature babies are now found working side by side with the medical staff in previously isolated intensive-care nurseries.

So, progress is being made. Old misguided policies are eroded by new ones which fit better the scientific knowledge base of normal and deviant child development. How they emerge as a result of (or in spite of) the policymaking process can make interesting case histories. This chapter will use several of these cases that illustrate the mental health systems ongoing policy processes.

Limiting the Focus to Mental Disorders

The limits and the structure of the information in this chapter are based on the observations of the authors, both research psychologists, who have worked with disturbed and normal children in academic, medical, social service, and educational settings. Further, since 1980, the authors have taken part in several of the extramural and intramural programs relevant to children at the National Institute of Mental Health (NIMH). Therefore, in this chapter, a type of research and policy supported by this Institute will be emphasized. It is consequently more directly related to mental disorders per se than to the equally important issues of normal healthy growth and development traditionally emphasized by the National Institute of Child Health and Human Development, the National Institute of Education, and the National Science Foundation.

We do not intend to provide a comprehensive review of all recent research and NIMH policy initiatives in the service of mental health similar to those prepared by the Research Task Force of the National Institute of Mental Health (Yahraes, Segal, & Boomer, 1975) or the most recent annual report of the NIMH Children and Youth Activities (Fishman, 1982). Instead, we will try to give the reader a visitor's perspective of science administrators engaged in the usually parallel, but sometimes interactive, worlds of child mental-health research, practice, domestic policy development, and shifting political mandates.

National Program and Policy Administration

Some of the attributes of and constraints on administrators in research-supported institutions have significant influences on the future of research applications. It is useful to explore a few of these before turning to the research and policies.

Science administrators with either policymaking or policy-supporting positions within government bureaucracies are often misunderstood. It has been convenient for those who do not know them to bundle them into a faceless collective stereotype seemingly borrowed from a Kafkaesque fantasy. We have all seen them used as favorite defenseless targets by elected politicians and special interest advocates. However, those who have had ample opportunity to observe them at their work know that they do not deserve such a negative stereotype. Instead, they are, as a group, dedicated career servants who conduct their business for the public under very much stricter rules of fairness and equal opportunity than apply in the private sector.

The rules of grants and contract procedures designed to promote fair competition also serve as restraints against science administrators' proceeding on any rapid new course of program development. Nor should one expect that a research proposal which is of particularly high interest to an administrator will receive any special treatment or exemption from competitive peer review for scientific merit.

Working within the rules, science administrators responsible for the development of the child mental-health research program will, of course, attempt to be progressive. Rolf and Read (1984) have expressed their views on how this progressive motive must be carefully exercised. They point out that in institutions such as NIMH, key staff which shape the research and training support programs must be responsive to the changing needs of the scientific community They are responsible for maintaining the health of their respective research areas and must detect signs of any significant shifts of energy levels. They are informed primarily through communications with senior field scientists who serve as advisers and by the competitive qualities of current grant applications.

How then does one generate administrative interest in adopting a new priority? The simplest answer is that it generally requires a slow and careful building of a consensus among trusted research scientist advisers in several related fields that the proposed new research activity has considerable merit and involves few risks either to the funding agency or to the viability of the scientific field. Only rarely will this careful, slow process be short-circuited. True emergencies call for more immediate actions. New research or services for children have been implemented within days of disasters such as a major earthquake in California or the threat of a melt-down at Three Mile Island in Pennsylvania. However, other than these emergency programs, attempts to further a policy objective by avoiding due process usually do not succeed.

THE EFFECTS OF RESEARCH ON POLICY

There are many types of research which are relevant to child mental health. They range from laboratory studies of child behavior to studies of the child in social interactions (i.e., family). They may focus on normal developmental processes, types of deviance and psychopathology, or their intersection. (Examples of the latter would be health promotion/prevention studies or diagnostic studies attempting to define the borders between normal problem behaviors and clinical cases of psychopathology.) In all types of studies, samples of children are drawn from one of many ecologically important subject pools: the home, the school, the clinic, the juvenile justice rosters, for example.

In all instances, research data about child mental health issues must pass through numerous filters before it can reach the ears or eyes of administrators, judges, or legislators whose decisions might influence public policy. These policymakers are probably interested in both the "facts" and in the motives of those who are interpreting them. Policymakers should ask, "Who speaks about what to achieve what personal or altruistic societal goal?"

Weber and McCall (1978) in their monograph entitled *Social Scientists as Advocates* address several important aspects of this issue. They point out that, like the legal professions, social scientists have increasingly become advocates for the disenfranchised. This is particularly true with the mental health of children, because children do not speak for themselves. Further, in many cases their parents are also disinclined to speak, because professionals and the lay public may target them for blame in their children's mental disorders. Consequently, self-appointed adults have chosen to become advocates, obstensibly in the name of the "public interest."

Weber and McCall (1978, p. 203) define three types of advocacy which concern social scientists: (a) *outcome advocacy*, where social scientists use scientific data to plead for the best final solution to a perceived policy problem; (b) *process advocacy*, based on the concept of mediation and conflict resolution where scientists balance the claims of all parties (regarding children and adults) to find the most just and equitable solution; and (c) *party advocacy*, where, by adopting the role of social activist and reformist, the scientist intervenes directly on behalf of an under-represented party in dealings with bureaucratic agencies.

"Outcome advocates" at research-supported institutions such as the NIMH most often take the form of expert research consultants who are hired on a temporary basis to staff topical advisory panels or to serve as visiting scientists in a developing program area. "Process advocates" are usually the professional staff at an institution such as NIMH. Their job, they believe, is to balance research priorities and budget allocations so that, for example, new policy for children does not seriously impede other programs (i.e., those for deinstitutionalized chronically mentally ill adults). "Party advocates," like other lobbyists, are by definition biased against competing programs. As such they are less welcome participants in the cycles of research-to-policy and policy-to-research decision-making process in governmental bureaucracies. Party advocacy, paradoxically, can conflict with the ethics of equal opportunity.

Research Based Knowledge Informing Policy

There are three ways that research either becomes involved in policy decision making or is found to be newsworthy by the media. They occur when: (a) new data are seen to significantly advance an important body of scientific knowledge; (b) a research-based consensus is used to justify a judicial ruling, a legislative change, or a shift in the ranking of existing programmatic priorities or budget allocations within an administrative unit; or (c) a policy decision leads to new research activities which is intended to produce more findings to justify, support, or extend this policy decision.

General Trends

There are several issues of single importance to child mental health which have been gaining momentum and greater recognition. They can be succinctly reduced to these seemingly unexciting phrases: (a) *mental health and disorders are multiply determined by complex interactions of biological, maturational, and experimental factors over time*; they are also more characteristically defined by rapid changes in children and by more gradual changes in adults; and (b) *the developmental perspective is critically important* for making valid any study of child mental disorders involving diagnosis, severity, duration, and outcome. Because of these complex interactive determinants and rapid changes inherent in the study of children, it is more difficult to study and to gain knowledge about mental disorders in children than in adults. Thus, the types of research training, methods, and data-analytic techniques which are appropriate for studying adult disorders are often insufficient or inappropriate for the study of disorders of childhood.

The issues of the complex determination of child mental health will be explored first, and the importance of the developmental perspective will then be discussed in the context of programs developed to foster the emerging fields of science that is being called developmental psychopathology.

From Simple to Complex Conceptualizations of Children

The history of the study of children is fascinating in that it reveals the great extent to which it has been shaped by the cultural, religious, and economic values held by adult historians (Aries, 1967). For all those centuries when child mortality rates exceeded 50%, studies on children were of a philosophical rather than an empirically scientific variety. With the advent of the Industrial Revolution which greatly enhanced the value of children as factory workers and with advancement of medical skill in coping with infectious diseases, the writing tended to shift to scholarly appraisals about whether or not children should be considered to function (intellectually, emotionally, and biologically) like miniaturized adults. In 1892, G. Stanley Hall, credited with the founding of experimental psychology as a science, established the first scientific journal of behavioral studies of children.

In the nine decades that have passed, thousands of books have been published on children. Hundreds of scientific journals containing tens of thousands of articles have been written on the myriad ways children differ from adults and from each other according to age, sex, cultural group, environmental, and genetic influences. Consequently, in the 1980s, children are considered to be extremely complex organisms for whom no single theory fully explains or predicts the causes or courses of the behavioral changes in any individual child. Modern academicians, in the spirit of specialization, divide this complexity into a number of content areas for study. Some of this categorized information has been put to practical use. For example, occasionally it has been translated into norms so that parents and teachers can compare the levels of skill attainment of a particular child in order to deliver rewards, punishments, and plan further training.

However, clinicians in the 1980s (i.e., child psychiatrists and psychologist practitioners) are still often uninformed about the complexities of the normal developmental processes in children. Their expertise, instead, concerns both the many problems children have in growing up and the problems that adults have in living with children. Clinicians traditionally group these problems into diagnostic categories and attempt to match each one with a type of therapy. Clinical researchers typically begin to study children from the perspective of these diagnostic groupings and then attempt to describe the differences in cause, course, and outcome between clinical samples and "normal" ones.

However, even though they have been primarily concerned with abnormal behaviors, clinicians too have gradually come to view children as more complexly determined than they were taught was the case. For example, over the past several decades, a number of diagnostic manuals have been developed and used. The most recent ones, *The Diagnostic and Statistical Manual of Mental Disorders, III* (1980) used in the United States and the *International Classification of Diseases* (ICD-9, 1978) used primarily in the rest of the world have dramatically increased the number and subtypes of official diagnoses of mental disorders and diseases. This increase in the number of subtypes over the few broad categories previously sanctioned testifies to the awareness of diagnosticians of the great complexity of child and adolescent disorders. Further, these newest diagnostic systems have become "multiaxial" which means that in addition to diagnosing the *type* of disorder, clinicians must now also rate the degrees of environmental stress impinging on the child and the child's general level of adaptation to his/her environment. These diagnostic manuals have also made some initial (and mostly inadequate) attempts to specify age ranges as part of the criteria which must be met to qualify a case for a diagnosis. The reason for this is because certain behaviors are judged to be normal at one age and not at others. For example, extreme shyness and avoidance of strangers is typical of healthy 8-month-old infants, but it would be diagnosable in an 8-year-old. Similar issues of age apply to wetting, soiling, language incompetence, activity and aggression levels, and so on. Unfortunately, most of the DSM III published age ranges (i.e., 2 to 18 years) are far too broad and still disregard current data on normal differences in roles of behavior during childhood and adolescence.

Clinical researchers, like clinical practitioners, are also rarely equally well-trained in both the developmental and clinical traditions. Nor do research teams studying mental disorders in children have optimum interdisciplinary training or skills to understand fully the relevance of a symptomatic behavior to a child's ongoing developmental processes. Thus, there are many instances when a child with problems is insufficiently understood both by the clinician delivering services or by the clinical researcher who intends to study the causes of the problems or to experimentally influence the child's behavior on a short-term basis.

The Case of Early Infantile Autism

It may prove helpful to use the diagnostic entity of early infantile autism as an example of how progress within speciality areas (i.e., child psychiatry, special education, and neurosciences) can be retarded by failure to promote interdisciplinary communication. A brief definition of the syndrome is that it involves a failure from birth for the infant to form normal social and emotional relationships with its caretakers; with advancing age during infancy, it also fails to develop communicative language skills, increasingly avoids social contact and often engages in self-referent, repetitive behaviors. Those who fail to acquire communicative language by early childhood rarely escape from a life characterized by intellectual and self-care incompetencies, custodial residential care, and a lack of peer relationships.

Early psychodynamic (Bettelheim, 1967) theories supposed these infants to be similar to immature adults who had been subjected to some form of extreme emotional deprivation similar to prisoners in concentration camps. Therefore, Bettleheim believed the cause of this psychosis was extreme parental "emotional refrigeration." Treatment, if followed, was designed to remove these victims from their often economically well-to-do but pathogenic parents and provide residential care and long-term psychoanalytic psychotherapy for the parents and child.

The types of clinical research on these children up to the late 1960s tended to be (a) observational studies to form interpretative case histories of the presumed symbolic significance of the autistic child's stereotyped and repetitive behaviors, and (b) studies of the autistic children's responses to psychoactive drugs which were being used with adult mental patients (Wolman, 1972). During the 1970s, the discovery and refinement by psychologists of behavior modification techniques led to its application in self-care instructional and child-management programs with autistic and other types of children in institutions. The highly structured staff training, compulsive data collection, and resulting publications of these behavior modifiers produced abundant evidence that autistic children could overcome some of their learning deficits, acquire positive habits, lose some of their most negative ones, and even be taught some socially communicative language skills. Of equal importance was the accumulating findings that many of the presumed cardinal features of the autism psychosis were also shared by nonpsychotic children in institutions for the retarded, the deaf, and those serving the handicapped who had suffered known brain damage affecting speech and language development. As communication increased between disciplines, it became clearer that autism overlapped with mental retardation and that neurological deficits in both groups probably accounted for many of the symptoms heretofore considered to be functionally psychotic and caused by nonorganic factors.

Most clinical researchers at the start of the 1980s recognize that autism (and probably other psychotic disorders) had multiple causes, the least of which is attributable to an all-powerful parental influence. For example, the list of interactive causes of autism include brain injuries, mental retardation, sensory handicaps, learning and language disabilities, and a host of presumed environmental and genetic influences (Bartak, Rutter, & Cox, 1974; Fish & Ritvo, 1979; Folstein & Rutter, 1978).

This admittedly simplified review is intended to demonstrate the progress that can occur when practitioners-researchers (in this case behavior modifiers) cross the boundaries of the too often isolated fields of mental health, mental retardation, and special education. It is also fortunate that advances in computer technology have permitted the rapid abstracting and categorizing of studies in these fields so that more cross-fertilization is taking place than ever before in the history of research with children. Consequently, today most clinicians working with severe forms of extreme child mental disorders are aware of the lessons learned from the history of the autism syndrome.

The Developmental Perspective as an Integrative Force in Child Mental Health

The idea of approaching the study of other types of clinical disorders of childhood from a developmental perspective is not new. A number of influential clinical investigators have attempted to integrate some developmental theory into their own writing. For example, E. J. Anthony (1956) discussed the importance of Piagetian theory to clinical understanding of the disturbed child. Peter Wolff (1960) endeavored to relate the Freudian stages of psychodynamic development to Piaget's cognitive developmental stages. Further, there were a moderate number of relatively naive and unsuccessful attempts to demonstrate that certain forms of adult psychopathological and schizophrenic thinking could be understood as arrested development or regressed development (Johnson, Rolf, & Bond, 1981).

While there were no real attempts to define an integrated orientation to research which could be called developmental psychopathology, crossover activities between the clinical and developmental camps continued at both the individual and institutional levels.

At an institutional level, there are a number of examples where applied and clinical research have been combined. Special education and the national Head Start program are illustrative. Both have tended to focus on the facilitation of intellectual and social skills acquisition in children who are at risk for mental retardation or other "developmental disabilities" and are thus expected to become special problems for the schools. Much important work has been accomplished in this applied developmental area over the past decade. Some of it has had considerable impact on national educational policies (e.g., P.L. 94-142 which requires the mainstreaming of handicapped children in regular classrooms). However, as these fields have advanced and their practitioners have become specialized, the feedback of new applied knowledge, techniques, and training curricula to the parent disciplines of clinical and developmental psychology has diminished. This probably is a result of several isolating forces. Restrictive journal editorial policies apply here as well as the nature of professional groups such as the American Psychological Association (which has 38 subspecialty divisions) and the intentionally nonoverlapping research support programs of key funding agencies such as NIMH, NICHD, and NIE.

There are a number of researchers who have attempted to remove these traditional topical and disciplinary barriers which impede the integration of the complex nature of child mental disorders. Two of these are Norman Garmezy (1983) and Michael Rutter (Rutter, Izard, & Read, in press). Together, they have had a major influence in drawing attention to developmental issues in clinical work. Both are psychopathologists and generalists in the renaissance sense of the term. They have come to advocate this position based on their respective types of risk research. Garmezy has searched for explanations as to why certain high-risk children (e.g., those with a highly stressed developmental history or with a psychotic parent) express their vulnerability through some developmental incompetencies, whereas others remain well-adapted and seemingly invulnerable to the most extreme stressors. Rutter through epidemiological studies has attempted to identify moderating variables which inhibit the pathogenic influences of risk factors on the developing child.

It is apparent that developmental psychopathology could become a legitimate scientific field of social and biological inquiry. As a field, it must be advanced on an interdisciplinary basis. If this were true, then do interdisciplinary teams already exist, or must they be created? Are there adequate opportunities for interdisciplinary research training? Is there an existing body of theory, methods, and research findings that could be viewed as providing the necessary foundation for developmental psychopathology? These were some of the central questions that stimulated recent activities at several national research-support institutions including, but not limited to, the MacArthur Foundation, the NIMH, the Society for Research in Child Development, and the Social Science Research Council.

Advancing Developmental Psychopathology

Rolf and Read (1984) report examples of activities that have been employed by these institutions to foster the creation of a developmental psychopathological research field. They believe that while no one type of activity need come first in a sequence, there must be a sequence, or their potent interactive effects will be lost and the movement will recede. The activities addressed included specific examples of: (a) consciousness-raising of the issues for key administrators of training and research institutions; (b) creating forums for research communication, evaluation, and planning; (c) building researcher networks; (d) shaping the priorities of funding agencies; (e) providing publication outlets; and (f) developing training possibilities for new investigators.

In their discussions they use, for example, the issue of defining and

understanding the roles that cognitive and affective developmental processes have on the timing, type, and duration of depressive disorders of
childhood. As was the case with early infantile autism, much psychiatric
practice and research on "child depression" have involved inappropriate
downward extensions of adult diagnostic, assessment, and treatment
procedures. They are inappropriate, because children don't always think
like adults. Depression in adults is largely an affective disorder characterized not only by sadness but also by distortions of thinking about
one's role in life, the probability for happiness and changes for the better
in the future, and one's perceived helplessness or adequacy to cope with
life's challenges. But a child younger than 8 years old, as compared to
adolescents and adults, has less cognitive ability to see him/herself as
others do, has only the vaguest concept of "future" to feel hopeless
about, and has more limited language and other symbolic skills with
which to express his sadness to adults, and thus won't be able to show
a classical adultlike depressive syndrome. Rolf and Read also show how
the various types of activities listed earlier have been used to integrate
both the developmental and clinical data and their theoretical models
to create new conceptualizations of affective disorders of childhood.

Developmental psychopathology is becoming a source of influence
in social-science research policy development. It is not yet a field; it may
now be a movement whose final definition and shape can not be known
at present. The recent promotional activities and sources of future support at national research institutes (e.g., NIMH and SSRC) suggest by
their very number that there will be a productive future ahead for those
who are willing to take the risks associated with being pioneers. It is
hoped that readers will be motivated to join this emerging field by
committing their resources to the fostering of closer collaborations between their clinical and developmental colleagues in research and service
institutions.

POLICY DECISIONS INFLUENCING CHILD MENTAL-HEALTH RESEARCH

In this section, we review a number of examples in the ways policy can
shape child mental-health research. These examples also reveal how
political considerations are involved in the process of making new national research policies and priorities.

There have been numerous efforts in describing the politization of
social science (e.g., Lynne, 1979; Mayer, 1979; Harris, 1970; Weiss, 1977)
and the obstacles to using research in policy making (Caplan, 1977;
Glaser, 1973; Rothman, 1980; Rodgers, 1967; Sharpe, 1975). There are

important issues discussed by these authors which are generally unfamiliar to most researchers studying mental health. For example, Carol Weiss (1977), editor of *Using Social Research in Public Policymaking*, provides a very concise and insightful overview of the myths and realities of the role research findings play in determining policy. "The basic premise of the research-for-policy literature," she writes, "is that it is a good thing" (Weiss, 1977, p. 4). This commonly held attitude is based on the intellectual community's affection for logic and the belief that knowledge (and its spokesperson) is neutral and nonpartisan. It is also generally held that government agencies (including research support institutes such as NIMH) are not making the best use of scientific data and that modest reforms in their administration, advisory board policies, or staffing would produce better, more useful research which would then be transformed by responsive decision makers into better policies.

Institutional Policy Shifts, Changes, and Effects on Research at the NIMH

Weiss's outline of assumptions seem to fit rather well the case of child mental-health research utilization within NIMH at the turn of the decade. A brief review of the recent history and milestones is instructive. In 1974, the first annual report on child and youth activities of the NIMH was prepared in order to provide information to the NIMH Task Force Report on Research (Yahraes, Segal, & Boomer, 1975). This task force then identified child-mental health as a top priority to b developed within the NIMH research, training, service, and dissemination missions. A coordinating position within the Institute, known as the Assistant Director for Children and Youth, was established in 1975. Staff from the relevant extramural and intramural research programs were then brought together to function as the Director's Child and Youth Activity Group. This group has continued to meet to share information, participate in policy development, and assist in the preparation of the annual reports which were used in budget appropriation discussions. The Center for Studies for Crime and Delinquency, established in the 1960s, was still devoting a major share of its resources to the causes and treatment of antisocial behavior among youth. Partly in response to the previously mentioned Task Force Report and one called *Toward a National Policy for Children and Families* (National Academy of Sciences, 1976), staff in the Center for Child and Family Mental Health within the Division of Special Mental Health Programs attempted to intensify its programs but without increased budgetary support. During its existence, this Center functioned primarily in advocacy and information dissemination capacities and funded relatively little direct research. Perhaps it was this "coordinating" rather than research-funding role that worked against its expansion. However, among the important NIMH publications produced during this period were the monographs *Families Today* (Corfman, 1979) and *Families, Social Service, and Social Policy* (Moroney, 1980) that summarize many of the dominant service issues and exemplary research projects concerning child and family mental health at NIMH during the 1970s.

Also, during the 1970s, child clinical mental-health service providers were identified as a manpower shortage area. Thus, increasing the number of child mental-health professional training programs was a definite goal for the Division of Manpower and Training. In 1976, the Mental Health Services Development Branch held a conference and published a state-of-the-arts monograph on "Defining Children's Mental Health Service Needs, Impediments to Services Delivery and Research Priorities" (Salasin, 1977). Also, in the 1970s, the Center for Studies of Schizophrenia, under the direction of Loren Mosher, through a series of conferences, and a grant awarded to Norman Garmezy, established a consortium of researchers funded by NIMH who were embarking on longitudinal studies of children of schizophrenic parents in order to observe the causes and course of this profound debilitating disorder.

These and other activities of the 1970s were promising changes in child mental-health policy that were propelled by two single conclusions. First, not enough known about children, and second, not enough was being done for children suffering from mental disorders.

In 1980 a special senior advisory group drawn from the research community recommended that a new unit be established with the responsibility of promoting, funding, and coordinating all NIMH research involving infant, child, and adolescent mental disorders. Coincidental with this recommendation, the directors of NIMH decided to dismantle the Center for Child and Family Mental Health in the Division of Special Mental Health Programs (the Center for Studies of Crime and Delinquency would continue its functions there) and to authorize the Division of Extramural Research Programs to establish a Center for Studies of Child and Adolescent Mental Disorders as part of its ongoing divisional reorganization.

To gain a better understanding of the importance of these recent administrative reorganizations to the resulting child mental health/research programs and policies at NIMH, we can turn again to Weiss's (1977) outline of basic principles influencing governmental organizations: "Not only courts but other governmental units have an enduring respect for order, but administrators, bureaucrats, and legislators as well as judges place a greater premium on negotiating differences and reconciling divergent views than on reaching scientifically elegant solutions" (p. 9).

In this specific instance, the new Child and Adolescent Research Center did not become an independent and coordinating developmental psychopathology unit within the Division. Instead, it was created as one component of five which comprised the Clinical Research Branch, one of six branches within the Division.

There were real checks and balances in this reorganization. By administratively placing this new center as a subcomponent within an existing branch of a even larger division, its ability to influence divisional or Institute policy and to compete strongly for any new funds was restricted. This is because funds were becoming increasingly limited, and other grants had to be paid first. The most numerous and influential research interest group supported by the Branch involved studies of adult clinical disorders which had a backlog of high quality, approved grants awaiting funding by the Branch. Conversely, there were many fewer high-quality, approved child projects and many fewer child clinical researchers to advocate for a disproportionally larger share of the pie in order to stimulate development in their special field. (This lack of child researchers is particularly true regarding research child psychiatrists who could be expected to speak a common language with the institutes medically trained top administrators. If we consider only those who spend the majority of their work days in research instead of service activities, then there are only about 20 research child psychiatrists in the entire nation who could serve as "outcome advocates" to the NIMH.)

External Events Restricting NIMH Child Research Programs

Similar to the promising beginnings of the 1970s, the new institutional changes in 1980 and 1981 for child mental-health research were to suffer a series of difficult challenges. Unpredicted, external exigencies seriously affected the expansion of child research programs at NIMH. The 1981 OMB recision (i.e., recapture) of approximately 15% during the current budget made it virtually impossible to fund any new or competing renewal research projects. With less to go around, grants already in progress had to be trimmed back in order to keep all of them operational during their continuation years.

If this recision were not enough of a stressor on developing new child mental-health programs at NIMH, President Reagan's goal of reducing the size of government resulted in an ordered hiring freeze and subsequent reduction in force (RIF) of the existing staff in the Department of Health and Human Services. This new reality made it impossible to recruit new permanent expert staff for the Child Center. Consequently, an optional and temporary solution was attempted through the Intergovernmental Personnel Agreement (IPA). Before HHS personnel policy was changed to terminate the IPA "loophole" as a viable option for staffing the new center, a child psychiatrist and a child clinical research psychologist were "borrowed" from their respective state supported universities. However, by December, 1981, the Center's IPA child clinical research psychologist was gone, and by January, 1983, its IPA child psychiatrist had moved to the Division of Manpower and Training to attempt revitalizing the NIMH clinical training programs which the President's 1983 budget would have terminated had not Congress intervened. In 1984, a pending RIF further interfered with the recruitment of expert staff for child research programs and the president's FY 1985 budget again projected no allocation for any clinical training.

Manpower Training in Child Mental Health

As has been mentioned, the Reagan Administration has recommended eliminating clinical training programs, including those relevant for child mental health. As many already know, Congress intervened in the fiscal year (FY) 1982 continuing resolution that was to serve in lieu of an FY 1983 HHS budget and made provisions for minimal clinical training and continued research training programs. Given the fact that HHS will operate on this continuing resolution, NIMH had for FY 1983 a much reduced pool of funds for professional clinical training grants in child mental health. Thus, this specialty training area must be placed on an endangered species list.

Child Mental Health Services

With regard to the development of mental health *services* for children, there was first a gradual decline; then during the recent past both the greatest promise of progress and the greatest setback in the past two decades. Following the conference on mental health service priorities for children, the Services Development Branch shifted funding from child and family projects in order to demonstrate mental-health service evaluation programs. The "most in need" (MIN) program which was intended to fund services for the most underserved children with mental disorders never received adequate budgetary support. What limited funds there were in the late 1970s and early 1980s went to programs for native Americans. Attempts to secure sufficient funds through legislative action were unsuccessful. Then, the mental health services advocacy community put its efforts into new legislation intended to replace the Community Mental Health Act of 1963. These efforts actually paid off, and the Mental Health Systems Act was signed into law during the final days of the Carter presidency. Within its various requirements were several state of the service arts stipulations which were intended to rectify the second class status of child programs within the expiring community mental health system legislation and its practice within the field. However, with the advent of the block grants system, the federal budgetary reductions for their subsumed programs, the virtual disbanding of a proactive services division at the NIMH as an advocate within the federal administrative structure, the anticipated child and adolescent mental-health service and evaluation programs died at birth. Further, given the subsequent severe economic recession across the country, many of the once-functioning services programs for children have been reduced or eliminated in CMHCs at a time when the need for them has dramatically increased due to greater stresses experienced by the family as a result of increased unemployment and marital disruption. Thus, the politics of the "new federalism" have terminated the research-informed federal service programs in child mental-health services, and the future does not look bright.

The Case of Prevention Research Policy

During the past two decades at NIMH, the fields of prevention research and preventive services development have generated relatively little programmatic activity, because the need for therapeutic services and more knowledge about etiological factors was so apparent. Until the Carter Administration, the Institute provided a very modest percentage of its budget for a rather broad spectrum of research which was intended to be related to the prevention of mental disorders. Much larger support was provided for studies of etiology, epidemiology, diagnosis, course, and treatment of mental disorders. Prevention, therefore, was always a popular future long-range goal rather than a pressing short-term programmatic objective.

Beginning in 1981 with the arrival of Secretary Schweiker and Assistant Secretary Brandt, prevention and health promotion became top policy priorities of HHS. This dramatic shift in policy was supported in part by a modest but growing knowledge base. That is to say, given the acquisition of considerable data concerning (a) etiological factors, (b) epidemiological indicators of risk for mental disorders, (c) a diverse armamentarium of tested therapeutic modalities, and (d) better methods of outcome assessment, prevention research appeared to be more scientifically feasible. Further, with the NIMH reduction in its manpower-training programs and virtual elimination of services activities, the area of prevention research became a highly visible and desirable program for NIMH career science administrators who had been staffing the terminating programs.

At the present time, bright prospects for child mental health research seem to lie in the prevention area. In April, 1982, the Center for Studies of Prevention was created in the Special Mental Health Services Division to serve as the new focal point of, and the coordinating unit for, the Institute's research activities and research-supported programs dealing with the prevention of mental disorders and the promotion of mental health. As descibed in its program notice (NIMH, 1982), it is currently promoting and supporting research in a wide range of programs for the study of prevention, involving infants, children, and adolescents as well as adults and the elderly. These include: (a) the causes of mental disorders and mental health as they are relevant to preventive interventions; (b) the development, testing, and replication of specific preventive interventions; (c) the elaboration of new developmentally relevant scientific models of prevention; (d) the design and implementation of prospective intervention and outcome assessment methodologies; and (e) the identification of specific groups at high risk for mental disorders and the detection of vulnerable individuals within these groups who could most benefit from preventive interventions.

During FY 1982, approximately $2.4 million was committed by the Center for Studies of Prevention and the Office of Prevention for prevention and promotion research activities, most of which involved infants and children. The next year at least $4 million was committed, again with most programs involving infants and children. Further, about the same time as the creation of this Center, the Institute published a Special Research Grant Announcement (Catalogue of Federal Domestic Assistance 13.242) which outlined a new program to support the development and maintenance of preventive intervention research teams of behavioral and clinical researchers in productive research environments. The basic concept underlying this special prevention research-centers program was to provide long-term support for interdisciplinary approaches to field testing and evaluating specific preventive interventions with groups already identified as being at statistically heightened risks for the development of mental disorders sometime in the near future. The majority of the grant proposal responses to this announcement have targeted infants, children or family units at risk. It is expected that by the end of 1984, four or more of these preventive intervention research centers will be funded to pursue their child-focused longitudinal studies.

The NIMH 1982 Research Highlights (1983) chose a child focus in summarizing three types of prevention studies for the public. These were preventive studies involving infants, preschoolers, and children at risk. However, in all cases, the summaries cautioned the reader that the cited findings from the ongoing research projects were preliminary and subject to change with additional data. Indeed, it is also anticipated that progress in this most difficult type of applied research will be slow, given the great methodological complexities which occur when developmental psychopathology, risk prediction, and preventive intervention research coincide. Thus, it is very important for preventive intervention research and policy advocates to avoid premature predictions of success. Failure to achieve any unrealistic goals will no doubt provide ammunition for those adult-oriented advocates who see prevention research in particular and child mental-health research in general as undesirable competitors for shrinking budgets providing research program support.

The departure of Secretary Schweiker from HHS in February, 1983, and the looming federal deficits will affect the rate of growth of prevention research at NIMH. It is certain that it will remain a priority area, but perhaps not the priority it had been during the first 2 years of Schweiker's administrative stewardship. However, for the near term, it is expected that his advocacy for prevention will continue to have a very supportive influence in interesting the scientific community in designing prevention research and the NIMH in funding the increased number of high quality research projects.

CONCLUSIONS

As is the case with most social systems encountered in life, things always seem simpler from the outside. Becoming immersed in national child mental-health research programs and policy development quickly results in a feeling of being caught up in a complex matrix of checks and balances that are understandable, only if one can acquire a historical perspective. Child programs and organizational structures within NIMH have been created on the basis of expert advice and the best of intentions. Frequently, their orderly growth rates are disrupted by exogenous forces, such as budgetary cutbacks and political pressures for or against a particular program. Sometimes such pressure is beneficial as has been the case for the now well-established programs on crime and delinquency and the rapidly emerging one for prevention research. But equally often, a dedicated science administrator is compelled to wait like an ancient mariner becalmed in the latitudes until another shift in the political breezes enables him or her to resume a programmatic course.

It does not seem likely that child mental-health research programs will be able to pick up much speed in the 1980s until the budget is restored at NIMH. Currently, there are not sufficient funds to expand the number of funded research projects. Instead, similar to the suggestions made by Brim (1982), policy can and is being subtly shifted to encourage greater communication and cooperation among research groups. Limited resources can be made to go a long way in network building (i.e., as in developmental psychopathology) and the fostering of research consortia (i.e., the Risk for Schizophrenia Consortium; Watt, Anthony, Wynn, & Rolf, 1984).

The research community itself can assist administrators by avoiding the type of expert advocacy that has as its primary goal the winning of a bigger piece of a shrinking budget for an exclusive, research interest group. The times no longer seem suitable for the traditionally vigorous competition over dollars for research in one diagnostic category at the expense of another. What is needed are more integrative, interdisciplinary efforts linking the basic behavioral and clinical sciences. "Linking agents" as described by Glock (1961) will be needed to improve attitudes and to encourage what Likert and Lippitt (1963) described as mutual associations. But others (e.g., Kochen, 1975; Rothman, 1980) have also pointed out that increased communication won't in itself be sufficient to insure viable working relationships. It will be the science administrators—the true professional process advocates—who hold the keys to the future. For now when they can't possibly satisfy the funding needs of the majority of the competing research groups, they may choose to advance an integrative model of cooperative science. It will be a tribute to the indefatigable commitment of these child mental-health administrators if they can again make less become more and take these progressive steps.

REFERENCES

Anthony, E. J. (1956). The significance of Jean Piaget for child psychiatry. *British Journal of Medical Psychiatry, 29*, 20–34.

Aries, P. (1967). *Centuries of childhood.* New York: Vintage.

Bartak, L., Rutter, M., & Cox, A. (1975). A comparative study of infantile autism and specific developmental receptive language disorders. *British Journal of Psychiatry, 126*, 127–145.

Bettelheim, B. (1967). *Infantile autism and the birth of self.* New York: Free Press.

Brim, O., Jr. (1982). Some implications for child policy of life span development research. *Social Policy Newsletter* (Society for Research in Child Development, Sprint, 4–5.

Caplan, N. (1977). A minimal set of conditions necessary for the utilization of social science knowledge in policy formation at the national level. In C. Weiss (Ed.), *Using social research in public policy making.* Lexington, MA: Lexington Books.

Corfman, E. (Ed.). (1979). *Families today: A research sampler on families and children* (2 vols.) (ADM 79-815). Washington, DC: U.S. Government Printing Office.

Diagnostic and statistical manual of mental disorders (3rd ed.). (1980). Washington, DC: American Psychiatric Association.

Fish, B., & Ritvo, E. (1979). Psychoses in childhood. In J. D. Noshpitx (Ed.), *Basic handbook of child psychiatry*, (Vol. 2). New York: Basic Books.

Fishman, M. (1982). Ninth annual report on NIMH child and youth activities. Washington, DC: National Institute of Mental Health.

Folstein, S., & Rutter, M. (1978). A twin study of individuals with infantile autism. In Rutter, M., & Schopler, E. (Ed.), *Autism: A reappraisal of concpts and treatment* (pp. 219–241). New York: Plenum Press.

Garmezy, N. (1983, February). Development, behavior and psychopathology: The search for risk and protective factors in mental disorders. Paper presented at the conference on Frontiers of Mental Health Research, NIMH, Bethesda, MD.

Glaser, Edward M. (1973). Knowledge transfer and institutional change. *Professional Psychology, 4,* 434–444.

Glock, C. Y. (1961). Applied social research: Some conditions affecting its utilization, in *Case Studies in Bringing Behavioral Science Into Use: Studies in the Utilization of Behavioral Science*, Vol. 1. Stanford, CA: Institute for Communication Research, Stanford University.

Harris, F. (Ed.). (1970). *Social science and national policy.* New York: Trans-Action Books, Aldine.

International classification of diseases (ninth revision) clinical modification. (1978). Ann Arbor, MI: Commission on Professional and Hospital Activities.

Johnson, J., Rolf, S., & Bond, L. (1981). Piagetian contributions to clinical psychology. Paper presented at the conference on Piagetian Theory and the Helping Professions. Los Angeles, CA.

Kochen, M. (Ed.). (1975). *Information for action.* New York: Academic Press.

Lazarsfeld, P., Reitz, J., & Pasanella, A. (1975). *An introduction to applied sociology.* New York: Elsevier.

Likert, R., & Lippit, R. (1963). The utilization of social science. In L. Festinger & D. Katz (eds.) *Research Methods in Behavioral Sciences.* New York: Dryden.

Lynne, L. (Ed.). (1979). *Studies in the management of social R and D: Selected policy areas.* Washington, DC: National Academy of Sciences.

Mayer, R. (1979). *Social science and institutional change* (ADM 78-627). Washington, DC: U.S. Government Printing Office.

Moroney, R. (1980). *Families, social services, and the issue of shared responsibility* (ADM 80-846). Washington, DC: U.S. Printing Office.

National Academy of Sciences. (1976). *Toward a national policy for children and families.* Washington, DC: N.A.S. Printing Office.

National Institute of Mental Health 1982 Research Highlights. (1982). Washington, DC: U.S. Government Printing Office.

National Science Foundation. (1969). *Knowledge into action: Improving the nation's use of the social sciences.* Washington, DC: U.S. Government Printing Office.

Pick, H., Jr., Leibowitz, H., Singer, J., Steinschneider, A., & Stevenson, H. (1978). *Psychology: From research to practice.* New York: Plenum.

Prevention research program notice. (1982). Washington, DC: National Institute of Mental Health, 1982.

Publication catalogue of the U.S. department of health and human services. (1982). Washington, DC: U.S. Government Printing Office.

Rogers, E. M. (1967). Communication of vocational rehabilitation innovations, in *Communication, Dissemination and Utilization of Rehabilitation Research Information: Studies in Rehabilitation Counselor Training.* No. 5. Washington, DC: DHEW.

Rolf, J., & Read, P. (1984). Programs advacing developmental psychopathology. *Child Development, 55*, 8–16.

Rothman, J. (1980). *Using research in organizations.* Beverly Hills, CA: Sage.

Rutter, M., Izard, C., & Read, P. (in press). *Depressive feelings and depressive disorder: A developmental psychopathology perspective.* New York: Guildford Press.

Salasin, J. (1977). *Important areas for children's mental health services development* (MTR-7481). McLean, VA: Meiter Corp.

Segal, J. (Ed.). (1971). *The mental health of the child* (PHS No. 2168). Washington, DC: U.S. Government Printing Office.

Sharpe, L. (1977). The social scientist and policy making: Some cautionary thoughts and transatlantic reflections. In C. Weiss (Ed.), *Using social research in public policy making.* Lexington, MA: Lexington Books.

Watt, N., Anthony, E. J., Wynne, L., & Rolf, J. (Eds.). (1984). *Children at Risk for Schizophrenia.* New York: Cambridge University Press.

Weber, G., & McCall, G. (Ed.). (1978). *Social scientists as advocates: Views from applied disciplines.* Beverly Hills, CA: Sage.

Weiss, C. (Ed.). (1977). *Using social research in public policy making.* Lexington, MA: Lexington Books.

White House conference on children. (1970). Washington, DC: U.S. Government Printing Office.

Wolff, P. H. (1960). The developmental psychologies of Jean Piaget and psychoanalysis. *Psychological Issues* (Vol. II).

Wolman, B. (1972). Schizophrenia in childhood. In B. Wolman (Ed.), *Manual of child psychopathology.* New York: McGraw-Hill.

Yahraes, H., Segan, J., & Boomer, D. (1975). *Research in the service of mental health: Report of the research task force of the national institute of mental health* (ADM 75-236). Washington, DC: U.S. Government Printing Office, (ADM 75-236).

EIGHT

FROM THE SOCIAL SCIENCE PERSPECTIVE: COMMENT AND CRITIQUE

ELI A. RUBINSTEIN
University of North Carolina at Chapel Hill

The three chapters in this section are intended to demonstrate the impact, directly or indirectly, of social science knowledge on social policy. It should be no surprise to the sophisticated reader that the connection between knowledge and action is complex and often strained. It is also not altogether an accident or perversity of edited volumes that each of the three chapters reveals markedly different attributes of this relationship between scientific information and public policy. Indeed, almost any other three topics relating to children could yield the same diversity in the hoped-for transition from social science to social policy.

TELEVISION AND CHILDREN

The chapter on television and children illustrates the special problems that arise when the topic is itself the media. When television is itself under scrutiny it responds, understandably, in much the same way any other large organization would do. It becomes defensive.

It would be inappropriate and misleading to assume that such defensiveness is without some justification. Social science research findings are rarely without some ambiguity. As Rubinstein and Brown point out, the television industry is now claiming that televised violence has not been conclusively identified as a cause of aggressive behavior. There is a middle ground between this industry position and the level of causal relationship inferred by the scientists in the field. (Ironically, that causal relationship is made to seem even more definitive by the headlines and stories in the print media.) Other scientists (Cook, Kendzierski, & Thomas, 1983) confirm the causal link, but believe that the relationship is at an even more modest level than is claimed in the literature. Thus, there is an honest difference of opinion among scientists on the level of causality in this matter.

Why are the television industry executives not willing to accept that middle-ground position? And what has pushed them from accepting the scientific conclusion as they seemed to have done in 1972 to the disavowal they now state publicly? Two related factors probably operate in this instance. First, the media interpretation, and probably the public interpretation as well, is likely to be a simplistic acceptance that causality is causality. That interpretation would require some direct policy response by the industry regarding televised violence. Second, there are serious legal implications in accepting the causal relationship. With increasing numbers of lawsuits against the print media and television for stories that were alleged to harm individuals involved in those stories, it is not unlikely that those legal implications influence the corporate response to scientific evidence. If the scientific evidence was accepted, it is not improbable that lawsuits would follow, claiming harm from watching certain television programming.

Thus, the legal implications relating to televised violence may be influencing the industry's response to the scientific findings. Ideally, of course, these are two separate matters. The scientific evidence should be judged solely on its own merits. The policy consequences of that evidence should be considered after the scientific judgment is made. While industry executives will not admit to this reversed consideration of truth and consequences, it could well be a factor in this case.

Perhaps the most unfortunate aspect of this interpretation of the effects of televised violence is that, as Rubinstein and Brown note, it ignores all the other scientific evidence on the effects of television on children. The major research emphasis is no longer on televised violence. In this shift away from the issue of violence and aggression, there are many positive possibilities in the conclusions of the newer research. Not the least is the opportunities in the field of health education, as discussed by Milio. Unfortunately, as Milio points out, the major activities in this direction are occurring outside the United States.

HEALTH EDUCATION

An important message in the chapter by Milio is the clear indication that health education need not come from intended efforts, but from program content which was produced primarily for entertainment. For example, as Rubinstein and Brown point out, the use of alcohol in entertainment programming in the United States is more prevalent than any other form of drink. Surely, children and adults watching such programs are influenced in subtle ways by this emphasis on alcohol as a beverage.

At the same time, it is clear from the studies reviewed by Milio that messages on television are, by themselves, unable to make major changes in health-related behaviors. What is needed is a social climate in which the health messages reinforce and are reinforced by public attitudes and public acceptance of the health information. At a certain point, public involvement plus the message plus media coverage may reach a combined intensity which induces change.

An example of this phenomenon now showing some effects is the national campaign against driving while under the influence of alcohol. States are beginning to enact stricter laws and the federal government is paying increased attention to the problem. Media coverage, both in print and on television, is extensive. In addition, major corporations such as General Motors are sponsoring public information messages on radio and television which dramatically describe the deaths caused by drunken drivers.

In retrospect, it is not easy to identify exactly why this combined campaign against drunken drivers is now more effective than ever before. It would be too simplistic to point out that a determined group of citizens—Mothers Against Drunken Drivers (MADD)—has organized in various states and has mobilized public opinion. After all, drunken drivers have been responsible for deaths on the highways for years. What, in recent years, has made the public, the politicians, and the media more concerned? In some way that still has not been fully documented, the social context in which these changes are occurring seems to be highly supportive of these combined efforts.

A health area of comparable long-term public concern, smoking and health, is discussed by Milio. As she points out, the nature of the national social climate is of central importance, if any long-term changes are to occur. The differences between the historical and social context in Finland and in the United States seem to be the critical variables resulting in greater success in Finland of an anti-smoking media health campaign. In essence, the public was more prepared to be responsive to such a campaign in Finland than was the American public.

There is an interesting parallel here to a conclusion reached in the first Surgeon General's Report on television and violence (Surgeon General's Scientific Advisory Committee, 1972). A key part of the conclusion that there was evidence of a causal sequence between televised violence and later aggressive behavior included an important qualification. It was emphasized that causality was probably applicable only to children "predisposed" to aggressive behavior. In a way, Milio seems to be saying that the public must be "predisposed" before health education messages can be effective. In this case, such predisposition is itself necessarily produced by various outside factors.

One important circumstance revealed in this examination of health education efforts through the media is the extensive work done outside the United States. The BBC productions are in striking contrast to the commercial programming in the United States. As Milio describes it, the BBC approach is not only one of full commitment to the objective of effective health education, it seems to be equally successful in holding audience attention and acceptance. It is small consolation, here in the United States, to note, as Milio does, that the Cable Health Network may have the potential to accomplish what is now being done in England and some of the other nations overseas.

Ironically, there is clear precedent that American audiences will watch more serious programming, if it is well done. News programs such as "60 Minutes" are obvious examples of this willingness by viewers in the United States to watch programs which go beyond mere entertainment.

CHILD MENTAL HEALTH

The chapter by Rolf and Johnson illuminates a different aspect of the triangulation connecting social science, the media, and social policy. Here the relationship is that more common to formal policy analysis: how social science leads to policy making and the role played by science administrators in this effort.

As the authors point out, social scientists can take varying positions in trying to show how knowledge leads to action. Rolf and Johnson are aware of the complexities and pitfalls that result from following the different approaches to the policy goal. "Outcome advocates," "process advocates," and "party advocates" are committed to somewhat different methods in achieving those policy goals. What is not clear from the authors' discussion is that the scientist does not always function in only one of these advocacy roles. Indeed, depending on the intended policy and the specific circumstances, the social scientist may adopt any or all of these advocacy roles.

And, by extension, the NIMH has, institutionally, served as an advocate in these varying ways. As the authors note, the Institute has a long history of involvement in both the initiation and support of policy relevant activities. Two special areas of Institute operations are especially relevant to the picture of science administration presented in this chapter.

First, the NIMH has had a long and productive record in translating and making available scientific information for public consumption. As noted in the chapter, a number of publications have provided important information on developments in the field of child mental health with policy implications. These publications have both informed the public and provided documentation to Congress of research progress in child mental health.

As an important corollary to this public information, and one also noted by Rolf and Johnson, the NIMH has been most sensitive to the need to demonstrate the applied value of research. Indeed, "applied research" has been a term formally used in the Institute long before it became a common phrase to emphasize scientific inquiry which is presumably more utilitarian than so-called "basic research." Since the early 1960s there has been an applied research program in mental health in which the goal has been to improve and increase the utilization of research results.

To those of us, such as this writer, whose experience with the NIMH goes back to the "good old days" in the 1960s, it is encouraging to read how today's science administrators are coping with budgetary limitations and other program constraints. At the same time, it is clear that major government programs in mental health no longer have the level of financial support that allows for vigorous growth in new areas and for what is always a necessary level of risk-taking in new research directions. Rolf and Johnson close on an important point when they urge a more "integrative model of cooperative science," in which the behavioral and clinical sciences more effectively find linkages of research activity. In other words, basic and applied research scientists need to combine efforts to increase the likelihood that research findings will have clear and meaningful utilization.

IMPLICATIONS FOR SOCIAL POLICY

Aside from the obvious generalization that there is no simple path from knowledge to social policy, these three chapters illustrate one other commonality. In all three instances, it is clear that only through long-term and continuous efforts do changes take place. In old child development theory it was believed that "all growth is saltatory." In social policy theory it is more realistic to believe that growth is gradual, sometimes painfully so.

If such policy growth is indeed gradual, then it becomes imperative that a continuous and institutional process must be established to nurture such growth. In the case of child mental health, that institutional process is so self-evident that it is paradoxically easy to miss. The NIMH has been the continuing resource for more than three decades. It is not just that important research has been fostered, it is not just that science administrators have stimulated new research directions, it is also that the NIMH has an institutional memory, which helps to keep the process of change moving forward. When Rolf and Johnson close with the hope that child mental-health administrators can continue to function effectively in adverse times, that hope is greatly enhanced because of the availability of that institutional memory.

On a lesser scale, the BBC health program series described by Milio is another example of the critical importance of an institutional process. In this case, the example is of a smaller institutional effort—the health series—inside a longer-term institution, the BBC. Here, again, the continuing mechanism allows for successful change.

Finally, to confirm by contrast, there is the example in the chapter by Rubinstein and Brown of an experimental effort in television programming to educate children against stereotypic attitudes about sex roles. As Rubinstein and Brown point out, as a one-shot effort this experiment was successful. The results, however, were short-lived with no lasting impact.

It would be too easy at this point to conclude that the simple solution to the problem of effective change is merely to establish long-term institutional mechanisms. While such a process may be necessary to translate knowledge into action, it is not, unfortunately, sufficient unto itself. As all three chapters note, in their closing statements, the direction toward successful change seems reasonably clear. The assurance that the direction will be followed is much less certain.

REFERENCES

Cook, T. D., Kendzierski, D. S., & Thomas, S. V. (1983). The implicit assumptions of television research: An analysis of the 1982 NIMH report on "Television and Behavior." *Public Opinion Quarterly, 47,* 161–201.

Surgeon General's Scientific Advisory Committee on Television and Social Behavior. (1972). *Television and growing up: The impact of televised violence.* Washington, DC: U.S. Government Printing Office.

PART THREE

FROM THE MEDIA PERSPECTIVE

Nine

Social Scientists and Journalists: Confronting the Stereotypes

SHARON DUNWOODY
University of Wisconsin

S. HOLLY STOCKING*
Indiana University

The instructor of a university-level continuing education course on "Medicine and the Media" had struck a raw nerve in one of her participants. "Reporters!" growled a white-haired physician. "You just can't trust them." He then detailed his strategies for dealing with the scoundrels: Have another individual present at the interview to act as a witness, tape-record the interview, and insist on seeing a copy of the story before it is published. What happens if the reporter does not agree to those terms? "No interview," retorted the senior academician.

As far as this physician was concerned, reporters have no respect for facts. They casually toss their stories together, not caring enough about the information to check back with the source to make sure the details are accurate. Even worse, the physician ominously warned the class, "they are never on time. You set up appointments with them, and they don't even bother to show up." The academician subsided in his chair after the outburst. And others in the room filed the information away for future reference.

Upon such a foundation are stereotypes built.

The relationship between scientists and journalists has often been characterized as tense. Media coverage of science is a frequent whipping boy among scientists who gather at conventions, and scientists periodically deplore the mass media's limitations in the pages of their journals.

*Currently self-employed writer, educator, and consultant, Bloomington, IN.

The most visible actor in the story production process—the reporter—is characterized as a sensation-seeker, with a primitive grasp of science and little or no respect for accuracy. Unable or unwilling to do more than stumble through a science story, he creates a "monster" that will haunt the scientist/source for the rest of his or her professional career.

Reporters also come equipped with their stock images of scientists. Many view scientists as individuals who do not really care about the public understanding of science and who react arrogantly to reporters' attempts to "translate" their work for general consumption.

In overly simple terms, the scientist sees the journalist as someone with a cavalier attitude toward the facts, whereas the journalist sees the scentist as a person with a cavalier attitude toward the public.

It is perhaps needless to say that neither image accurately describes these two groups. So why are these images so firmly embraced?

We believe that such images, like most stereotypes, survive because they are functional to those who possess them. Stereotypes "work" partly because they help individuals to simplify their world, to cope. Created from a "kernel of truth," they help order perceptions and guide behavior. The problem, of course, is that stereotypes also work against the understanding of complexity. Morever, they often work to create the very behavior that is despised. A young girl's father is a male chauvinist, and so she develops an image of men as male chauvinists. Subsequently, all men, regardless of individual differences, are seen and treated as if they were male chauvinists. In the process, the woman elicits the very behavior she so despises in men and lessens the probability that she will ever meet a warm, sensitive male who defies her stereotype.

In a similar vein, the hostile scientist at the "Medicine and Media" seminar may have adopted his images of the press after one or two negative encounters with reporters. Or, he may have formed his images from listening to the "horror stories" of his seniors. In any event, he has long since given up on the possibility that any journalist can be redeemed. Now, he treats all journalists as untrustworthy. Whenever a ringing telephone brings an interview request, he reacts cautiously, even scornfully. In the process, of course, he reinforces any stereotypical images of scientists held by reporters. And should the reporters respond badly to this perceived "arrogance," the scientist interprets these reactions as proof that his original assumptions about journalists were correct. What is so insidious about this kind of feedback, says psychologist Mark Snyder (1981), is that it turns stereotypical assumptions into self-fulfilling prophecies.

It is probably much too late to try to change this particular scientist's view of journalists. As Elliot Aronson (1980) has noted, "A deeply prejudiced person is virtually immune to information" (p. 201). However, for scientists who lack well-developed views on the press or who may have been exposed to stereotypical thinking but have not yet hardened in their attitudes toward the media, it may NOT be too late. At the very least, Hamilton (1981) argues, "increased knowledge of and familiarity with a group results in the fragmenting of a global stereotype of that group into differentiated conceptions of subgroups" (p. 340). While such categorizations may simply serve to create many stereotypical generalizations where once there were few, Hamilton suggests that these subgroups constitute less sweeping characterizations and, if they have at least some basis in reality, they may be more accurate than the more global stereotypes they replace. For the scientists whose attitudes toward the press are still in the making, then, a little bit of information about how journalists work—and the complexity of mass media operations—may help minimize stereotypical thinking and the negative feedback loops that it can create.

With the foregoing thoughts in mind, we undertake several tasks in this chapter. First, we discuss why scientists stand to benefit from informed views of the press. Second, we attempt to acquaint scientists with what is known about journalists and mass media organizations. More specifically, we examine some popular images of journalists held by scientists, measuring them against available research findings and, where research is wanting, against the authors' experiences as science writers and professional observers of mass media coverage of science. Finally, we briefly note some more formal educational efforts that might be—and in some cases are being—undertaken to acquaint scientists with the public communication process.

As we have noted, the dangers of stereotyping exist for both scientists and journalists. Journalists too must learn more about the scientific process and scientists. However, given that scientists may have more to learn about journalists than journalists have to learn about scientists (Carter, 1958), we devote ourselves here to the scientific part of the equation.

RATIONALES FOR INCREASED MEDIA KNOWLEDGE

Research on scientists' knowledge of the media is scant. We do know, though, that formal scientific training rarely includes information about the mass media (Dunwoody & Ryan, 1982). We also know that scientists and journalists alike believe that scientists do not "understand the problems reporters face in writing for the public" and "should have some training in the fundamentals of news communication" (Ryan, 1979).

Not only is there a perceived need for information, but the need seems to be growing. As media coverage of science increases, many more scientists are interacting with the press. The plethora of new general science magazines that have made their way onto the newsstands since the late 1970s, the slow but steady growth in the number of science communicators filtering from university classrooms into the mass media and various institutions, and the somewhat tenuous but continuing interest of the federal government in public understanding of science issues all have contributed to a rise in the *amount* of scientific information moving into the public domain.

Social scientists, who conduct the bulk of policy-related research on children and families, may be particularly susceptible to this new media appetite for scientific information, for the few studies that have examined scientific content in the mass media find social science information to be a media staple. Cole's (1974) analysis of the scientific content of four large daily newspapers from the 1950s to the 1970s showed an increase in coverage of the social sciences relative to coverage of other types of scientific information. And several researchers studying coverage of general scientific meetings have found that social science information gets a disproportionate share of attention from both reporters and newspaper editors (Chivilo, Staniford, Unkovich, & Webb, 1980; Dunwoody, 1980b).

Finally, at least one survey has indicated that social scientists are more likely to encounter journalists than are other types of scientists. Dunwoody and Ryan, in a national survey of scientists, found that social scientists were twice as likely as physical or biological scientists to interact with a "large" number of journalists (three or more) within a year (Dunwoody, in press).

So we are suggesting that learning more about journalists and the production of news has survival value for social scientists. But this is not the only reason social scientists should learn about the press. One also could argue that social scientists who are committed to the public understanding and use of their research stand to benefit from learning to interact with journalists for the simple reason that media are major sources of social science information for people.

Some scholars suggest that, once formal education is completed, the mass media constitute the main sources of scientific information for nonscientists (Patterson, 1982; Wade & Schramm, 1969). And least two studies offer evidence that policymakers also use the mass media as sources of information. Caplan, Morrison, and Stambaugh (1975), in one study of governmental policymakers, found that, along with government reports, newspapers were the most frequently mentioned source of social science information. And Weiss (1974), in a survey of a more varied group of opinion leaders in the United States, found that the most frequently mentioned sources of information about issues relevant to them were the media: "They (the media) seem to serve as a link among members of different sectors, reporting news, ideas, opinion, even purposeful leaks, when other communication channels are closed or clogged" (Weiss, 1974, p. 17).

Finally, although the evidence is scant, it seems that even scientists themselves depend upon media accounts of science to help them remain current in their own or other fields. Shaw and Van Nevel (1967) found that a sample of physicians utilized the mass media to keep up with the most current medical information. And one sociologist offers anecdotal evidence of the ability of media coverage to, in a sense, help set the scientific "agenda" of other scientists. Walum (1975) presented a paper at a sociological meeting, and a resulting newspaper story based on the paper topic received wide national publicity. One surprising result was the attention devoted to that piece of research within the sociological community. Walum received numerous requests for reprints, and the paper was ultimately anthologized in several books. She feels the paper received more attention from colleagues than it perhaps deserved, *because* other sociologists were using the mass media to monitor happenings in their own field.

Now, let's take a look at some of the images that scientists have of journalists.

IMAGES OF JOURNALISTS

Image 1: Journalists Are Largely Ignorant of Science

This particular image contains a large element of truth. Although journalism students typically take a large percentage of their courses in subjects outside journalism, those outside courses rarely involve science. Like most college students, journalism students need only dip lightly into science to satisfy university requirements (Committee on the Federal Role, 1982). And one study (Becker, Dunwoody, Tipton, & Fruit, 1981) indicates these students are most likely to concentrate their nonjournalism coursework primarily in political science and English.

However, one particular subgroup of journalists does come fairly well equipped to understand science, and the training of this group is increasing both in quantity and quality. The group is science reporters.

Although few in number relative to all journalists, science reporters do exist on major newspapers, magazines, and on national network television news crews. They are exceedingly rare on smaller media outlets and in radio, with the exception of National Public Radio. There is no accurate count of their numbers within mass media, although in 1983 the National Association of Science Writers, the leading professional organization for this specialty, listed among its members some 550 mass media and free-lance communicators.

Science reporting is a fairly young specialty area within journalism; mass media actively nurtured the specialty only after the launching of Sputnik in the late 1950s and during NASA's manned space shots in the 1960s and early 1970s. Many of the well-known science reporters on major media in the United States date their science-writing careers from that period.

This "older" group of science communicators typically moved into science reporting from other areas of journalism; for instance, a general reporter for a newspaper may have been tapped by his editor in the early 1960s to cover the moon shots. And studies of the educational backgrounds of this group (Ryan & Dunwoody, 1975) show relatively minimal academic grounding in science. However, Dunwoody (1978) found that the average reporter had, by the mid-1970s, covered science for some 15 years. And in those 15 years individuals had picked up a tremendous amount of scientific knowledge.

Newer "generations" of science reporters have begun adding a formal scientific component. Able to identify science communication as a professional goal while they are in school, this group has grounded itself as well in science as in journalism. It is not unusual to find a young science reporter with the equivalent of a double major in science and journalism. And one even runs across M.D.s and Ph.D.s in science who have gone on to training in journalism and ultimately to science communication jobs in the media.

Most recently, universities have begun to acknowledge the existence of a science communication specialty area and have begun gearing courses and entire programs to preparing individuals for such careers. A recent, national directory of such courses and programs lists more than 40 programs and 127 courses in 67 colleges and universities (Verbit, 1983).

Today's rosy picture of the scientifically literate science journalist is tarnished, however, when it comes to coverage of the social sciences. There are two problems inherent in such coverage: (a) science reporters skilled in covering the physical/biological sciences rarely have been formally exposed to social science theories or methods, and (b) much social science research may be covered not by science journalists but by general reporters, whose grounding in any type of scientific training is likely to be minimal.

Consider these points one at a time. First, although most media science reporters are charged with the responsibility of covering everything related to science and technology, including the social sciences, many of the elite reporters profess little interest in the "softer" sciences, and their formal training in the area is nil (Dunwoody, 1980a). This does not prevent them from covering the social sciences, but it does seem to make them more reluctant to pick social science topics for stories. Thus, those science writers, whom one might expect to be the best equipped to report the social sciences, lack both interest and training to do so.

Second, some evidence suggests that editors assign such stories to general reporters rather than to scientifically trained reporters (Tichenor, Olien, Harrison, & Donohue, 1970). Why? One possibility is that journalists do not perceive social science to be, well, scientific. An editor wanting a story about new advances in solar-heat collectors is likely to acknowledge the technical aspects of the topic and look for a journalist with some technical expertise to handle it. On the other hand, a sociological study of two-career couples who live apart and commute from their jobs to be together may sound to the editor like a good old-fashioned feature story about *human nature*. And as far as the editor is concerned, any of her reporters can handle stories about the human condition.

So the image of the scientifically illiterate journalist is an accurate one in many ways, particularly when it comes to the social sciences. But as with all generalizations, this one will not fit everybody. A handful of media outlets have hired social science reporters. Teachers of science communication are becoming sensitized to the need to incorporate the social sciences in their training of reporters (Stocking, 1981). And even general journalists may be exposed to more social science training in school, particularly in the area of survey research, than they have in the past.

Image 2: Journalists Aren't Interested in "Good Science"—They're Simply Interested in a Good Story

On the surface, good science and a good story are not mutually exclusive categories. But the intended message of this generalization is that journalists will emphasize the colorful, sensational aspects of a piece of research, even when it means distorting the intent of the research or the findings of the scientist.

Do journalists evaluate information differently than do scientists, using criteria that do not take scientific evaluations into account but instead emphasize color and emotion?

The answer, not surprisingly, is complex. Available research seems to indicate that journalists—particularly science reporters—do evaluate scientific information in ways similar to scientists. In other words, they can be just as skillful at selecting "good" or "important" science as are scientists. But research also indicates that the constraints of journalistic work sometimes make other criteria more important to selection of scientific information. To put this another way, given complete freedom to pick and choose, reporters will select "important" science to write about. But the job setting ensures that no reporter is completely free to make such choices.

A number of studies over the years have assessed the comparative judgments of scientists and journalists in selecting science news. Tannenbaum (1963) found that experts in mental health and news media personnel communicating about mental health (writers, producers, directors, and performers in television productions) held similar views on the subject. Similarly, Johnson (1963) found little difference between scientists' and reporters' criteria for evaluating science news stories, although he did find disagreement between scientists and editors.

In the same vein, three other studies have found that scientists and journalists perceive larger discrepancies between their respective attitudes about science news than actually exist. Two studies (Carter, 1958; Tichenor et al., 1970) concluded that reporters' rankings of news values were more similar to scientists' rankings than they were to scientists' estimates of reporters' values. And a recent study (Ryan, 1979) found that attitudes of scientists and science journalists toward various statements relating to science news coverage were "remarkably" similar, although, again, each group perceived a larger gap than actually existed.

But all these studies assessed the comparative criteria and attitudes of scientists and journalists in what amounted to a vacuum. Journalists were able to select topics in these studies without worrying about deadlines, newsroom pressure, or the vicissitudes of competition. More recent studies suggest that, once such "work" variables are factored in, they have a great deal to say about reporters' selection patterns.

Sociologists in recent years have become interested in describing news selection in terms of journalists' work settings (Tuchman, 1978; Gans, 1980; Fishman, 1980). One of their major arguments is that news criteria are not so much the products of individual minds but instead emerge from the demands of the production process, from the way in which media are organized and from the way in which daily work gets done. These criteria set the *boundaries* for what information is available to become news and what information is not. Among the more important criteria investigated to date are organizational constraints, newsroom relationships, and the journalist's perception of the reader or viewer.

Organizational constraints. Most media are engaged in the daily production of information. To that end, a finite number of reporters must be deployed to geographic locations where "news" is likely to occur. These reporters must act quickly to gather information, and they must meet continuous, inflexible deadlines for processing that information. In one study of science writers' coverage of a national science meeting, Dunwoody (1979) found that constraints imposed on reporters' information selection by the production process were strong predictors of what became news about the meeting. For example, the presence of one and sometimes two deadlines a day meant that reporters were likely to gather information at certain times during the day. Deadlines also forced reporters to concentrate on gathering information in places where "getting a story" was more likely; in this case, that place was a press conference. This one organizational constraint alone, in other words, may have meant that "what's news" about the meeting for a reporter on any one day could only be defined as what had occurred in press conferences between 9 a.m. and noon. Deadlines set the boundaries within which the reporter could operate.

Newsroom socialization. In a seminal study, sociologist Warren Breed (1955) found that reporters quickly learned that "surviving" in a newsroom meant assimilating the news values of their editors. In most news operations, the reporter works under an editor who hands out news assignments and evaluates the resulting products. Even when a story originates with a reporter, an editor has final say over whether or not the story actually gets published or aired. In such situations, Breed discovered, reporters are reinforced for producing news that meets the criteria of their editors. In other words, a reporter's most important reader is the editor. Although science reporters perceive themselves as being more autonomous than other reporters (Dunwoody, 1978), they, too, are subject to the decisions of editors. One science reporter for a large metropolitan newspaper, for example, charged that his editor was more interested in "far more flamboyant stuff" than the science he writes about:

> We had a front-page story on pickles. Everything you want to know about pickles. I did one on the bureaucratic dismemberment of one of the largest mental health research centers in the country, and that was on a split page (inside the newspaper). That's what I'm up against.

Perceptions of the audience. Journalists' major responsibilities are to their readers or viewers. At least that's what all journalists-in-training are told. The problem is that a number of studies of reporters find that they have no accurate picture of their audience (cf., Gans, 1980); without any systematic feedback from audience members, journalists resort to generalizing from such bad samples as their colleagues, family, and friends. One science writer argued that his readers had an intense interest in archeology, because every archeology story he wrote brought a small flurry of letters. "Readers love it, the editors like it, and so we run a lot of archeology stories," he explained.

In lieu of any real knowledge of audience needs or desires, a set of news criteria has emerged over the decades that serves as a standardized road map for picking one's way through the welter of possible stories. These criteria appear in nearly every basic news writing text published in the United States. Among the more common criteria are:

- Audience impact: Stories that are thought to be relevant and useful to readers are more newsworthy than are stories that appear to have no audience application.
- Proximity: Local happenings typically are more newsworthy than events that occur far away. At a scientific meeting, for example, scientists from "home" are more newsworthy than other scientists.
- Prominence: Individuals with public reputations usually are more newsworthy than individuals whom no one knows.
- Timeliness: Since media publish information frequently, information that can be pegged to a current and specific time (today, yesterday) is more newsworthy than information that is timeless. At a scientific meeting, again, a reporter can turn someone's research into "timely" news by starting the story: "A psychologist said *today* that . . ."
- Conflict: Conflict in any form—from physical warfare to a clash of major scientific theories—is newsworthy.
- Uniqueness: One-of-a-kind events or happenings may be more newsworthy than predictable events.

Such criteria do not guarantee that the "most important" information will be published in a newspaper on a given day. But they do offer journalists some assurance that they have selected information that, a priori, has a chance to attract and hold the attention of their readers or viewers. Functionally, the journalist has to work hard to lure the audience; a story ignored is a story wasted.

So journalists *do* employ criteria that are very different from those of scientists. Scientists and journalists both publish, but their vastly different publishers and their correspondingly different audiences dictate such differences.

But do the different criteria employed by journalists necessarily mandate that scientific information be selected and written about in a distorted and sensational way?

Journalistic products have been labeled sensationalistic for decades. And historically, at least, working conditions fostered such an approach to information. In an analysis of the working conditions of journalists in the 19th century, Smythe (1980) found that many newspapers, instead of paying regular salaries to reporters, paid only by the published story. In other words, a reporter in those days made nothing unless he convinced an editor to use his story. And the more spectacular the news, the more likely it was to get printed. Consequently, there was a distinct reward for emphasizing (and perhaps "creating") glamorous aspects of stories.

Today, reinforcement for exciting, colorful stories is more subtle. But it exists. Johnson (1963), for example, found that newspaper editors evaluated the newsworthiness of science stories on the basis of color and excitement. And former *New York Times* science editor William Stockton (1982) argues that the limited news space available in newspapers forces journalists to "oversell" a science story to their editors: "The reporter has had to take this routine, but interesting, finding in science, or this finding in science that is a step above routine, and turn it into a major discovery to get it into the newspaper" (p. 24).

But another group of studies indicates that at least some science topics are being rationally treated in the media. In other words, despite use of various news criteria that would seem to conflict with evaluations of the intrinsic importance of scientific information, scientifically important information *is* being published.

Rubin and Hendy's (1977) analysis of press coverage of the swine influenza inoculation campaign, for example, found that, although coverage was generally superficial, "it was rarely inaccurate or sensational, as had frequently been assumed" (p. 769). Similarly, the national task force that analyzed media coverage of the 1979 nuclear power plant accident at Three Mile Island (Stephens & Edison, 1982) concluded that coverage by the major American media offered a balance of perspectives on the accident. Additionally, the task force argued that its analysis does not support the conclusion "that coverage leaned toward the alarming or negative. The tone of the coverage was predominantly reassuring or positive" (1982, p. 259).

Shepherd (1979), in an analysis of media coverage of the potential health risks of smoking marijuana, found that reporters did not often turn for information to scientists conducting marijuana research, but despite that problem he concluded that "the press has done a respectable job in reporting the marijuana issue . . . (and) the scientific repute of most studies publicized by the press, relative to scientific studies not publicized, was very high. Likewise, the general scientific status of authorities quoted (as opposed to their specific credentials as marijuana researchers) was also, on the average, very high" (p. 25). And perhaps most importantly, Shepherd (1979) concluded that "the similarities between the press' interpretations of marijuana as a scientific question and the assessment of marijuana derived from the scientific literature itself appear to be more pronounced than their differences" (p. 26). In other words, despite the information-gathering problems that Shepherd found, the final media accounts indeed accurately represented the state of scientific findings and scientific opinion regarding the health risks of marijuana.

Finally, a recent study by Stocking (in press) also supports the contention that journalists are using scientifically acceptable criteria to evaluate scientific information. Stocking was interested in the criteria that could best predict the visibility of U.S. medical schools in news media accounts of medical research. And she found that a strong predictor of such visibility was the faculty members' publishing record in referred journals. In other words, research that had been deemed by the scientific community to be valid was also the research being picked up by journalists.

In summary, journalists do employ criteria in selecting "good" stories that scientists would never use when selecting "good" science. Some of those criteria are tied up with the production process; some are related to journalists' best estimates of the interest and needs of their audience; some, unfortunately, are mandated by editors who seem to utilize criteria that differ from those of both scientists *and* science journalists (Johnson, 1963).

But those criteria do not necessarily prevent "good" science from getting covered. Scientific and journalistic criteria need not be mutually exclusive; rather, for the good science reporter *both* sets of criteria must be satisfied before a piece of scientific work becomes "news." This could happen in two ways. Sometimes journalistic criteria will constitute the frame within which the universe of story choices exists, as in the scientific convention situation studied by Dunwoody (1979). But once that universe is defined, science reporters then may utilize scientific criteria to make their selections. In other situations, the reverse may be the case: A journalist may select a topic that is scientifically good and then drum up ways of making it journalistically sound as well. For example, one newspaper science reporter noted that she tries to select stories that will help readers understand the "process of science." But to convince her editors to attend to such stories, she must build into them journalistically valid criteria: She must come up with a "news peg." Doing so "is not too tough," she asserts. "You can always find news in something. And if not, put it in your drawer, and wait a bit and try to do a trend piece or an analysis piece."

The ability to select good science to cover requires some understanding of what constitutes good science. And that implies that the best predictor of good reporting of science may be the level of a journalist's science education. But regardless of that, the simple stereotype of the journalist as sensation-seeker is not an accurate one. Again, it would make sense for a scientist to assess journalists as individuals, with some consideration for the complex demands that journalists must satisfy each time they produce a product.

Image 3: Journalistic Accounts are Notoriously Inaccurate

Among all complaints about media, this is perhaps the most common one voiced by scientists. Nearly every scientist knows a colleague who has sworn off all interactions with the press because of a bad experience with an inaccurate reporter. And all science reporters have been confronted at some point in their career with the scientist/source who precedes an interview with the grim prediction that the story inevitably will be inaccurate.

Because this problem has been around for some time, perhaps more science communication research has been devoted to studies of the accuracy of science news than to any other area. And the findings indicate that, yes, science news has accuracy problems. But the same studies also point to inaccuracy complaints as being heavily dependent upon how the "complainer" defines accuracy. In this section, both elements will be considered.

First, however, it is important to note that the studies available to us get mixed results when they ask scientists to evaluate the accuracy of journalistic accounts. For example, among 73 scientists involved in the Tichenor, et al. study (1970), 59% agreed with the statement that science news is "generally accurate." Tankard and Ryan (1974), in a survey of 193 scientists, also found that 56% agreed with the statement that "science news coverage is generally accurate." And a survey of 111 scientists at two Ohio universities by Dunwoody and Scott (1982) found that half (51%) cited accuracy as a reason for being critical of mass media coverage.

Certainly, in all these cases a substantial proportion of respondents were critical of the accuracy of science accounts in the media. But it is also important to realize that a large proportion of respondents in each case either found media coverage to be generally accurate or maintained positions of neutrality on the issue.

Additionally, two of the studies point out inconsistencies among respondents' evaluations of accuracy. In the Tichenor et al. study (1970), whereas 59% of the sample rated science news as "generally accurate,"

95% rated an article quoting themselves as "generally accurate." Similarly, in the survey by Dunwoody and Scott (1982), scientists rated the accuracy of stories about their work more highly than they did the accuracy of science news in general.

A third study bolsters this contention that scientists may be more critical of general media science coverage than they are of stories about themselves. Pulford (1976) asked scientists to rate the accuracy of media stories about their own work and found that 73% of the 143 respondents found the articles to be generally accurate.

The point here is that scientists do not universally condemn media accounts on the grounds of accuracy. Rather, accuracy assessments seem to be situational, with scientists rating the accuracy of accounts in which they have been quoted more highly than they rate the accuracy of science coverage in general.

Are science accounts more error-prone than other types of journalistic accounts? The answer depends on the study you examine. Tankard and Ryan (1974) found that respondents in their study located about twice as many errors per story as had been found in previous studies of general media news. However, Pulford (1976) suggested that the higher number of errors per story in the Tankard and Ryan study might have been a result of the method used by the researchers to elicit comments from the sources; Tankard and Ryan had provided sources with a list of 42 possible errors from which to choose, compared to lists of about 14 errors in the earlier studies. Pulford replicated the Tankard and Ryan study using the shorter list, and this time the number of errors identified by scientists was quite close to the perceived error rates of the earlier general news studies.

More interesting, perhaps, than the number of errors found in these studies are the types of errors found. Tankard and Ryan divided their errors into two groups: objective and subjective. Objective inaccuracies, sometimes referred to as "inaccuracies of fact," are mistakes that can be recognized as such by all parties. For example, everyone will agree that a name has been misspelled once the correct spelling is divulged. And everyone will readily acknowledge the error when a number has been transposed—say, from 15% to 51%. Subjective inaccuracies, on the other hand, are defined as errors of meaning. The charge that something is inaccurate in this case is based upon individual interpretation, and it is likely that not all individuals will agree with the call. For example, a scientist may suggest that a story is inaccurate because "relevant information has been omitted." One would not expect all individuals to agree on what is or is not "relevant information."

Literally all of the accuracy studies found that when scientists complained about errors, they were talking primarily about subjective ones.

In the Tichenor et al. (1970) study, scientists mentioned "overemphasis on the unique" as the greatest accuracy problem. The next most serious criticism was "omission of relevant information." In the Tankard and Ryan (1974) study, "relevant information about method of study omitted" ranked as the most serious problem, followed by "relevant information about results omitted." Pulford (1976) concluded that "a large portion of errors which occur seem to deal with omission of information from stories." And in a study of the accuracy of science articles in mass circulation magazines, Borman (1978) found the major criticism to be omission of relevant information.

These studies lead to the conclusion that the most common inaccuracy problem in science news accounts is omission of information. Scientists are protesting that journalistic accounts are *incomplete*. Borman (1978) underscores this in her study by finding a strong correlation between article length and the number of omission errors; the shorter the article, the more errors of omission the evaluator perceived. And one experimental study indicates that scientists, when given the opportunity to assess the accuracy of stories about themselves, are more likely to add information than to modify existing information in the story. Broberg (1973) analyzed the corrections and additions that a group of scientists made to press releases prepared by university public information personnel about their research. Of all the changes made, Broberg found that additions accounted for the highest proportion. And as the material in a press release became more complex, the scientist tended to add more details to it.

If "incompleteness" is indeed the major problem that scientists encounter with media accounts, then it may be the case that their quarrels with accuracy stem more from their lack of understanding of what constitutes a media account than from inaccuracy per se. In fact, the problem may be a tendency of scientists to use the same criteria to evaluate media accounts that they use to evaluate their own research reports. They may demand the same level of precision and the same amount of detail in both. And since the journalistic account is dramatically different from the scientific one, the media version comes off the worse for the comparison.

The differences between the two accounts are many. But at least two differences deserve mention because they affect the amount of information a media story contains: (a) media accounts must be brief; a 500-word story literally must eschew details and can communicate only the main points; (b) media stories are aimed at nonscientists, so they must reduce complex scientific languages to plain English equivalents. The process of doing this often results in some information loss.

But does such loss of detail really mean that media accounts are inaccurate? If one accepts the proposition that media coverage of science at best communicates main points, then at least one study indicates that media stories *do* communicate those points accurately most of the time. Tichenor et al. (1970) asked a group of nonscientists to read newspaper science stories and then to summarize each article. Scientists quoted in the articles were then asked to judge the accuracy of the audience summaries. Nearly two thirds of the audience recall of the average article in the study was generally acceptable to the scientist quoted.

In other words, when considering the problem of "accuracy" it is important to define what one means. What constitutes an inaccuracy to the scientist may be considered a perfectly acceptable writing strategy by the journalist. To acknowledge these differences is to take the first steps toward abolishing the stereotype of the "inaccurate journalist" and toward acknowledging that accuracy is a subjective judgment over which good scientists and good journalists can respectfully disagree. The media contain much poor reporting of science, and it is important to take to task those journalists who, in an objective sense, clearly are inaccurate. But it is also important to start separating those accounts from science stories in which the differences between scientist and journalist are *subjective*. In these cases, there is room for differences of opinion.

CONCLUSIONS

In this chapter, we have examined in some detail the data underlying three images that many scientists have of journalists. The first—that journalists generally know little about science—contains a large element of truth. The second—that journalists utilize different criteria to select science news than that used by scientists to select good science, thereby promoting sensationalistic coverage of science—is generally true in the first part, but not necessarily true in the second. Journalists do utilize a variety of criteria that scientists would never use in selecting scientific information. But those criteria do not eliminate additional judgments based on the quality of the scientific information. And, in fact, good journalists will use *both* journalistic and scientific criteria when selecting science topics. Sensationalism is not an automatic byproduct of the journalistic process. And finally, the third image—that journalistic accounts are inaccurate—is not supported by existing data. In many cases, accuracy disagreements between journalists and scientists can be reduced to conflict over the amount of detail incorporated in a news story. And because both sides can muster logical reasons for the inclusion or exclusion of such details, the "inaccuracy argument" may amount to a difference in value judgments.

As a social scientist, how does one deal with these three images in order to make them useful components of an overall strategy for interacting with journalists? Our response would be to give some credence to the first one, and let your knowledge of journalists and the journalistic process help you modify the other two.

Assuming little understanding of social science theory and methods on the part of journalists (Image 1) gives the social scientist the opportunity to become an active part of the story production process by educating journalists with background information. In his study of the accuracy of science stories, Tichenor et al. (1970) found that stories based on written materials such as press releases and journal articles were judged by scientists to be more accurate than were stories based solely on information derived from an interview. This means that scientists who provided background information prior to, during, or following an interview with a reporter found the resulting stories to be more accurate than did scientists who did not provide such materials. So providing background information works. It helps explain basic concepts to a reporter, reinforces statements made in an interview setting, and provides the journalist with reference materials that can be referred to when writing the story back in the newsroom.

Strategies for providing background information to journalists vary. Some scientists offer citations by phone or mail published studies to the reporter prior to the interview; indeed, some individuals make the reporter's perusal of these materials a prior condition for the interview. Others make sure studies are on hand during the interview itself. And still others go to greater lengths to make sure that their work has already been described in simple English. This latter strategy most often means that scientists ask their institution's public information office to prepare a story regarding their research. But in some instances, the scientist will prepare the materials; in one case, a researcher listed and defined terms that would be used in the interview and also wrote out the hypotheses that were undergoing tests in the research.

Regardless of strategy, "educating" the reporter via background material does seem to work. And we find it an appropriate response to the necessary conclusion that the "average" journalist will know very little about a specific research project or about the scientist's field in general.

We have used much of this chapter to provide knowledge that we hope will help social scientists modify their responses to the other two images of journalists and journalism. It seems obvious to us that the more scientists know about journalistic work, the more realistically they will be able to interact with reporters. And vice versa. Increased understanding does not guarantee harmony. But it can lead, as we noted earlier, to a more individualistic response to journalists, to a sorting out of the "good" reporters from the "bad," rather than a wholesale dumping of the entire profession.

Scientists interested in increasing their levels of knowledge about journalists and about mass media coverage of science have a number of options available to them these days. Formal scientific training, for the most part, still eschews any mention of the public communication of science. But other components within society are beginning to take up the slack.

- Since 1975, the American Association for the Advancement of Science has offered a media internship program to scientists-in-training. Individuals spend a summer working for a newspaper, TV station, radio station, or magazine and then either return to their studies and eventually move into science or—as has occurred in a significant number of cases—enter the science communication profession.
- Many institutions—both public and private—are beginning to acknowledge the importance of scientists and journalists understanding one another. These institutions stage seminars of their own, bringing in local reporters to talk about science news coverage. A recent program for faculty of the University of Wisconsin-Madison Medical School, for example, featured medical reporters from around the state as well as physicians with some experience in dealing with the media.
- The National Science Foundation in 1980 added a new course to its offerings in its Chautauqua Short Courses for College Teachers. The course, titled "Science, the Media, and the Public," is geared to helping scientists get a better grasp of the quantity and quality of science coverage in the mass media, as well as helping them understand *how* the coverage got there in the first place. As with other Chautauqua courses, "Science, the Media, and the Public" is offered at two university sites each year and is open to science teachers at 2- and 4-year colleges.
- A small number of universities are beginning to incorporate media information into their formal science training. M.I.T., for example, has begun offering science communication courses at both the undergraduate and graduate levels. Johns Hopkins in 1982 began offering a media course for graduate students in the biological sciences.
- Finally, scientists at most large universities will be able to locate science communication courses and programs on their own campuses. Most will be situated in journalism or communication de-

partments, although a few have found homes within science departments.

We do not mean to suggest that undermining stereotypes and educating scientists to ways of the media will solve all problems between scientists and journalists. Some scientists will continue to avoid the press. Some journalists will continue to err and distort research findings. Problems are inevitable when two such diverse systems come into contact with one another.

But we do mean to suggest that communication of social science information via mass media has an impact on nonscientists, be they policymakers or individuals seeking ways of dealing with their own life situations. And we do not think that social scientists can afford to simply write off the mass media as a rather large annoyance. Rather, we think it is time scientists became active, knowledgeable participants in the public understanding process. With such participation, the portrayal of social science in the mass media stands only to benefit.

REFERENCES

Aronson, E. (1980). *The social animal* (3rd ed.) San Francisco, CA: Freeman.

Becker, L. B., Dunwoody, S., Tipton, L. P., & Fruit, J. W. (1981). A survey of graduates of three universities: Preliminary report. Mimeo. Columbus, OH: The Ohio State University School of Journalism.

Borman, S. C. (1978). Communication accuracy in magazine science reporting. *Journalism Quarterly, 55*(2), 345–346.

Breed, W. (1955). Social control in the newsroom. *Social Forces, 33*, 326–335.

Broberg, K. (1973). Scientists' stopping behavior as indicators of writer's skill. *Journalism Quarterly, 50*(4), 763–767.

Caplan, N., Morrison, A., & Stambaugh, R. J. (1975). *The use of social science knowledge in policy decisions at the national level*. Ann Arbor, MI: The University of Michigan, Institute for Social Research, Center for Research on Utilization of Scientific Knowledge.

Carter, R. E. (1958). Newspaper "gatekeepers" and the sources of news. *Public Opinion Quarterly, 22*, 133–144.

Chivilo, E., Staniford, M., Unkovich, M., & Webb, J. (1980). Newspaper reporting of the 49th ANZAAS Congress. *Search, 11*, 243–245.

Cole, B. (1974). Science conflict: A content analysis of four major metro newspapers, 1951, 1961, 1971. Unpublished master's thesis, University of Minnesota.

Committee for a Study of the Federal Role in the College Science Education of Non-Specialists. (1982). *Science for non-specialists: The college years*. Washington, DC: National Academy Press.

Dunwoody, S. (1978). *Science writers at work*. Center for New Communications Research Report No. 7. Bloomington, IN: Indiana University School of Journalism.

Dunwoody, S. (1979). News-gathering behaviors of specialty reporters: A two-level comparison of mass media decision-making. *Newspaper Research Journal, 1*(1), 29–39.

Dunwoody, S. (1980a). The science writing inner club: A communication link between science and the lay public. *Science, Technology, & Human Values, 5,* 14–22.

Dunwoody, S. (1980b). *Tracking newspaper science stories from source to publication: A case-study examination of the popularization process.* Paper presented at the meeting of the Society for the Social Studies of Science, Toronto, Canada.

Dunwoody, S. (in press). The scientist as source. In S. Friedman, S. Dunwoody & C. L. Rogers, eds. *Scientists and journalists: Exploring the connections.* New York: Macmillan.

Dunwoody, S. & Ryan, M. (in press). Scientific barriers to the popularization of science via mass media. *Journal of Communication.*

Dunwoody, S. & Scott, B. T. (1982). Scientists as mass media sources. *Journalism Quarterly, 59*(1), 52–59.

Fishman, M. (1980). *Manufacturing the news.* Austin, TX: University of Texas Press.

Gans, H. J. (1980). *Deciding what's news: A study of CBS Evening News, NBC Nightly News, Newsweek, and Time.* New York: Vintage Books.

Hamilton, D. L. (1981). Stereotyping and intergroup behavior: Some thoughts on the cognitive approach. In D. L. Hamilton (Ed.), *Cognitive processes in stereotyping and intergroup behavior* (pp. 333–353). Hillsdale, NJ: Erlbaum.

Johnson, K. (1963). Dimensions of judgment of science news stories. *Journalism Quarterly, 40,* 315–322.

Patterson, J. (1982). A Q study of attitudes of young adults about science and science news. *Journalism Quarterly, 59*(3), 406–413.

Pulford, D. L. (1976). Follow-up study of science news accuracy. *Journalism Quarterly, 53(1),* 119–121.

Rubin, D. M., & Hendy, V. (1977). Swine influenza and the news media. *Annals of Internal Medicine, 87*(6), 769–774.

Ryan, M. (1979). Attitudes of scientists and journalists toward media coverage of science news. *Journalism Quarterly, 56*(1), 18–26, 53.

Ryan, M., & Dunwoody, S. (1975). Academic and professional training patterns of science writers. *Journalism Quarterly, 52*(2), 239–246, 290.

Shaw, D. L., & Van Nevel, P. (1967). The informative value of medical science news. *Journalism Quarterly, 44,* 548.

Shepherd, R. G. (1979). Science news of controversy: The case of marijuana. *Journalism Monographs, 62.*

Smythe, T. C. (1980). The reporter, 1880–1900. Working conditions and their influence on the news. *Journalism History, 7*(1), 1–10.

Snyder, M. (1981). On the self-perpetuating nature of social stereotypes. In D. L. Hamilton (Ed.), *Cognitive processes in stereotyping and intergroup behavior* (pp. 183–212). Hillsdale, NJ: Erlbaum.

Stephens, M., & Edison, N. G. (1982). News media coverage of issues during the accident at Three-Mile Island. *Journalism Quarterly, 59*(2), 199–204, 259.

Stocking, S. H. (1981). Don't overlook the "social" in science writing courses. *Journalism Educator, 36,* 55–57.

Stocking, S. H. (in press). Public relations efforts and news-value characteristics of organizations: An exploratory study of their relative influence on media visibility. *Journalism Quarterly.*

Stockton, W. (1982). Making editorial decisions for Science Times. *Annals of The New York Academy of Sciences, 387*, 23–27.

Tankard, J., & Ryan, M. (1974). News source perceptions of accuracy of science coverage. *Journalism Quarterly, 51*(2), 219–225, 334.

Tannenbaum, P. H. (1963). Communication of science information. *Science, 140*, 579–583.

Tichenor, P., Olien, C., Harrison, A., & Donohue, G. A. (1970). Mass communication systems and communication accuracy in science news reporting. *Journalism Quarterly, 47*, 673–683.

Tuchman, G. (1978). *Making news: A study in the construction of reality.* New York: Free Press.

Verbit, L. P. (1983). *Directory of science communication courses, programs, and faculty.* Binghamton, NY: Department of Chemistry, State University of New York at Binghamton.

Wade, S., & Schramm, W. (1969). The mass media as sources of public affairs, science, and health knowledge. *Public Opinion Quarterly, 33*, 197–209.

Walum, L. R. (1975). Sociology and the mass media: Some major problems and modest proposals. *The American Sociologist, 10*, 28–32.

Weiss, C. H. (1974). What America's leaders read. *Public Opinion Quarterly, 38*, 1–22.

TEN

COMMUNICATING DEVELOPMENTAL RESEARCH TO THE GENERAL PUBLIC: LESSONS FROM THE BOYS TOWN CENTER

ROBERT B. McCALL, THOMAS G. GREGORY, and BARBARA LONNBORG

Boys Town Center, Nebraska

In his presidential address to the American Psychological Association (APA) almost 15 years ago, George Miller (1969) admonished his colleagues to "give psychology away," not only by providing services to society but by communicating the fruits of psychological research to benefit individuals and society at large. While the message was well received in theory, very little action was taken to implement the appeal. It was soon forgotten—an idea proffered before its time.

But during the last few years, a chorus of APA presidential candidates have advocated a closer relationship between psychology and society in their statements to the voting membership, and William Bevan, in his presidential address (1983), reiterated Miller's petition for psychology to distribute its knowledge to society.

It is likely that the recent appeals to bring psychology closer to society will be better received than Miller's request, because the bleak funding climate for social and behavioral research makes the need for improved public relations more urgent and tangible.

WHY COMMUNICATE?

Besides helping to build a public constituency and providing information that is useful to people, communicating research results to the public serves both of the common public-service activities of psychologists—clinical service and influencing legislation (Good, Simon, & Coursey, 1981). McCall (1983), for example, has argued that increased public communications would assist community mental-health agencies in making people aware of their services, helping people to help themselves, and securing funding and volunteers for publicly operated service units.

In addition, the dissemination of information to the general public is an important component of the legislative process. Public priorities are crucial to legislation. The media are chief suppliers of science information to nonscientists after their school years (Schramm & Wade, 1967), and "there are no good laws without good public awareness" (Steinem, 1978). Mass communications creates awareness about issues, raises or lowers the importance of a topic in people's minds, reinforces attitudes that people already hold, and implants attitudes if none existed (McCombs & Shaw, 1977; McQuail, 1969; Schramm, 1973). Further, policymakers themselves use the media as major sources of information (Weiss, 1974). In one study of high-level bureaucrats in Washington, 81% reported obtaining job-related social science information from newspapers, 70% from magazines, and approximately half from television and radio (Caplan, Morrison, & Stambaugh, 1975).

Oil and water?

Despite these and other apparent needs and benefits of public communication (McCall & Stocking, 1982), scientists in general have not been eager to communicate with the general public. Many are quite antagonistic toward journalists and the media (Goodfield, 1981), some with understandable contempt (Herrnstein, 1982), and many deliberately avoid interacting with the popular press (Rubin, 1980). Indeed, it has been fashionable to consider the media and science to be something like oil and water—they do not mix (McCall & Stocking, 1982).

Researchers, for their part, frequently dismiss the popular press as incompetent and irresponsible. They imagine that many, if not most, articles written about science are oversimplified, inaccurate, and "hyped" with grabby headlines and leads that suggest results and implications that are light years beyond the data. As one scientist reportedly summarized the schism (Goodfield, 1981), "the public prefers a simple lie to a complicated truth."

The antagonism is not one-sided. Journalists sometimes regard scientists as irrelevant, obfuscatory, arrogant, and incapable of forming a simple declarative sentence. One editor who works closely with child development researchers commented that "most scientists cannot write their way out of a wet paper bag."

To be sure, instances can be cited to support such accusations (e.g., Herrnstein, 1982; Rubin, 1980; Weigel & Pappas, 1981; Wallum, 1975), but research on science communication indicates that each profession perceives the other as being more extreme than is actually the case (Ryan, 1979; Stocking & Dunwoody, 1982; Tankard & Ryan, 1974).

McCall and Stocking (1982) have recently summarized these issues, especially with respect to psychological science. Accuracy of popular accounts seems to be the major concern of scientists, but researchers often do not appreciate the values, procedures, and constraints of journalism. The two communities really do operate under different sets of principles, and while those principles serve their respective professions well, some accommodation must be made if the two professions are to cooperate with one another. This chapter reports the attempt of one project—the Boys Town Center's Communications and Public Service project—to make that accommodation in a way that will satisfy the criteria of both developmental science and the media.

Existing Communication Channels

As background for the Boys Town project, it is helpful to consider briefly the advantages and limitations of existing communication channels.

Mass media.　The mass media communicate more information on social and behavioral science to more people faster and at less cost than any other means of communication. But they make this considerable contribution, however, at some cost. For one thing, the mass media represent a shotgun approach to communications. They send the message indiscriminately to everybody. In some cases, though, a message should go to some people (e.g., teachers) but not to others (e.g., pupils).

Then, too, for all their efficiency at reaching large numbers of people, the mass media may be inefficient at reaching particular groups of individuals (e.g., parents of underachieving pupils) who might be contacted best through service professionals (e.g., school counselors).

Another problem with the mass media is that very few writers and producers are trained in behavioral science. Most science writers concentrate on the physical, biological, and medical sciences (Herbert, 1980; Ryan & Dunwoody, 1975). Such specialists are often excellent, but most do not regard the social and behavioral sciences as part of their "beat."

This may be a special problem for child development researchers, because the journalistic profession tends to view child development as "life style" or (still) "woman's page" news. Thus, psychology and child development research tend to be covered by reporters who have little or no training in behavioral research, have less understanding of scientific values and methods, and may not know much about the content of the field (e.g., general assignment reporters). Sometimes the result is less competent than it should be.

Mass media coverage of behavioral science also suffers from journalism's heavy emphasis on news. Generally speaking, news is information not known before (by the public). It is often counterintuitive, or it is tied to an event (e.g., the hostage crisis, the publication of a technical paper, the holding of a conference, a speech). Since every reader fancies him- or herself a psychologist, journalism is biased toward behavioral findings that are unexpected or surprising. For example, research that shows divorce can increase the problem behavior of young children would not make much news (people know that already). But a research finding that says it doesn't would make news. The fact that such a result is only one study against a background of many often does not seem to matter.

Another problem is that except at major newspapers and television networks, journalism is under great time constraints. What scientists do in three years, a journalist may summarize and communicate in an afternoon. Researchers know that behavioral science "truth" peeks through countless studies reported over many years, but journalists do not have time to review the literature and do not favor citing a review article as much as a report of a single study. And they do not have time to send out their articles for critiques before publication. The result is sometimes inaccuracy, lack of balance, or a superficial treatment of a topic deserving more careful reporting.

Another issue of concern is the de facto definition of accuracy in journalism. Some newspapers and magazines are very concerned with accuracy and employ "fact-checkers" to verify every factual statement in every article. But basically they are verifying reliability, not validity (McCall & Stocking, 1982). They check that Jones said what the reporter writes, but they do not determine if Jones speaks the truth. As Paul Newman accused journalist Sally Field in the film "Absence of Malice," "You don't print the truth, you print what people say is the truth." Thus, since most journalists are not in a position to judge good from poor science or odd from mainstream conclusions, some rather atypical, occasionally bizarre research gets into the newspaper.

Of course, science writers and behavioral science specialists at large, well-heeled newspapers, news services, and magazines often do have the time and resources to research, validate, and write balanced reviews, but there are too few of them.

Other communication avenues.   Mass media journalism is not the only means by which behavioral science and child development news are communicated to the public. Some other approaches can be taken to remedy two of the major limitations of mass media journalism—problems of accuracy and the inability of the mass media to reach specific groups of individuals who need specific information.

For example, university information bureaus attempt to generate news about university activities, including faculty research. They might write press releases; tape radio news spots; produce films; write speeches; publish magazines, newspapers, and newsletters; and act as a reference service for media and the general public seeking information about a particular subject. Many bureaus now have people designated as "science writers" who are hired specifically to keep up with research on the campus and to communicate it to the public.

Extension services, sometimes administratively linked with information bureaus, are a leading source of "targeted" communications —pamphlets, booklets, brochures, and other small publications or films aimed at specific groups of individuals. The prototype was the agricultural extension service which provided the latest research information useful to farmers, but the coverage of such services is now much wider and often includes materials on child-rearing and family services.

The news bureaus and extension services presumably have the asset of greater accuracy, although no systematic validation of this assumption is known to us. Many such services check their press releases with the scientist sources before distribution, and extension services often rely on academics to provide the basic information or even write their targeted materials. Whether such materials are reviewed by researchers who are not sources is unknown.

But these services also have some limitations. First, only a small part of the bureaus' time can be devoted to covering and reporting research. Further, except for a small number of large universities, the audience for the news generated by these bureaus is usually only regional, perhaps statewide at best. Similarly, extension services are located at state universities and distribute their materials primarily within the state. Also, when writing about research, these bureaus often cover only one study or one faculty member's work. There is usually no overview of the existing state of knowledge in the field and no critical comments by other professionals.

A variety of private organizations also attempt to disseminate developmental research to the general public. For example, the Guttmacher

Institute publishes materials that communicate research on teenage pregnancy; the Children's Defense Fund distributes a variety of materials pertaining to issues of children and families that have social and legislative importance; the March of Dimes Birth Defects Foundation produces materials on birth defects and other disabilities; and the High/Scope Project distributes a variety of materials on early education and related topics.

These organizations typically focus on a single issue or topic and become specialists in that area, and they may communicate both through the mass media and through targeted channels. But most of these organizations do not cover the broad range of issues in child development and family life, and some are advocates of certain social or political stances rather than unbiased sources of objective information.

The mass media, university news bureaus and extension services, and most private organizations each have their advantages and limitations. In the next section we describe a major effort by a private institution to disseminate objective information on children, youth, and families through a variety of mass media and targeted communications. It was an attempt to overcome some of the major limitations and disadvantages of existing communication efforts.

BRIDGING THE GAP BETWEEN THE SCIENTIST,
THE MEDIA, AND THE CONSUMER

In 1974 Father Flanagan's Boys' Home, popularly known as Boys Town, established three largely autonomous Centers for the Study of Youth Development located at Catholic University of America in Washington, DC, Stanford University, and on the main campus at Boys Town in Nebraska. In addition to its research program, the Center at Boys Town included a division devoted to developing information materials such as brochures, books, and television programs to meet the information needs of audiences concerned with issues or problems in child and youth development. Some years later the three Centers, at the initiative of Boys Town, were dissolved for legal reasons. However, the dissemination program on the Boys Town campus, now officially called Communications and Public Service, was retained to continue its original mission.

Philosophy and Operating Principles

The Boys Town communications program is a unique blend of the thinking of scientists, science writers, and members of Boys Town manage-

ment and board of directors who were intrigued with the idea of applying
principles of marketing in an effort to help troubled youth.

Assumptions. Four basic assumptions underlay the development
of the program and the process by which it is carried out.

1. It was assumed that the presentation of research results from child
    and youth development would stress information and alternative
    courses of action rather than advocate a social or political theme.
    The information would help the consumer better understand an
    issue and find new ways to solve a problem.
2. The purpose of any communication would be to help others indi-
    rectly or directly help troubled children or prevent such problems
    from emerging. Consequently, it was essential that the message be
    designed and distributed in such a way that it filled the information
    need of the consuming audience to which it was directed.
3. The scientific information would have to be accurate and valid, rep-
    resenting the best research data and professional opinion available.
    Data would be drawn from work generated anywhere in the world,
    not just at the Boys Town Centers. Conclusions would be based
    upon relative consensus in scientific literature.
4. It was assumed that the effect of most communication would be to
    increase awareness of or sensitivity toward a given issue. The pri-
    mary objective was to inform, not to change behavior, so formal
    scientific studies of effects were not conducted.

Together, these assumptions and operating principles pushed the
Boys Town dissemination program in a direction that was quite different
from traditional university-based public relations or information programs. Its emphasis on the audience placed it more in the context of
marketing (e.g., what information do you need?) than public relations
(e.g., here is the information we want you to know). The significant
involvement of sources—scientists and service professionals from across
the country—in shaping the content of the product also placed the program outside the tradition of journalism where the journalist retains sole
editorial control over content, interpretative comments, and emphases.

Specifically, the communication of science information to nonscientists usually is seen as a linear model (Gregory & Stocking, 1981). In this
model, the process begins with the generation of knowledge by scientists. This knowledge—usually presented in professional journals or ac-
quired during an interview—is interpreted and rewritten by journalists
for dissemination to nonscientist publics. In contrast, the dissemination
of social science information at Boys Town was carried out largely as an

interactive process with consumers (potential readers, viewers, and listeners) directly or indirectly interacting with information sources (scientists and service professionals) and communicators (writers and producers) in the development of the content of the message as well as the selection of its format and its mode of distribution.

Staff. The emphasis on the interactive process had considerable influence on staffing the dissemination unit. Not only did Boys Town look for experienced science writers and producers, but there was an equally important need for senior-level, experienced research scientists to serve on staff. Six years of producing research-based science materials for nonscientists have reinforced the view that the scientist–communicator position is vital to the success of such a program. Ideally, this individual should have won his or her spurs as a research scientist in the field of child development. He or she should know the dimensions of content areas, be acquainted with major researchers in a variety of areas, and be able to mediate between communicators, sources, and advisory boards of scientists who review and evaluate the dissemination products. It is also important that the staff scientist have interest in and knowledge of communications, a sense for the public interest, and skill in interpreting scientific information for the general public.

The role of the science writer or producer in the development of dissemination materials is twofold: (a) to package information in a format and in language or pictures appropriate for the intended audience, and (b) to ensure that the content and format of the message accurately reflects the interests and needs of the audience, the information sources (e.g., scientists), and sponsoring agency. The communicator in this process, unlike counterparts in the traditional model, does not insist upon exercising independent, final control over content. These decisions come out of an interactive process that can be influenced by external factors (such as deadlines, space and time limitations, and budgets) as well as the desires of sources and the audience (Gregory & Stocking, 1981).

Operating steps. Once the staff was in place, the dissemination process evolved into the following steps:

1. *Determination of significant needs for information on the part of those who work with children, youth, and families.* This is accomplished through formal (e.g., national surveys of parental problems) and informal "needs assessments" of specialized groups. All proposed programs are evaluated by staff in terms of their consonance with institution-wide objectives, relationship to research data, need, and cost.
2. *Selection and synthesis of appropriate research results.* Depending on the

specific project, up to four groups have been used to summarize or review research information: visiting scientists, staff scientists, outside consultants, and advisory committees of scientists and consumers.

3. *Packaging of information into a format (brochure, film, conference) and language that will be useful and understandable to specialized audiences.* To ensure that materials are both accurate and useful, each product is evaluated at various stages of its development by members of the intended audience and by scientists and relevant professionals, including those who provided the information and outside reviewers.

4. *Selection of cost-effective methods of distributing materials to specialized audiences.* When Boys Town's interest in a topic area is shared by another national organization serving youth, Boys Town might produce the communication product (e.g., a brochure) and the allied organization may distribute it. Otherwise sample publications may be sent in mass mailings to target groups—teachers, school counselors, family therapists—who may then request additional copies. Also, the availability of some materials, particularly those of wide appeal to parents, has been publicized via press releases to the media or by producing materials for the mass media.

Using this four-step process, almost 30 books, brochures, posters, and films have been produced for targeted audiences (McCall, Lonnborg, Gregory, Murray, & Leavitt, 1982). At the end of 1984, more than 1.8 million copies of these materials, 300,000 in 1984 alone, have been distributed nationwide—most of them free of charge. Thus, more people received Boys Town materials last year than have subscribed to the journal *Child Development* in its 52-year history. In addition, our mass media materials reach approximately 2 million households each month, probably more people than have ever subscribed to all the professional child journals.

Specific Targeted Communications Projects

Three specific targeted communications projects illustrate how the general process has been implemented in different circumstances.

Friendship skills.   In 1978, research had suggested that the inability to get along with peers was a serious problem for many children, one that could lead to later adjustment problems. A formal survey of existing research literature on the topic revealed that a good deal was known that would be of use to teachers and parents who could help friendless children. But little was written especially for parents or teachers. An informal needs assessment showed that teachers and parents were interested in the subject and wanted to learn how to help these children, but they had no particular thoughts about how that should be accomplished. In fact, both teachers and parents often felt that "there is nothing we can do."

An advisory committee was formed that included several nationally recognized researchers in the area of social skills training for children. The committee and staff decided that there were two major needs: (a) to increase awareness of the importance of social relationships for children and the possibility that friendless children could be helped, and (b) to provide parents and teachers with explicit research-based guidelines they could use to help children learn how to make friends.

Several formats were chosen for the awareness campaign. One product was a $16'' \times 20''$ color poster featuring an engaging picture of two children, arms around one another and smiling. The message on the poster read: "Friends are not luxuries . . . they are necessities. You can help children learn how to make friends: Teach them how to cooperate, share, and take turns. Show them how to ask for what they want. Help them learn to solve problems without insults or fights." The poster was chosen on the basis of an informal survey that suggested that an effective way to communicate brief messages to teachers was through posters hung near the coffee pot in the teachers' lounge.

A second product was a 16-page booklet, selected to carry explicit "how-to" information for parents and teachers. Approximately 500 booklets were printed and distributed to the largest school districts in the country. Plans for a more extensive distribution were halted when a commercial publisher asked the authors to expand the booklet into a book for publication and national distribution through trade book stores and educational outlets (Stocking, Arezzo, & Leavitt, 1979). A total of 25,000 copies were printed.

Subsequently, the National Association for Children with Learning Disabilities wanted to offer its members a modified version of the poster, together with a smaller, fold-over brochure highlighting some of the important guidelines in the booklet. These additional formats were produced. As of December, 1983, 73,000 copies of the poster and 74,000 copies of the brochure had been distributed.

School problems.   National surveys indicated that corporal punishment is still being used in many schools, and professionals believe its use is probably not in the best interests of children or society. Staff scientists and advisers felt that physical punishment might be used less frequently, if teachers and counselors were more aware of effective nonphysical methods of discipline. Interviews with teachers revealed that such information would be most helpful if presented in a brief, succinct, fold-over brochure that concentrated on techniques that research has demonstrated to be effective. A specialist in classroom disciplinary methods (Daniel O'Leary) was asked to summarize the research literature in approximately 10 pages. Based on this review, McCall (McCall & O'Leary, 1982) wrote a 1-page brochure.

A draft of the brochure was reviewed by more than 100 elementary and high school teachers and several professionals in behavioral management. Their comments prompted a number of changes. For example, the teachers emphasized that parental involvement was crucial to solving children's academic and behavior problems in school. As a result, two companion brochures were written for parents—one suggesting ways for them to work cooperatively with the school if their child was acting up in class or underachieving, and the other, with Rex Forehand, explaining how to use a periodic progress-report system to change behavior (McCall, 1982; McCall & Forehand, 1982).

A set of the three brochures was mailed to the counselor or principal of the 3,600 largest junior high schools in the country. Within a few months, requests were received for an additional 95,000 copies for use by teachers and parents.

Children and television.   Perhaps no innovation has changed the home environment and the experience of children as pervasively and in so short a time as television. The effects of TV on children are hotly debated. So, a staff member with research experience in the subject (John Murray) first compiled a bibliography of 25 years' worth of studies on the effects of television on children and the conclusions of this research in a book written for professional and academic audiences (Murray, 1980).

Parents were then interviewed to find out how they handled their children's television viewing and if they considered it a problem. A number of informational and advice books had been written for parents, and some training programs were available. However, there appeared to be a need for a short booklet that would do three things: (a) summarize what research had discovered about children and television; (b) suggest what parents could do to monitor their children's viewing and control its effects; and (c) list other resources, activities, and organizations for parents who were interested in doing more.

A 16-page booklet was written by Murray and Barbara Lonnborg, staff science writer (Murray & Lonnborg, 1981), and press releases announcing its availability were sent to the national media. Articles or notices appeared in magazines such as *Parents, Families, Health, Ladies Circle,* and *U.S. News & World Report;* major newspapers such as the

Chicago Tribune and *Washington Post*; and many other daily and weekly newspapers, journals, and newsletters. More than 100,000 copies of the booklet have been distributed in response to requests generated from these reports; the *Parents* article alone drew more than 9,000 letters.

In addition, the National PTA, long interested in the topic of children and television, offered to distribute to its members a 1-page fold-over brochure that summarized the booklet's content (Lonnborg & Murray, 1981). Within 9 months, the PTA had distributed 150,000 copies and requested another 150,000 brochures.

Specific Mass Media Projects

While targeted materials can be produced and distributed by almost any organization, access to the mass media is controlled by a group of professionals—specially trained and experienced journalists, editors, and producers. Scientists do not expect a journalist to be able to conduct research and publish it in technical journals without some help or special training. Similarly, communications professionals do not expect scientists to write articles or produce television programs of acceptable quality. Therefore, our attempts at mass media communications had to rely on the media skills possessed by our staff and consultants plus a strategy for gaining access to the media.

Television news feature project.   Our first mass media project capitalized on our staff—a health-science film and TV producer–director (Gregory) and a research developmental psychologist (McCall). With the help of funding from the National Science Foundation, we produced a set of 20 television news features, 60- to 150-second episodes on research findings pertaining to children, youth, and families designed to be aired on the local news of television stations across the nation (McCall & Gregory, 1982; McCall, Gregory, & Murray, 1984).

Our approach to the project, called "Science for Families," was very different from that typically followed by local TV news and was roughly patterned after the general procedural steps outlined earlier. For example, we used several criteria for selecting content. First, the information had to have high public interest and satisfy some public need. This meant that we favored topics that (a) provided information for personal decision making, (b) contributed to the public understanding of a social issue, or (c) were simply intrinsically interesting.

A second criterion was that the information had to be based on a substantial research literature. Thus, we preferred conclusions that emerged from a variety of studies rather than the findings of a single project. However, science frequently follows society rather than leads it, and so there were occasions when topics of major public interest and need did not have extensive research literatures. In these cases, we read the primary literature itself and contacted people in the field for informal reviews before proceeding. Some of these topics were approved, and some were not.

We had other criteria as well. Our intention was not to be political advocates or to provide a platform for individual theorizing but to emphasize balanced and representative conclusions. We also emphasized diversity in content, scientific discipline (mostly psychology, but also sociology, education, and pediatrics), production style, and geographic location of the researchers portrayed in the series. Further, because this was a television project, topics had to lend themselves to visual portrayal. Finally we wanted to make several miniseries of two or more episodes on a single topic, both to cover the material more adequately and allow stations to advertise the series in their promotions for the local news.

With the help of research colleagues, McCall listed 60 topics for possible news features. Then, 25 leading researchers in child development were selected to represent these topics, and McCall and Gregory conducted 1- to 2-hour interviews with these professionals. The interviews were tape-recorded and transcribed, and 60 possible news features were outlined. These outlines were then rated for public interest, scientific basis, and "general appeal" by project staff and by a national advisory committee (Jerome Kagan, psychology/education; Roberta Simmons, sociology; Michael Cohen, pediatrics; William Melson, communications/psychology). We discussed each of the leading topics until 15 were selected.

The researchers representing the 15 topics were shown an outline of the proposed news feature; they criticized the proposal, and it was discussed until a mutually satisfactory plan was achieved. The outline was again reviewed with the researcher at the time of filming, which sometimes led to changes in the content and even the number of news features. Ultimately, after editing, 20 features were produced. Scripts of these penultimate versions were sent for review to the featured researcher and to at least one outside reviewer. Only one episode required some change.

To illustrate the news features, Table 1 gives the titles and main themes of the 20 episodes, and Table 2 presents the transcript of one of the features. "Getting to Know You" followed the "typical" style of a science news feature—a report of research findings illustrated with pictures of scientific equipment, an interview with a leading researcher, and relevant pictures of an infant in the research context. This episode followed the script outline closely, was filmed in a matter of hours, and

TABLE 1:   The Television News Features*

1. *Getting to Know You—What Newborns See in You.* Marshall Haith. Describes the visual capabilities of babies in the first two months of life.
2. *Waterbeds for Premature Babies.* Anneliese Korner. Describes the benefits for premature babies of special oscillating waterbeds and cautions against home use.
3. *Attachment is a Long-Term Process.* Robert N. Emde. Suggests that early contact between parent and infant is a good beginning, but it is neither necessary nor sufficient for attachment.
4. *Preparing Your Daughter to Achieve—Part I.* Jeanne Block. Illustrates how parents behave differently toward their sons and daughters with respect to problem solving and achievement.
5. *Preparing Your Daughter to Achieve—Part II.* Jeanne Block. Illustrates with a case study behaviors in a father that promote achievement in his daughter.
6. *The Effects of Working Mothers on Children.* Ivan Nye. Suggests the effects of working mothers depend on the woman's feelings about her role, the management of the added stress by the entire family, and the quality of the care for the child.
7. *Divorce—It Was Worse Than I Expected.* Mavis Hetherington. Attempts to counter the popular notion that divorce leads immediately to a cessation of conflict and a new, exciting life.
8. *Divorce—Attachments Die Hard.* Mavis Hetherington. Points out that attachment to a former spouse dies hard and often produces confusing behavior in the newly divorced individual.
9. *Divorce—It's Family Conflict That Hurts Children.* Joan Kelly. Suggests that conflict, within marriage or following divorce, has harmful effects on children.
10. *Divorce—School Problems.* Mavis Hetherington. Describes some of the school problems of children of divorce.
11. *Divorce—Helping in the Classroom.* Joan Kelly. Illustrates an attempt by school teachers to help divorced children.
12. *Before Minimum Competency Testing.* Sanford Dornbusch. Suggests that the emphasis on building up self-confidence and positive social relations with disadvantaged pupils is creating a false notion of adequate standards of academic performance which then leads to failing minimum competency tests.
13. *Teenagers and Alcohol: Set a Moderate Example.* Ronald Akers. Shows that parental drinking habits have an effect on the drinking patterns of their children and that parents who use alcohol moderately and appropriately have teenagers who have the fewest problems with alcohol.
14. *Teenagers and Alcohol: Avoid Overreacting.* Ronald Akers. Reports that overreacting to a young person's experimentation with alcohol either by being disinterested or by becoming terribly upset may lead to undesirable drinking habits in the adolescent.
15. *House Calls for Families-in-Crisis—Part I.* Jill Kinney. Shows a family about to break up because of a problem teenager helped by a crisis intervention service.
16. *House Calls for Families-in-Crisis—Part II.* Jill Kinney. Describes the process by which a unique crisis intervention service keeps families together.
17. *Adolescents are Abused Too.* James Garbarino. Makes the point that infants and young children are not the only ones who are abused; adolescents are also mistreated.

continued

*From "Communicating developmental research to the general public" by R. McCall and T. Gregory, 1982, in J. deWit (Ed.), *Perspectives in child study.* Lisse, The Netherlands: Swets and Zeitlinger. Copyright 1982 by Paedologisch Instituut, Amsterdam and Swets and Zeitlinger B.V., Lisse. Reprinted with permission.

18. *It's Risky to Love.* James Garbarino. Adolescent abuse victims tell how it is difficult for them to establish a close, personal relationship with other people.
19. *Advice to Runaways.* James Garbarino. An adolescent abuse victim tells other teenagers about the perils of running away.
20. *Abused Youth as Parents.* James Garbarino. Makes the point that adolescent abuse victims have learned a poor lesson in parenting.

TABLE 2: Transcript of a News Feature: Getting to Know You—What Newborns See in You (Marshall Haith)*

Audio	Visual
Suggested Lead-In	
Parents often wonder whether their newborn babies can see or recognize them. Only a decade ago, many doctors told parents that their newborn babies were essentially blind. But now Dr. Marshall Haith, a psychologist at the University of Denver, has created a clever system for studying what new babies see—and they can see us.	Read live by local announcer
Dr. Haith	
What we designed here is a system for measuring exactly where the baby is looking. The baby lies in this comfortable crib and looks up at the mother's face through a mirror. Behind the mirror is a television camera that records the baby's eye as he looks at his mother's face. Newborn babies definitely can see. They probably can see a little bit of color. They do not see the mother's face as a whole until about 7 weeks of age. They tend to look mostly at the sharp contrast borders around the face.	Dr. Haith in front of electronic equipment

Baby in crib of apparatus
Mother and baby looking in mirror of apparatus

Research assistant at video console

Black and white closeup of baby's eye

Color closeup of baby's eye
Zoom in on another baby's face
Face of woman |
| We don't really know why babies tend to concentrate on light and dark edges rather than the eyes. We think, however, that looking at light/dark edges may send messages to the brain which could be critical for development of the whole visual system. | Dr. Haith |

---

*From "Communicating developmental research to the general public" by R. McCall and T. Gregory, 1982, in J. deWit (Ed.), *Perspectives in child study*. Lisse, the Netherlands: Swets and Zeitlinger. Copyright © 1982 by Paedologisch Instituut, Amsterdam and Swets and Zeitlinger B. V., Lisse. Reprinted with permission.

At around 7 weeks of age, however, the baby begins to become social, looking at the mother's eyes when she talks to him.	Dr. Haith and baby playing

Mother and Father with Baby

At first I had to look into her eyes and move her around so she could see me. Now it seems as if she can look into my eyes and sees me and sees my husband and we're more of a family now.	Mother
	Mother and father
	Mother, father, and baby

Suggested Tag

While newborn babies can see, Dr. Haith says they do not see as clearly as adults do, especially objects that are far away. So, if you want your baby to see how cute and adorable *you* are, stay close by.	Read live by local announcer

edited in a half day. It looked like "science," and sample viewers thought it was among the most informative of the news features.

In contrast, "Preparing Your Daughter to Achieve—Part 2," reflected a totally different style. The information was communicated by having a young girl and her father talk about their relationship, their family, and the daughter's career choice. Their statements closely matched the main themes in the research literature on achievement in women. The episode was introduced and concluded by a professional who referred to research, but the body of the feature was a personal story in which research was not mentioned at all. This episode took considerably longer to film and edit, and the father–daughter material was filmed before the professional so that the professional's comments could relate specifically to this material. Sample viewers found this episode more interesting, but considerably less informative than others.

Distribution was conducted privately by selecting the leading stations in the nation's largest cities, contacting news directors by phone to determine if they would be willing to review the materials for possible use on their news programs, and sending them the features, transcripts with introductions and closes, and background material on the content of each news feature. If a station refused the materials, the next leading station in that city was contacted.

As of 1981, 28 stations had broadcast some or all of the features one or more times, and 23 additional stations had not made a decision. The number of households capable of receiving the news features for confirmed stations was 14,788,300. Assuming 2 persons per household, the potential audience was approximately 29.6 million (plus the audience for the 23 unconfirmed stations). By making a few assumptions (McCall et al., 1984), we roughly estimate that at least 6.2 million people actually saw any one episode, and approximately 12.4 million saw at least one of the news features (plus viewers from the unconfirmed stations).

Although we did not conduct formal evaluations of viewer response, we did perform informal surveys of viewers in controlled situations that were crude by psychological research standards but were substantially more extensive than are usually conducted for production projects (McCall et al., 1984; Murray, 1983). These surveys indicated that the "Science for Families" features were at least as interesting, stimulating, and informative as the best control news features broadcast during a three-week period in Omaha, Nebraska, by the three network affiliate stations.

Another method of evaluation was to submit the series to award competitions. "Science for Families" won national media awards from the American Psychological Association/Foundation and from the American Academy of Pediatrics.

Other video projects.   Gregory, with the help of James Garbarino, produced a film for high school audiences on adolescent abuse entitled "Don't Get Stuck There" (Gregory, 1981) which has been sold to or used by more than 700 schools across the country and which won two national film awards.

In addition, we have worked with free-lance professionals to produce a half-hour television program on the abuse of adolescents ("Adolescent Abuse—The Chorus of Pain"; Keidel, 1983) and a series of fifteen 90-second features similar to "Science for Families," except that the same on-camera host appears in all episodes ("Parent-to-Parent"; McCall & Harrington, 1982).

Our experience with these several TV and film projects indicates that scientists and producers can work cooperatively to generate television material that researchers regard as scientifically responsible and that news directors, viewers, and media award reviewers regard as interesting, stimulating, and of high production quality. But such cooperation requires accommodation by scientists to the requirements of the media (e.g., short format, visual portrayals, illustration of research themes by a single case, repeated "takes" to achieve clear communication and a conversational style, and final authority vested in the producer/director). Similarly, producers must accommodate to the penchants of researchers (e.g., the addition of qualifiers, reluctance to draw simple declarative conclusions, desire to control content, and avoidance of practical prescriptions).

Writing for the public.   Early in the development of our program, we consulted with several prominent journalists specializing in science, behavioral science, and child development. Although our staff included journalists, we were told that it was difficult to break into newspaper and magazine writing on a free-lance basis. Editors are inundated with free-lance articles, and to cope with the deluge they rely on a quick screening policy: Deal only with writers known to the editor or who have a substantial list of newspaper and magazine credits. This presents something of a "Catch 22"—a person can not write for newspapers and magazines unless he or she has written for newspapers and magazines.

Our first task, then, was to acquire more national journalistic credits, especially magazine placements, and become known to editors. We followed a deliberate strategy. First, we were advised that it was easier to publish a book aimed at the general public than a magazine article. Further, promoting the book would involve publishing excerpts in major magazines, thus providing the author with magazine credits. Second, most newspapers have "op-ed" pages where they publish short articles from readers or free-lancers. This is a way to build up credits, starting with the local newspaper and working toward national publications. A third task was to jointly author magazine articles with an experienced magazine writer who would rewrite our first draft and place the article with editors whom the writer knew. We, in turn, would then become "known" to the editor of that publication.

We pursued all three strategies. McCall wrote a book on infants for parents with the help of Holly Stocking, an experienced journalist specializing in behavioral science, (McCall, 1979, 1980), and excerpts were published in several magazines. In addition, an article was written with Patrick Young, an experienced science reporter (McCall & Young, 1979), Stocking and McCall wrote newspaper articles placed with editors known to Stocking, and several op-ed pieces were published locally.

It also helps to have a little luck. As part of the promotion for McCall's trade book on infants, galleys were sent to *Parents* magazine with the hope that they would publish a portion of it. The timing was fortuitously propitious, because *Parents* needed a columnist to cover the first year of life, and they asked McCall to write a monthly column on infants. This has led to nearly 50 columns and 8 additional feature articles for *Parents* which reaches an estimated 2 million plus families each month.

Implications for other professionals.   While not every researcher has the time, inclination, skills, or opportunity to learn to write for lay audiences, it can be done, and a variety of cooperative efforts are possible. For example, Michael Lewis, a developmental psychologist specializing in infancy, is a consultant to *Mothers Manual* magazine and frequently provides information for articles co-authored with a professional writer. Other child development researchers are consulting editors for publications aimed at parents, although the task of a consulting editor for a popular magazine is different than for a scholarly journal (e.g., articles are not reviewed in the same way).

Researchers are more likely to be sources of information than actual writers. That experience can vary depending on the publication and the writer. Local newspapers, for example, are written very quickly and there is usually time only for a short interview, because the article appears one to three days later. National newspapers have more time to research an article, and they frequently have reporters who specialize in science, in behavioral science, or in education or child development and family life. Researchers may be interviewed once and possibly called back again, and more than one source will be contacted. National magazines have even more time, and many are even more careful. Articles may be written in a week or over several months. Depending on the publication and the writer, who may be a staff writer for the magazine or a free-lancer, a very cooperative arrangement may emerge. Further, once the article is submitted to the editorial process, many national magazines check all the facts and quotes in the article with their original sources.

Researchers who anticipate being a source for a journalist or free-lance writer or being on radio or television might benefit from some guidelines designed especially for psychologists or child development specialists to improve their effectiveness and to make the experience more satisfying (e.g., McCall, 1983; McCall et al., 1984; McCall & Stocking, 1982; Hilton & Knoblauch, 1980).

CONCLUSIONS

Social and behavioral science in general and child development research and practice in particular need to improve their relationships with society. These disciplines and professions need a public constituency for continued funding of research, support from universities, and money and volunteers to continue to provide professional services. Society, in turn, needs these disciplines. For example, approximately half of the deaths associated with the leading causes of mortality in America are associated with behavioral circumstances and life style (Institute of Medicine, 1982), many of which begin during childhood or in the family. In addition to issues of mortality, most of society's most pressing problems are directly or indirectly behavioral and developmental.

Our experience has shown that it is possible to communicate accurate and balanced information in a manner that is also interesting and useful to the general public. It is not necessary to forego accuracy and balance to gain an audience. Instead, we have tried to select information that is useful, topical, and interesting. Once you strip away methodological details, p values, esoteric theory, and topics that are not interesting to the public, the fruits of developmental disciplines are remarkably interesting and useful to people without requiring a great deal of "translating" or "hype."

Our enterprise has attempted to involve child and family scientists across the country from a variety of disciplines. With only a few exceptions, they have been generous in giving their time, cooperative in attitude, and respectful of the enterprise. In this context, "going public" is not something researchers have shunned; instead, they have been a great help to us.

Not every scientist can or should become a communicator or a disseminator, but *some* should, and all should support attempts at responsible, accurate, balanced dissemination of information. Further, many researchers will be sources for the mass media or targeted communications, and they should approach that task with an attitude of cooperation and accommodation to the requirements of the media and with some knowledge and skill in being a source.

If researchers want public support, it is best to give the public something they can use—to show the public that their support returns dividends to them. It is a function most researchers have not eagerly adopted in the past, but one that can no longer be ignored.

REFERENCES

Bevan, W. (1982). A sermon of sorts in three plus parts. *American Psychologist, 37*, 1303–1322.

Caplan, N., Morrison, A., & Stambaugh, R. J. (1975). *The use of social science knowledge in policy decisions at the national level.* Ann Arbor, MI: The University of Michigan, Institute for Social Research, Center for Research on Utilization of Scientific Knowledge.

Good, P., Simon, G. C., & Coursey, R. D. (1981). Public interest activities of APA members. *American Psychologist, 36*, 963–971.

Goodfield, J. (1981). *Reflections on science and the media.* Washington, DC: American Association for the Advancement of Science.

Gregory, T. G. (Producer). (1981). *Don't get stuck there* [Film]. Boys Town, NE: Boys Town.

Gregory, T., & Stocking, S. H. (1981). Communicating science to the public through targeted messages. *Children and Youth Services Review, 3*, 277–289.

Herbert, W. (1980, October). Humanities and journalism: Akin but worlds apart. *Humanities Report*, 4–8.

Herrnstein, R. J. (1982, August). IQ testing and the media. *The Atlantic Monthly,* 68–74.

Hilton, J., & Knoblauch, M. (1980). *On television! A survival guide for media interviews.* New York: AMACOM.

Institute of Medicine. (1982). *Health and behavior: Frontiers of research in the biobehavioral sciences.* Washington, DC: National Academy Press.

Keidel, D. (Producer). (1983). *Adolescent abuse: The chorus of pain* [Film]. Boys Town, NE: Boys Town.

Lonnborg, B., & Murray, J. P. (1981). *Children and television.* Boys Town, NE: Boys Town.

McCall, R. B. (1979, 1980). *Infants: The new knowledge.* Cambridge, MA: Harvard. Also released as *Infants: The new knowledge about the years from birth to three.* New York: Vintage.

McCall, R. B. (1982). *What to do if your child is an underachiever in school.* Boys Town, NE: Boys Town.

McCall, R. B. (1983). Family services and the mass media. *Family Relations, 32,* 315–322.

McCall, R. B., & Forehand, R. (1982). *Parent's guide to the periodic progress report.* Boys Town, NE: Boys Town.

McCall, R. B., & Gregory, T. G. (1982). Communicating developmental research to the general public. In J. deWit (Ed.), *Perspectives in child study.* Lisse, The Netherlands: Swets & Zeitlinger.

McCall, R. B., Gregory, T. G., & Murray, J. P. (1984). Communicating developmental research results to the general public through television newsfeatures. *Developmental Psychology, 20,* 45–54.

McCall, R. B., & Harrington, K. A. (Producers). (1982). *Parent to parent* [Film]. Boys Town, NE: Boys Town.

McCall, R. B., Lonnborg, B., Gregory, T. G., Murray, J. P., & Leavitt, S. (1982). Communicating developmental research to the public: The Boys Town experience. *Newsletter of the Society for Research in Child Development,* Fall, 1–3.

McCall, R. B., & O'Leary, D. (1982). *Tips on discipline in the classroom.* Boys Town, NE: Boys Town.

McCall, R. B., & Stocking, S. H. (1982). Between scientists and public: Communicating psychological research through the mass media. *American Psychologist, 37,* 985–995.

McCall, R. B., & Young, P. (1979, March). Make room for daddy. *American Way,* American Airlines.

McCombs, M., & Shaw, D. (1977). The agenda-setting function of the press. In D. Shaw & M. McCombs (Eds.), *The emergence of American political issues: The agenda-setting function of the press* (pp. 1–18). St. Paul, MN: West.

McQuail, D. (1969). *Toward a sociology of mass communications.* London: Collier-Macmillan.

Miller, G. A. (1969). Psychology as a means of promoting human welfare. *American Psychologist, 24,* 1063–1075.

Murray, J. P. (1980). *Television and youth: 25 years of research and controversy.* Boys Town, NE: Boys Town.

Murray, J. P. (1983). *Controlled viewer surveys for the "Science for Families" television newsfeature project.* Unpublished manuscript.

Murray, J. P., & Lonnborg, B. (1981). *Children and television: A primer for parents.* Boys Town, NE: Boys Town.

Rubin, Z. (1980). My love-hate relationship with the media. *Psychology Today*, *13*, 12–13.

Ryan, M. (1979). Attitudes of scientists and journalists toward media coverage of science news. *Journalism Quarterly*, *56*, 18–26, 53.

Ryan, M., & Dunwoody, S. L. (1975). Academic and professional training patterns of science writers. *Journalism Quarterly*, *52*, 239–246, 290.

Schramm, W. (1973). *Men, messages, and media: A look at human communication*. New York: Harper & Row.

Schramm, W., & Wade, S. (1967). *Knowledge and the public mind*. Stanford, CA: Stanford University Press.

Steinem, G. (1978, August 28). Invited address. American Psychological Association, Toronto, Canada.

Stocking, S. H., Arezzo, D., & Leavitt, S. (1979). *Helping kids make friends*. Allen, TX: Argus Communications.

Stocking, S. H., & Dunwoody, S. L. (1982). Social science in the news media: Images and evidence. In J. Sieber (Ed.), *The ethics of social research: Fieldwork, regulation, and publication*. New York: Springer.

Tankard, J., & Ryan, M. (1974). News source perceptions of accuracy of science coverage. *Journalism Quarterly*, *51*, 219–225, 334.

Walum, L. R. (1975). Sociology and the mass media: Some major problems and modest proposals. *The American Sociologist*, *10*, 28–32.

Weigel, R. H., & Pappas, J. J. (1981). Social science and the press: A case study and its implications. *American Psychologist*, *36*, 480–487.

Weiss, C. H. (1974). What America's leaders read. *The Public Opinion Quarterly*, *38*, 1–21.

Eleven

A Workshop Approach to Building Communications Bridges with Journalists

JOSEPH SANDERS
Auburn University at Montgomery

JAMES J. GALLAGHER
University of North Carolina at Chapel Hill

INTRODUCTION

The mass media provide an essential link between the worlds of the academician and the policymaker. As Gallagher and Sanders (1981) have noted:

> those in decision-making positions—in industry and in the executive, judicial, and legislative branches of government—learn about the work in the professional fields through the media. The busy legislator will read the newspapers or watch the 11 o'clock news; he or she will not, in all liklihood, read technical reports by professors. What the media relay about these technical reports is often all the decision makers receive. (p. 22)

It becomes important, therefore, for academicians to find ways to communicate effectively with the representatives of the media. One communication device is an annual workshop on public policy that has been conducted for journalists by the Bush Institute for Child and Family Policy at the University of North Carolina at Chapel Hill. This chapter describes the four workshops that have been held—their rationale, content, and outcome.

JOURNALISTS AND SOCIAL POLICY

The social scientist who takes on the role of policy analyst occupies a more difficult position than his or her colleagues in dealing with the mass media. On one hand, those colleagues who choose to teach and conduct research do not need journalists to help them communicate with students and researchers. On the other hand, those colleagues who become advocates for social causes seek exposure and media promotion. In the middle is the social policy analyst, who can neither ignore the media nor stage media events but who seeks instead an interdependence.

What is the role of journalists in public policy that makes relationships with them both unavoidable and desirable? It is no great revelation that the mass media have come to occupy a central position not only in transmitting information to citizens but also in determining which information reaches them and which they find salient (Gans, 1980; McCombs & Shaw, 1972). Citizens include not only John and Jane Doe, but also those decision makers who make and shape policy: elected officials, corporate executives, and lobbyists. Although these leaders have access to a wealth of detailed policy reports, they are often influenced heavily by information provided by journalists. The Westinghouse Report (Cicirelli et al., 1969) on Head Start and the Coleman Report (Coleman et al., 1966) on segregation were debated by many more politicians and government officials who had received their information through the mass media than those who had read the reports themselves.

Even when policy makers rely on their staffs to digest the literature for them, they often find themselves scurrying to investigate policy issues thrust upon them unexpectedly by journalists. An example of agenda-setting by the media is offered by Thomas Birch (1980), former counsel to the Subcommittee on Select Education in the U.S. House of Representatives. He points out that the passage by Congress in 1977 of an act to ban the use of children in pornography resulted not from a legislative initiative but from articles about "kiddie porn" carried in California and New York newspapers. "When we saw the publicity," Birch said, "it occurred to staff and Congressmen that we ought to take this up." Several journalists subsequently provided information and recommended witnesses to Subcommittee staff who were setting up hearings.

Most journalists see their role in reporting proposed policies as neither advocate nor antagonist but merely that as a "watchdog" on government activities (Dyer & Nayman, 1977; Miller, 1978). Nevertheless, many a policy analyst has seen a carefully studied list of policy options torpedoed or circumvented by a barrage of publicity and editorials. Recent examples can be drawn from proposed rule-making by the Federal Trade Commission and the Food and Drug Administration. Two effective publicity campaigns are recalled by Edie Fraser (1979), president of Fraser/Associates, a Washington-based counseling firm:

> Probably the most massive effort ever undertaken was the grass roots campaign on the labor law reform legislation. We were engaged to conduct an editorial program throughout the U.S. . . . We insisted that the strategy be placed at the grass roots level. We concentrated on the news media, believing we could develop a swell of editorial comment. . . . We orchestrated grass roots activities through press conferences, press releases, forums, special presentations, and one-on-one contact . . . which would cause individuals and groups to contact their senators in opposition to the legislation.
>
> By forming the Nitrite Safety Council, leaders of the meat industry followed a similar approach. . . . The Council's campaign was successful because the industry was organized with its allies and had the ability to reach out to millions of Americans who love their hot dogs at ball games and bacon for breakfast. (p. 11)

It is therefore incumbent upon the social scientist who enters the field of social policy to recognize the strength and dimensions of the relationship between journalists and policymakers. By merely doing their jobs, journalists influence the consideration, modification, passage, or rejection of policy options. It is the job of the social policy analyst to build relationships with both policymakers and journalists, balancing the often contradictory requirements of each for accessability, confidentiality, and trust.

THE SOCIAL POLICY ANALYST'S POSITION

This recognition leads the social policy analyst first to study his or her proper position in the journalist's marketplace of news and then to take up that position. To ignore the first step is to invite frustration. In *Deciding What's News*, Herbert Gans (1980) observes that:

> Experts who would like to communicate their ideas and findings to the nation are often stopped short when reporters tell them that stories which may be highly newsworthy within the expert's circles cannot be sold to a producer or editor who must consider the lay audience. In recent years, many social science disciplines have tried to bring their findings to the attention of that audience, only to discover that journalists are unable to help. (pp. 137–138)

Social scientists would meet with greater success if they would understand and utilize their position in the marketplace. Social scientists work in the realm of "soft news"—science, the family, children—as opposed to "hard news"—political contests, presidential action, disasters, and immediate happenings. Soft news occupies a significant amount of space in newspapers, news magazines, and the electronic media, but its characteristics are distinct. Soft-news topics usually gain coverage not because of their inherent news value, but because they can be incorporated into what Gans (1980) refers to as "complexes" of interest:

> Thus, the nation is made up of such symbolic complexes that have also become sections in the news magazines. New complexes are added as new actors and activities come to the fore. . . . Since 1975, stories about child abuse and wife beating have appeared in the news, not because they are new or even rapidly increasing phenomena, but because they relate to concerns about maintenance of the Family. (p. 19)

Occasionally a soft-news topic will be transformed into hard news. This happens when elements of the topic itself combine with outside events to create "newsworthiness" (Gatlund & Ruge, 1970). Child pornography became a newsworthy event, because it met several criteria: it violated widely held values, it was shocking, it involved "human interest," it was unambiguous, it was related to an ongoing story of the relationship of pornography to organized crime, and public officials began to talk about it. The introduction of this topic to Congressional attention created for those social policy analysts who had previously established relationships with journalists an atmosphere in which to raise some broader concerns about the abuse of children.

In occupying the realm of soft news, the social scientist can utilize some advantages. First, journalists who cover soft news tend to be specialists in their topics, many with training in a social science or several years' experience. Second, Gans (1980) points out that, "Journalists are not immune from familial problems, and . . . their existence creates a ready interest in stories about the problems of two-career families, child-rearing difficulties, and adolescent 'dropouts' " (p. 127). Third, the absence of the daily deadlines that accompany hard news allows some journalists more time to delve into a policy and digest its complexities. Fourth, the social scientist can develop long-term relationships with journalists that give the scientist influence and access to public debate when appropriate issues are taken up by public bodies and thereby are transformed into hard news.

This approach to media relations is recognized in the policy analysis model adopted by the Bush Institute for Child and Family Policy at the University of North Carolina (UNC) at Chapel Hill. Part of UNC's Frank Porter Graham Child Development Center, the Bush Institute has since 1978 trained doctoral students and professionals for policy careers. The Bush model of policy analysis consists of six steps; the last two steps require access to the media and good communication skills (Haskins & Gallagher, 1981).

THE BUSH POLICY MODEL

Restatement of the Problem. First, the social policy analyst states the problem in terms of its causes, variables, and possible remedies. The agitation of public officials over welfare, for example, might be translated into policy questions such as "What are the disincentives of a guaranteed annual income," or "What are the comparative effects of service and income strategies?" The key element of this step is to distill a question that can be addressed out of what is often merely a vague concern.

Criteria for Analysis. Each discipline has a set of criteria it tends to emphasize in analyzing a given policy: Law is concerned with due process and rights, economics with efficiency and optimization, child psychology with provision of optimal environments for development. A policy analysis must identify and specify the criteria by which alternative policies are to be weighed. These criteria must go beyond a mere aggregation of those offered by various disciplines; rather, the criteria must represent an ordered set of values that can be applied to the analysis of all policies that affect children and families. The choice of criteria by the social policy analyst represents his or her own value system. Some may believe that vertical equity, or the reduction of income spread in the society, is a critical element by which to weigh strategy. Others may not. The criteria must be spelled out, so that the reviewer of the analysis knows the analyst's values and orientation.

Synthesis of Information. No single discipline can offer a broad enough perspective to synthesize information into a comprehensive policy on major social issues. For example, welfare reform strategies must take into account data from the fields of health, psychology, sociology, law, and education. To be effective, a social policy analyst must be schooled in the miltidisciplinary approach in order to both identify the professional specialities that contribute to a solution and organize the contributions of these disciplines into a coherent statement.

Alternative Strategies. The problem under analysis can yield four or five possible solutions. For example, policies to make day care more affordable range from employer incentives to vouchers. The criteria chosen in "Criteria for Analysis" must be applied to identify the most feasible strategy. Criteria such as cost, political feasibility, and evidence of effectiveness can then be applied to reach a decision. A successful analysis will produce a decision matrix with quantitative and qualitative information that allows for a choice among options.

Communication of Analysis. The goal of a policy analysis is not only to choose between alternative strategies but also to assure the results of the analysis are communicated to the appropriate decision makers. A careful academic analysis will be of no use, if it does not find those who must act on the issue. The media provide one avenue by which such communication takes place. Part of the task of the social policy analyst is to employ media channels to reach the appropriate decision makers.

Implementation Strategy. If the analysis has proven successful and a strategy chosen, there is still the task of deciding how best to implement the strategy. Must laws be passed? Budgets rewritten? Institutions reorganized? Persons who are faced with change grow nervous and resistant, unless the process by which the change takes place is understood and agreed upon. A new policy of treating delinquents or providing counseling services for families with handicapped children will require some definite changes in how professionals work or what they do. Strong communication skills are important to pave the way for successful implementation.

Planning for Communication

The 27 fellows who enrolled in the Bush program from 1978 through 1982 had a wide range of academic and professional backgrounds. Of the 27, 13 were doctoral candidates working toward degrees in such disciplines as psychology, public health, special education, and economics; the rest were professional fellows who prior to entering the program had gained work experience in some policy or service position related to children and families.

Familiarity with the mass media varied greatly among the fellows. Two of the fellows had worked for a short time as journalists. One was working toward a doctorate in mass communications, but 20 of the 27 fellows had no course work in the field. Five reported that prior to entering the Bush program they had extensive contact with journalists, but 14 claimed little or no previous contact.

In an effort to increase the fellows' familiarity with journalists (and journalists' familiarity with policy analysis), the Bush Institute sponsored a series of four annual workshops beginning in 1978. This format, which brought approximately 20 journalists together with Bush faculty and fellows over a 2-day period, was chosen for its inherent advantages. First, the workshop format encourages an exchange of information and viewpoints, unlike a press conference. Second, the Bush faculty and fellows could meet more journalists at once than through a guest lecture by a journalist. Third, person-to-person communication is more effective than print or audiovisual for influencing attitudes and actions.

The workshops were therefore seen as a device for achieving four main goals:

1. To create a forum for the exchange of information and viewpoints among journalists, Bush faculty and fellows, and invited policy professionals;
2. To present background information on a small number of policy topics being addressed by the Bush fellows;
3. To establish the Bush Institute as an information source for journalists who cover child and family issues; and
4. To contribute toward constructive relationships between social policy analysts and journalists, thereby improving both the formulation of policy and its reporting.

A committee of three Bush faculty and a faculty member in the UNC School of Journalism began each fall to plan for a workshop in the following spring. The committee was charged with setting the workshop agenda, selecting the topics and presenters, recruiting appropriate journalists, and securing a workshop site. The committee was guided in each of these tasks by the workshop goals.

Workshop agenda.   The committee recognized that a collection of lectures on policy topics would not accomplish the goal of creating an exchange of information and viewpoints. The agenda were designed instead to provide both structured and unstructured exchanges between fellows, faculty, and media representatives. The first evening's session of the 1981 workshop included a presentation by Judy Randal, who was a journalist on leave from the New York *Daily News* to work for a year as a Congressional fellow. Her presentation on "Social Policy from a Reporter's Perspective" was followed by an open discussion designed to create an atmosphere that would encourage the journalists to speak freely during the remainder of the workshop. On the final day of the workshop, a panel discussion was led by three journalists on "Press Problems in Covering Child and Family Issues." This session gave the Bush faculty and fellows an opportunity to hear from journalists about the ways in which social scientists can better meet their information needs. Informal discussion time was scheduled around meals and in the evenings.

Topics and Presenters. Each workshop featured three or four policy presentations as a means of attracting journalists and providing Bush fellows with practice in communicating with the media. Although six or more policy issues were under study each year at the Institute, some had a wider appeal for journalists. The committee tried to meet the criteria of topic appeal, whether the study had progressed enough to produce policy recommendations, and willingness of the fellow to take part. Table 1 shows the policy topics covered in the four workshops.

The fellows who agreed to serve as topic presenters took responsibility for developing approximately 45-minute presentations. To round

TABLE 1:   Policy Topics Covered at the Four Workshops

1979

What We Know About:
- Day Care
- Family Violence
- Income Redistribution

How to Analyze a Proposed Policy or Program.
Supplemental Security Income.
Children, Families, and the Legal System.

1980

Divorce Law and Child Custody.
Sexual Abuse of Children.
Television Advertising Aimed at Children.

1981

Adoption and Foster Care.
Teenage Pregnancy.
The Findings of the Select Panel on the Promotion of Child Health.
Sex on Television.

1982

Mothers in Prison.
Family Stress Induced by Parental Unemployment.
Mental Health Treatment Needs of Children.

out some topics, the fellows recruited outside experts in service or policy positions. Outside experts included a Congressional staff attorney, a staff director of the Federal Communications Commission, the executive director of the N.C. Governor's Advocacy Commission on Children and Youth, and a family planning counselor from a county social services department. Each presentation was intended to provide a statement of the policy problem, some recommendations for reform, and implications for service to children and families.

Each fellow worked under the guidance of an Institute faculty member. In addition, the committee held two briefing sessions to prepare the fellows for dealing with the media. An orientation session was held early in the planning process, followed by a dress rehearsal in outline form approximately a week before each workshop.

Recruiting Journalists. In the committee's view, the journalists who would most benefit from the workshops were editors, editorial writers and columnists, family section editors and their staffs, television producers, and public affairs directors in radio and television. For the first year, recommendations for journalists to invite were collected from Bush faculty and fellows and other institutions (including the UNC and Duke University news bureaus, UNC School of Journalism, and the Southern Newspaper Publishers Association). In subsequent years, journalists who had previously attended or expressed an interest were invited and asked for recommendations. The pool of invited journalists grew by this method to about 100.

A mix of 10 North Carolina journalists and 10 from out-of-state was sought as a balance between the Institute's state and national focus. This number was viewed as large enough to make the workshop worthwhile but small enough to allow each journalist a chance to ask questions and participate. To support recruitment, the Institute covered the journalists' costs of room, meals, and workshop materials; the journalists' employers were asked to cover travel expenses. As is implied by this arrangement, recruitment of out-of-state journalists was more difficult than in-state recruitment. Each November, a committee member began to invite journalists through a series of letters and follow-up telephone calls. Over the 4 years, representatives from more than 32 different media outlets attended the workshops. National media such as National Public Radio, *Woman's Day* magazine, and *U.S. News and World Report* sent producers and editors. Local or state newspapers most often sent staff writers, or in some cases, editorial writers or columnists. Over the course of the workshops, *Parents* magazine was represented by a staff writer, an associate editor, and the managing editor. Local television stations were represented by their producers, special projects directors, or public affairs managers.

Workshop location. The University of North Carolina's conference center, Quail Roost, was chosen for the workshops. Quail Roost's location 35 miles from Chapel Hill removed the faculty and fellows from daily distractions. Most participants spent the two nights of each workshop at the conference center. The center still retains the atmosphere of the country estate that it was before being donated to the University; sitting rooms and dining areas are arranged for small groups, and the center's management encourages guests to be relaxed and informal.

Execution and Follow-up

Execution has been defined as a byproduct of the planning process. Certainly some of the Institute's small staff spent more time preparing for the workshops than they spent in the workshops themselves. Logistics—delivering equipment and providing transportation for out-of-state guests—was handled by the Institute's communications director, his assistant, secretary, and two work-study students, with help from three or four faculty and fellows. Packets of materials containing outlines and statistics used in presentations were assembled and distributed to the journalists at the beginning of each workshop. The packets contained evaluation forms that the journalists completed at the end of the workshop. Results were compiled and distributed to all Bush faculty and fellows.

Following each workshop the Institute's communications director, assistant, and a writer from the UNC News Bureau each wrote a feature story on a workshop session. The features were distributed to North Carolina newspapers by the News Bureau; the Institute staff mailed the features to journalists who attended the workshop and those who had expressed an interest but could not attend. An issue of *Developments*, the quarterly national newsletter of the UNC Child Development Institute, was devoted to each workshop.

Benefits of Conducting the Workshops

The journalists' evaluations and follow-up interviews with Bush fellows indicate the workshops achieved some of their objectives. Only one of the Institute's 27 fellows did not attend a workshop; of the 26 who did, 13 reported that the workshops significantly increased their knowledge of how to interact with journalists. Fourteen of the fellows agreed that the workshops "have helped me work with journalists," 5 disagreed, and 7 were equivocal (said one, "[I've had] no opportunity [to work with journalists] . . . I suppose it would help"). One former fellow said, "I have a greater appreciation for the way journalists secure a story," and another added, "I'm much more aware of journalists and enjoy contact with them."

The Institute had some success in establishing itself as a source of information for the journalists to call upon in the future. Ten of the fellows reported that following the workshops they were contacted for information by media outlets including National Public Radio, *Time*, *McCall's*, *Woman's Day*, *The New York Times*, and numerous North Carolina newspapers and television stations. *Time* flew three workshop presenters to its New York office to brief its staff on child custody, and *U.S. News and World Report* asked for information to help prepare a cover story on the status of American children.

The workshops were held to build relationships and not to secure immediate media coverage. Yet coverage of the workshop topics is an indication that the journalists found them relevant. Of the 32 media outlets that sent representatives to the workshop, 20 published information based on one or more of the workshop sessions.

Problems With the Workshops

The Bush workshops were refined over their 4 years, based on journalists' evaluations and faculty discussions. For example, service providers were asked to help with presentations in response to criticism that presentations were too academic. Some problems remained after four workshops, however. These fell into categories of preparation and presentation, the journalists who took part, and follow-up.

Preparation and Presentation. The journalists' evaluations indicated that the choice of Quail Roost and the logistical preparations were wholly successful. Reception of the workshop content was mixed, however.

It is clear that more attention must be paid to preparing for the roundtable discussion of press problems led by journalists themselves. It was assumed that the journalists leading the discussion would spark reaction from the other journalists simply by describing how they tried to cover social policy issues, and that the Bush faculty and fellows would learn from the discussion. In 2 of the 4 years, however, the journalists giving presentations concentrated so heavily on the details of their work that discussion was slow to follow. When Bush faculty and fellows criticized press practices, some journalists were resentful. "There was agreement," said one journalist, "that we can talk until we're blue in the face about how we have to consider reader interest . . . but that doesn't mean that anyone on the outside will understand or accept our limitations." The fact that the roundtable discussion was well-received one year, however, indicates that it can work when discussion leaders are selected carefully and are fully prepared.

The topic presentations also varied greatly in their reception. Those sessions that were ranked lowest were criticized on two grounds. First, they were seen as "academic and conceptual," as one journalist remarked. Said another, "There is a need to more clearly understand the type of information needed on a topic by journalists. This showed up in the inability of many speakers to impart their knowledge in a meaningful way to the audience." Second, some outside experts were unable to integrate their perspective into the policy topic. For example, an economist gave a presentation on deficit spending that the journalists could not relate to the topic at hand, which was the effects of unemployment on children. Given the inexperience of many Bush faculty and fellows in dealing with the media, more concrete information on the journalists' needs should have been provided ahead of time.

Journalists.   Journalists were recruited from a range of media outlets. The committee believed that variety would encourage discussion from different perspectives. While this objective might have been reached, the journalists came to the workshops with differing expectations. Representatives of parent-oriented magazines, in particular, wanted presentations to include practical tips and "solutions for our readers," which was too great a leap for some policy topics. There was also a divergence of interest between the national and North Carolina journalists, and between large publications and small. While a journalist representing a large national publication complained that "there was too much data presented that applied just to North Carolina," a North Carolina journalist wrote that "I don't feel that its (the workshop's) topics are all that applicable to a small daily at which such specialization is impossible." It is possible that this problem could be overcome by scheduling concurrent workshop sessions tailored to meet different needs, thereby preserving the overall variety of journalists who attend.

An interesting mystery remains surrounding journalists' decisions as to whether to attend the workshops. Representatives of small newspapers, radio, and television networks declined to attend, because they said the small size of their staffs would not allow one member to be absent. But a more intriguing question is why *Time* sent a representative to three workshops when *Newsweek* declined each year on grounds that they could get policy information through their own channels. Why

Woman's Day and *Parents'*, but not *Ladies Home Journal*? The answer lies perhaps in the working "culture" of each organization: Some have a management style that encourages attendance at "backgrounder" type workshops while others look for more immediate results and products, especially when dealing with an organization unfamiliar to them, such as the Bush Institute.

Some Bush faculty believed that the workshops should reach a new group of journalists each year. At least one public relations professional sees repeat participation as a virtue, however. John Stokes, director of Medical Center Public Affairs at UNC, conducts annual workshops for medical and science writers. He says, "You don't build a relationship with one shot, so it's good to keep them coming back."

Follow-up. If long-term relationships are to be built between academia and the media, communication must continue. At the Bush Institute, fellows complete their programs in one or two years and move on; continuing their relationships with journalists is their responsibility. For the Institute, however, more could be done to keep in touch with journalists following the workshops. Each journalist is mailed a packet of materials and placed on the *Developments* mailing list. An effective added effort would require that policy studies completed by the fellows be abstracted and selectively mailed to journalists who expressed an interest in specific topic areas. This activity would require a resetting of work priorities that we have not yet chosen to make: Achieving one desired objective usually requires trading off another. But such a follow-up activity should not escape consideration by others who consider a workshop approach to building communication bridges with journalists.

CONCLUSIONS

Successful workshops result from a commitment by faculty, fellows, and staff. There is no question that the Bush Institute made a commitment to the workshops: Each workshop required the Bush Institute to expend approximately $4,000 plus staff time, supplemented by the UNC School of Journalism's contribution of approximately $500 and a faculty member's help. On balance, the comments by fellows and journalists lead us to conclude that the workshops were worth the money and effort.

The workshops revealed some of the continuing problems in establishing communications relationships. Journalists are often unable to change or modify the policies of their own institutions. Therefore, stories that they would like to present or write on social science topics are sometimes not viewed with approval by editors or producers. Many academicians still have difficulty communicating without using technical language. And while journalists seek unambiguous conclusions, academicians speak cautiously and qualify their comments. It is unrealistic to believe that academicians or journalists could completely overcome their tendencies and remain effective in their professions. It is realistic, however, to strive for mutual respect for each other's methods.

REFERENCES

Birch, T. (1980, May 13). Personal communication.

Cicirelli, V. (1969). *The impact of head start: An evaluation of the effects of head start on children's cognitive and affective development.* Athens, OH: Westinghouse Learning Corp.

Coleman, J. S., Campbell, E. Q., Hobson, C. J., McPartland, J., Mood, A. M., Weinfeld, F. D., & York, R. L. (1966). *Equality of educational opportunity.* Washington, DC: U.S. Government Printing Office.

Dyer, C. S., & Nayman, O. B. (1977). Under the capitol dome: Relationships between legislators and reporters. *Journalism Quarterly, 54,* 443–453.

Fraser, E. (1979). Public policy issues: a bold, new challenge for communicators. *Journal of Organizational Communication, 9*(1), 10–11.

Gallagher, J. J., & Sanders, L. J. (1981). The social scientist, the media, and public policy. *The Educator, 23*(1), 20–27.

Galtung, J., & Ruge, M. H. (1970). The structure of foreign news. In J. Tunstall (Ed.), *Media Sociology.* Urbana, IL: University of Illinois Press.

Gans, H. J. (1980). *Deciding what's news.* New York: Vintage.

Haskins, R., & Gallagher, J. J. (1981). *Models for analysis of social policy: An introduction.* Norwood, NJ: Ablex.

McCombs, M., & Shaw, D. (1972). The agenda-setting function of the mass media. *Public Opinion Quarterly, 36,* 176–187.

Miller, S. H. (1978). Congressional committee hearings and the media: Rules of the game. *Journalism Quarterly, 55,* 657–663.

TWELVE

FROM THE MEDIA PERSPECTIVE: COMMENT AND CRITIQUE

JANE D. BROWN
University of North Carolina at Chapel Hill

Social scientists are increasingly aware of the need to communicate with the world outside their own. In one sense, the need to communicate is a very pragmatic one. Social scientists depend to a large extent on public monies for their survival. They must work for good public relations in order to ensure continued financial support. Much of the work of social scientists has social policy implications as well, and if the work is to be worthwhile, it should be made available to relevant decision makers. And finally, much of the research being conducted has practical implications which might improve the quality of children's lives.

But social scientists have a problem. In order to communicate with these various publics, they must contend with the media. And most often that means they must first contend with a journalist. To most scientists that is an uncomfortable, if not downright scary, proposition. The scientist most likely expects that the journalist knows little about the social sciences and almost certainly knows nothing about the scientist's speciality. The scientist probably expects that the story will end up inaccurate and incomplete and will sensationalize some aspect of the research findings.

But the individual journalist isn't the only problem. Sometimes the message the scientist wants to communicate is relevant to only a small segment of the population, e.g., abused adolescents or the parents of infants. Large newspapers and network television generally are not interested in messages of this sort, however, and are not the most effective means of delivering the message in any case. The scientist needs to be able to target the message to the particular audience but often is at the mercy of the larger media outlet.

These problems and their potential solutions are addressed in the preceding three chapters. Dunwoody and Stocking have approached the topic with a sympathetic look at the stereotyped journalist covering social science stories. They find that a part of the stereotype is justified, but greater understanding from the scientist of the constraints of the news business is necessary. Sanders and Gallagher then describe a series of workshops especially designed to promote such understanding of the journalist's world. And finally, McCall, Gregory, and Lonnborg describe a series of media projects that circumvented the usual problems encountered in communicating social science findings through the mass media.

Each of these chapters assumes that public communication is a necessary and important aspect of today's social science. Each also finds the task a difficult although not impossible one. It is pertinent to examine the first assumption of the need for public communication and then look at the remedies proposed for the perceived lack of adequate coverage.

NEED FOR PUBLIC COMMUNICATION

The mass media in this country have always been faced with issues of representation and fairness. The mass media are challenged with the task of communicating among a multitude of factions and interests. They are supposed to not only keep track of what is going on in each of the various institutions in the society but also to tell their audiences what they should do about the issues and controversies that arise. Over the years, the media system that has developed is a complicated yet primarily efficient mechanism for communication. Its flaws become apparent, however, as soon as we begin to look more closely at its track record for any one of the institutions or interests it is supposed to be monitoring.

These three chapters are implicitly and sometimes explicitly critical of the role the media have played in conveying information about social science issues, especially those relevant to children. Basically, the Bush Centers and Boys Town are criticizing the media for inadequate and incomplete coverage. They think the media have not represented these issues or the institutions of social science (and their own, in particular) fairly. The programs they describe are their remedies for previously bad treatment by the media.

These are not the first groups to try to improve media representation with these methods. In fact, much of what is described here could simply be called good press relations. Business and industry have understood the need for such activities at least since World War II, when large-scale "public information" campaigns were developed to create a more favorable opinion climate for big business. Since then we have seen other general as well as specific public relations campaigns which have used the media to influence public opinion and public policy. One public relations firm, for example, claims credit for the successful campaign against the Food and Drug Administration (FDA) and its efforts to ban cyclamates. Another firm worked hard to keep the FDA from banning television advertising directed at children (Gandy, 1982).

These kinds of claims and other more comprehensive studies by mass communication researchers suggest that such activities are worthwhile. The media do play an important role in the shaping of the political scene. Numerous studies (McCombs & Shaw, 1972; Shaw & McCombs, 1977) now have shown that the media are important in setting the public agenda or in specifying which issues will be debated. The media probably are less important in changing the attitudes, opinions, and behaviors of their audiences, but in some situations, especially with new issues (or new candidates or products), even these changes can result. It is no wonder, then, that institutions are not content to leave the process up to the media.

Gandy (1982) calls the techniques used in these efforts to influence the media agenda "information subsidies" and defines an information subsidy as "an attempt to produce influence over the actions of others by controlling their access to and use of information relevant to those actions" (p. 61). Having reporters come to a background workshop on child and family policy research or producing news features are all information subsidies, because they reduce the cost of the information for the media. Basically, the source (in this case, the Bush Centers and Boys Town) are making it easier for journalists to acquire information. In the case of the news features from Boys Town, the cost to the media is practically nil. How could a television station refuse?

As all three chapters point out, however, the media can refuse such information subsidies, if they do not adhere to certain structural and organizational traditions. Dunwoody and Stocking describe certain basic constraints which set boundaries on which information will become news. First, stories must be obtainable before deadlines. That means that the reporter must be able to get there and get the story in time to write it. Second, the story must satisfy the editor. That generally means that the story must meet at least some of the standard news criteria of audience impact, prominence, conflict, uniqueness, etc.

The credibility of the source should be added to these criteria. Reporters and editors make decisions about the accuracy and reliability of information, depending to some extent on the status and perceived trustworthiness of the source of the information. This is particularly relevant when the information is subsidized (i.e., handed out at a press conference or a workshop; provided in broadcast-ready form). Then the journalist, in the interests of the presumed objectivity of the media in the United States, will want to make sure that the source does not have some vested interest in the information that is being so generously provided.

THE BUSH CENTER AND BOYS TOWN SUBSIDIES

So, with those constraints in mind, how will the Bush and Boys Town programs for providing subsidized information fare? While the two programs are different, their goals are basically the same—keep child and family policy issues on the public agenda. The Bush approach is somewhat akin to a long press conference or a backgrounding session for reporters. It is interesting to note that over the course of the sessions, journalists insisted that more information be presented that could immediately be made into stories. Backgrounding goes only so far. If you are going to provide information subsidies, they said, in effect, abide by the rules and make it relevant, timely, newsworthy.

It also is clear that journalists, as ignorant as they may be about the social sciences, do not want to be preached at or criticized for the job they do. While many of today's science writers are being trained in the social sciences, as Dunwoody and Stocking point out, you're still not worth your salt as a reporter unless you can cover just about any story that comes up and in a hurry. The social scientist probably is going to learn more about journalism than the other way around at one of these give-and-take mutual critique sessions, and that is a reasonable goal. What these workshops seem to be best designed for is to set up a pool of sources for future stories (which may indeed have been suggested by the topics presented). The journalist goes away with a credible source list which can be referred to when the story does get on the agenda.

In terms of gaining control over media representation, the Bush program faces two problems which the Boys Town program has sought to overcome. First, Bush has relatively little control over the kinds of audiences which receive various messages. They are at the mercy of the media representatives who come to the meetings to decide which messages are most suitable for the audience they serve. Second, the Bush program cannot control the accuracy or completeness of the stories that do get written or broadcast. They can only hope that by establishing the source's trustworthiness, the journalist will listen more carefully and perhaps will take the time to check out the story with the source. But time is exactly the problem in many situations, and so it is unlikely the story will get checked.

The Boys Town program is composed of three different approaches, but all have the advantage of at least some amount of control over sources, messages and channels. This is subsidized information in its most direct form. The Boys Town program leaves almost nothing for the journalist to do. In fact, the targeted messages (friendship skills, school problems, and television and children) were sent directly to the relevant audiences, and the mass media were completely (and competently) circumvented.

With the television news feature project, some control was relinquished, however, since individual television stations could decide simply not to run the shows. In producing these shows, Boys Town adhered to all the criteria as outlined earlier for newsworthiness. They also made "good television," and it would be difficult to imagine why a station would not accept this information subsidy, except perhaps on the grounds of credibility. Even that is difficult to understand, since the messages were deliberately designed to "stress information and alternative courses of action rather than to advocate a social or political theme."

Boys Town's attempts to get messages directly in the mass media were apparently a little less successful, although they did have luck on their side, as they say, and were able to get a column in *Parents* magazine. But they did their homework and wrote a book first and then a magazine article with an experienced science writer, which helped to establish their credibility with the rest of the media.

While these appear to be very efficient methods for increasing the visibility of issues relevant to children, they also are more expensive than other, less controlled approaches. McCall and his colleagues do not discuss the cost of these efforts, but it is clear that extensive resources (personnel, time, and money) were expended by Boys Town. Other less well-endowed research institutions may not have these resources and may have to go with the less impressive and less expensive versions of information subsidizing, such as the Bush workshops.

CONCLUSION

In sum, it is clear from these three chapters that better communication between social scientists and journalists is needed. Social scientists need to understand how the mass media work, so they can have more control over how their stories get presented to the various publics they need to communicate with. On the other hand, journalists need to know more about the social sciences so they will know a good story when it is presented to them.

But one final word about information subsidies. While it appears that more and more information of all sorts that appears in the media is managed or subsidized, we must be careful not to abuse the process. I personally favor the less well-managed approach of the Bush Centers, because they still allow the journalist to make decisions about news-worthiness, story content, and tone, etc. While the Boys Town process did include writers and producers in some stages of the production of materials, they basically have obviated the need for journalists to make decisions, except about whether or not to run the materials. Journalists are trained to be fair and accurate and complete as they construct their stories. Sometimes they do not do such a good job. But I am not con-vinced that I would rather have the institution telling me what the story is. Social scientists need to continue to improve communication with journalists so their story gets heard along with the other stories in the political world. It would be accomplished better through cooperation rather than circumvention.

REFERENCES

Gandy, O. H. (1982). *Beyond agenda setting: Information subsidies and public policy.* Norwood, NJ: Ablex.

McCombs, M., & Shaw, D. (1972). The agenda-setting function of mass media. *Public Opinion Quarterly, 36,* 176–187.

Shaw, D., & McCombs, M. (Eds.). (1977). *The emergence of American political issues: The agenda-setting function of the press.* St. Paul, MN: West.

Author Index

Italics indicate bibliographic citations.

Subject Index

A

ABC, 109
Accuracy of journalism, 179–182, 190, 191
Action for Children's Television, 113
Administrations, impact of change of, 85
Administrators, science, 138–139, 162
Advertising, health messages and, 123–124
Advocacy, types of, 140–141, 161
Affective aspects of television, 103–104
Agenda-setting by media, 211
Aggression. *See* Violence on TV
Alcohol, Drug Abuse, and Mental Health Administration (ADAMHA), 63
Alcohol, Drug Abuse, and Mental Health Block Grant, 72–73
American Association for the Advancement of Science, 184
American Educational Research Association, 32
American Medical Association, 97–99
Analysis of social policy, 212–222
Apathy over TV violence, 97–99
Arousal, concept of, 103–104
Audience, perceptions of, 175–176
Australia, media experiments in health instruction in, 120–123
Autism, early infantile, 143–145

B

Behavior and beliefs, TV and social, 105
"Bill of rights" for mentally ill, 69–70, 73
Block grant scheme for mental health services, 72–73
Bourne, P., 61, 86–88
Boys Town Center communication project, 193–206, 227–228

mass media projects, 199–206
philosophy and operating principles of, 193–196
targeted communications projects of, 196–199
British Broadcasting Corporation (BBC), health message from, 126–130
British Health Education Council, 128–129
Bryant, T.E., 53, 61, 62, 65, 71, 86, 88
Bureaucracy, competitive drives in, 12–13
Bush Institute for Child and Family Policy, 214–222, 227–228
Bush model of policy analysis, 214–215
Busing, 27–29. *See also* Coleman Reports
Butler v. Michigan, 39

C

Cable Health Network (CHN), 133–134
Califano, J., 18, 62, 65, 86
California, media experiments in health instruction in, 120–123
Carter, J., 52, 53, 59, 60, 86
Carter, R., 51–52, 53, 60, 61, 62, 65, 71, 86
Carter Administration, 61–63
Celler, E., 6
Center for Studies for Crime and Delinquency, 148
Children
    conceptualizations of, 141–143
    distribution of sexual materials to, 47, 49
    TV and. *See* Television, children and
Civil Rights Act (1964), 6–7
Civil Rights Commission, 22
Clark, K.B., 15
Coffin, T., 96
Cognitive aspects of television, 103–104

235

DATE DUE

DEMCO 38-297